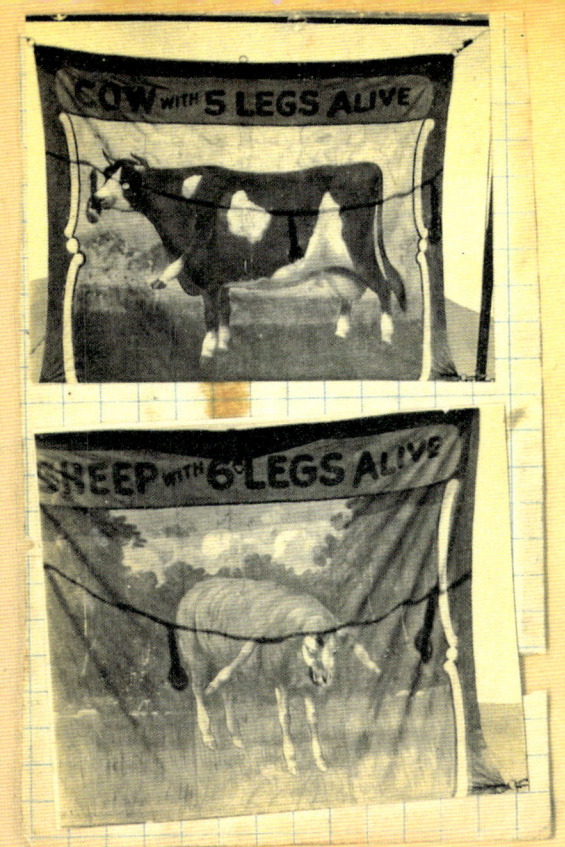

Ackley's Independent Shows

RANDY JOHNSON
JIM SECRETO
TEDDY VARNDELL

CONTRIBUTIONS FROM
Glen C. Davies · Steve Gilbert · Johnny Meah · John Polacsek · Dale Slusser · Lisa Stone

Freaks · Geeks & Strange Girls
Sideshow Banners of the Great American Midway

HARDY MARKS PUBLICATIONS · HONOLULU

This book was published by:
Hardy Marks Publications · P.O. Box 90520 · Honolulu, Hawaii 96835

Designed by: Randy Johnson

Edited by: Lisa Stone

ISBN 0-945367-15-5

© 1995 Hardy Marks Publications

All rights reserved

Every effort has been made to contact copyright owners of material in this volume – in case of oversight, please contact publisher for correction in a future edition.

Printed in Hong Kong

PREFACE

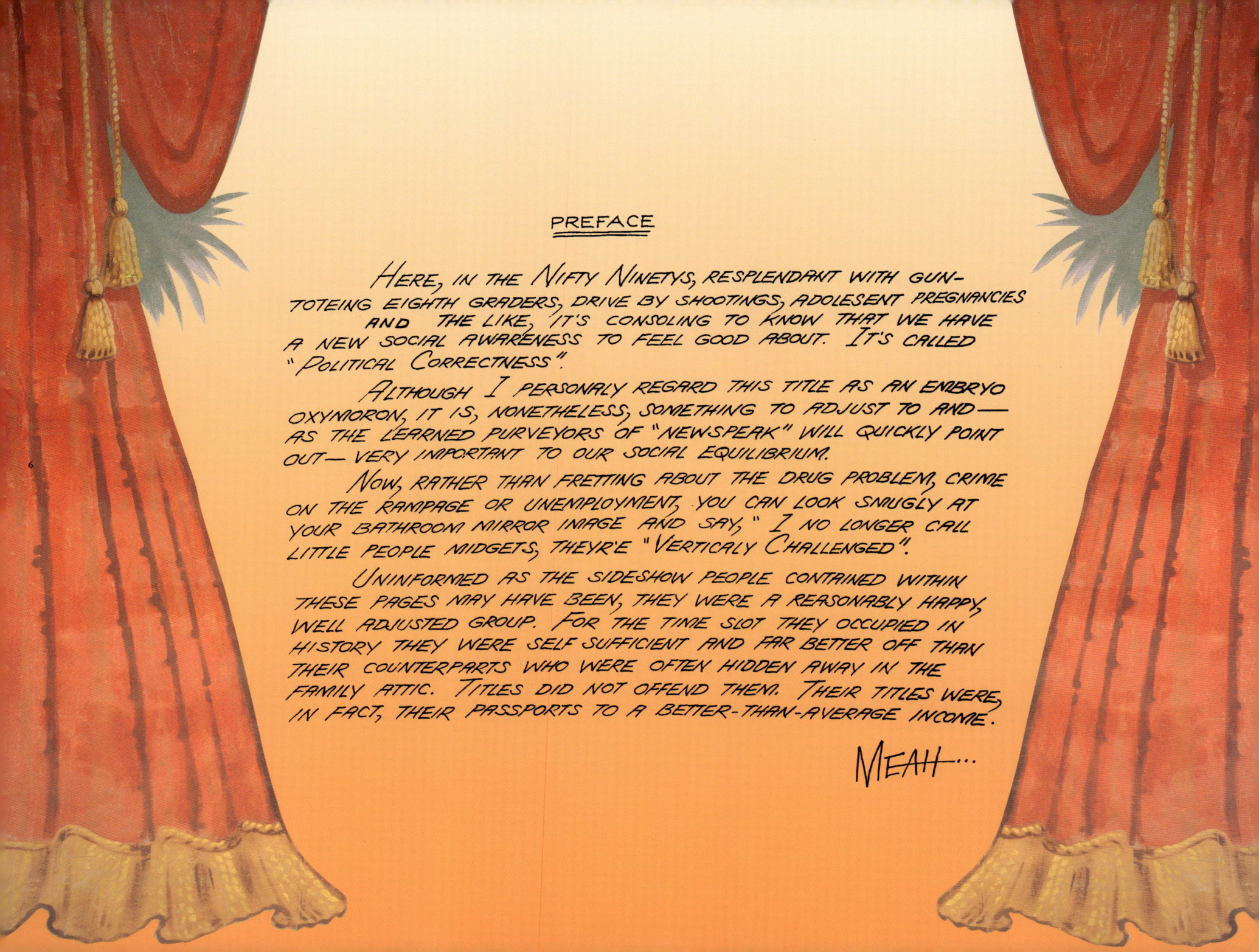

Here, in the Nifty Ninetys, resplendant with gun-toteing eighth graders, drive by shootings, adolesent pregnancies and the like, it's consoling to know that we have a new social awareness to feel good about. It's called "Political Correctness".

Although I personally regard this title as an embryo oxymoron, it is, nonetheless, something to adjust to and — as the learned purveyors of "Newspeak" will quickly point out — very important to our social equilibrium.

Now, rather than fretting about the drug problem, crime on the rampage or unemployment, you can look snugly at your bathroom mirror image and say, "I no longer call little people midgets, they're 'Vertically Challenged'".

Uninformed as the sideshow people contained within these pages may have been, they were a reasonably happy, well adjusted group. For the time slot they occupied in history they were self sufficient and far better off than their counterparts who were often hidden away in the family attic. Titles did not offend them. Their titles were, in fact, their passports to a better-than-average income.

MEAH...

TABLE of CONTENTS

11
Introduction: Depicting the Demons, Inside and Out · *Lisa Stone & Randy Johnson*

17
The Truth *Is* Stranger than Fiction · *Johnny Meah*

31
Alive and on the Inside: Historical Notes on Sideshow Paintings & Banners · *John Polacsek*

47
Cunning Crafters of Dreams · *Johnny Meah*

63
Memorial to the Milestones · *Glen C. Davies*

87
Larger Than Life: Positively Fat · *Jim Secreto*

101
Totally Tattooed: The Self-Made Freaks of the Circus and Sideshow · *Steve Gilbert*

125
Lure of the Sideshow: Denial/Desire · *Dale Slusser*

135
The Dope Show · *Teddy Varndell*

153
Banner Notes & Captions

161
Other Publications of Consequence

163
Literary Freaks·Computer Geeks & Strange Contributors

165
Unbelievable Beings of Strength: World's Greatest

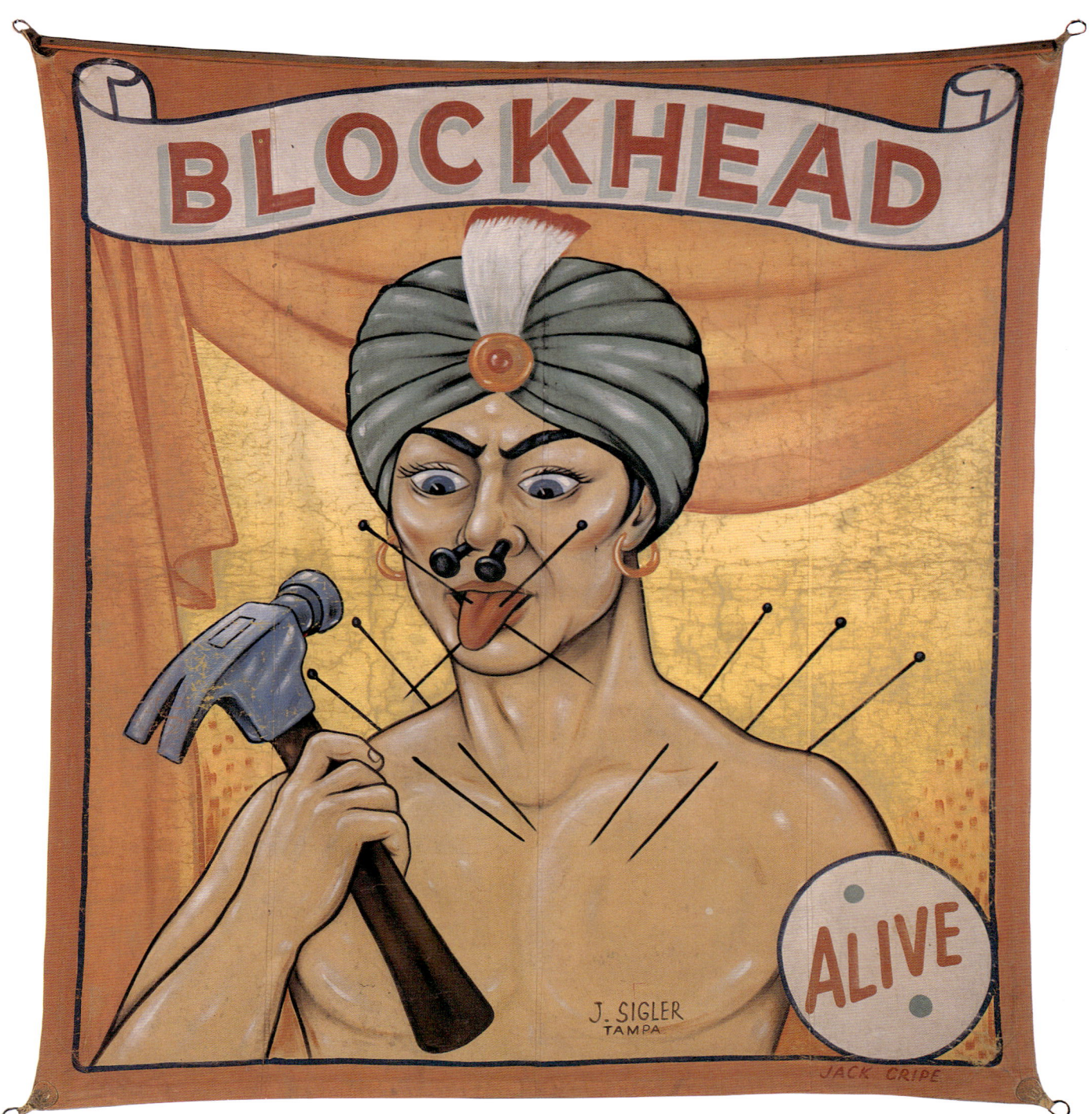

Left: Bee Boy, 1981, Right: Melvin Burkhart: Human Oddity, 1985
© Joel-Peter Witkin
Courtesy Pace MacGill, N.Y.C. and Fraenkel Gallery, San Francisco

INTRODUCTION
DEPICTING the DEMONS · INSIDE and OUT

Lisa Stone & Randy Johnson

It's comforting to think you're normal, and it does much to stay back the demons, because being human comes with a price—history, imagination, fate, and the unexpected. On the other hand, you've got your Freaks, Geeks, and Strange Girls. These descriptions, used freely in the past, conceptualize social attitudes towards "things," mostly real people, who were placed on display for the shock, revulsion, and/or amusement of observers who believed that they themselves were normal, in fact, they were dead-sure of it. Words like freaks and geeks are now taboo. We're not allowed to say them, though by not saying them the social history they transmit has not been erased entirely. Visual art forms more easily sidestep the caprices of language restraints, reflecting cultural undercurrents of the moment. One of these, the sideshow banner, unfolds an eye-dazzling and outrageously literal panorama of America's idea of freaks and geeks, not to mention the phenomena of "strange girls," and a parade of other extra-ordinary beings. A contemporary view of sideshow banners also provides an incisive backwards glance at the observers.

The sideshow banner is no longer needed to hawk sideshows, but this genre of monumentally depicted freaks 'n' geeks has resurfaced in a new context, wavering on the high wire of fine art/folk art, creating its own precarious balancing act in the process. Though you're reading this in an art book of great flash and beauty, it's important to realize that sideshow banners weren't always perceived as art. They emerged as cheap advertisement. They hung in the wind. They earned their keep. Once the show folded or the attraction bolted, they were instantly obsolete as paintings (unless they were recycled for other shows), and were used instead for their value as tarps. They sopped up oil under trucks, they were cut up for scrap, discarded. When the sideshow evolved beyond its traditional form and amusement parks like Chicago's Riverview closed for good (1967), countless sideshow banners joined the flow of lost objects from our material culture, waiting to be rediscovered. Unsurprisingly, a handful of artists and a few collectors and dealers initially gravitated toward orphaned banners, riveted by their visual and conceptual power, recognizing in them an essential aspect of American painting that had been predictably overlooked by the Big-Top Art World. Banners found their place in artists' collections and were viewed as art, unqualified, for the most part, by art-world designations. They soon filtered from antique shops into art galleries, presented first as folk art and more recently as outsider art.[1] Now they're in a different sideshow ...modern American culture on the brink of millennium.

Sideshow banners document an aspect of our culture that we don't all want to face: people would (and will) flock like flies, they'll pay good money to see freaks—aberrations of nature and culture—representations of the grotesque, real or fabricated. Sideshows originally offered a glimpse at things the general public might not normally encounter, such as erotica, exotica (generally people of color), animals from afar, hybrid creatures, and human artworks tattooed from head to toe—offering the folks a "museum-quality" educational experience, and pretty cheap, right there at the edge of town. Soon the arena expanded and big bucks were made by promoters who offered brief and isolated face-to-face encounters with the human figure in all its contorted aspects, and other oddities that exhilarated infrequently explored areas of the psyche. Compassion and etiquette, false or genuine, could be checked at the door, and an ocean of human flesh, for instance,

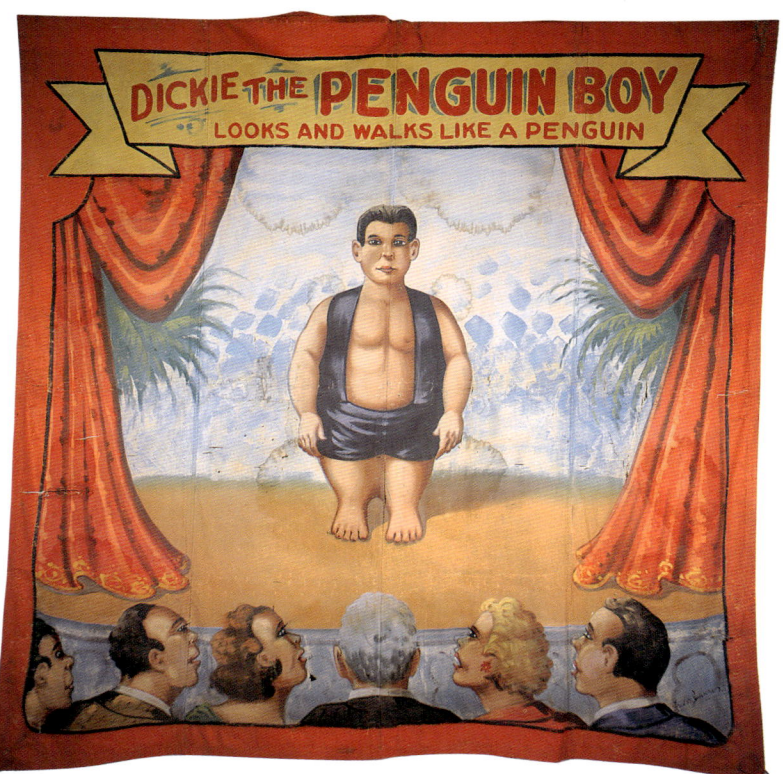

In this introduction we present images from traditional sideshow culture alongside works from contemporary art world – all by artists who share in the same art/history – visualizing encounters with distortion and exaggeration, found inside and out.

Ed Paschke, *Wanda*, 1973, oil on canvas, 55.5" x 45.75", photo: William H. Bengtson, courtesy Phyllis Kind Gallery, private collection.

Snap Wyatt, (detail), *Zoma Depraved*

It's easy to generalize about people who flocked to sideshows and why—the common assumption being that these venues primarily served the "regular Joe" whose life was starved for a little stimulation from the underworld. Countless artists hit side shows and other so-called seedy attractions for the similar reasons. Ed Paschke, Karl Wirsum, and other Chicago Imagist painters plumbed the depths of said attractions, polishing the facets of titillation and taboo into an enduring aesthetic tradition.

could be gawked at with complete social impunity. But in many cases the attraction—fat man, thin man, half girl, geek—was a dismal overdose of sad reality, striking chords of depression and uncertainty. For some, the inventively rendered compositions of flash on canvas outside must have provided both the draw *and* the gratifying moment at the sideshow.

Sideshow acts plumbed the depths of the social psyche and the extant images send us crawling for explanations. What was the "FAT SHOW" really about? Why the magnetism to gargantuan distortion—the physical, visceral, human face and body of total excess? How does this relate to continually evolving popular ideals of the body, or the American obsession with consumption, gratification? How did Strange Girl acts correspond with attitudes toward women at the time? These acts depicted variations of a primal transformation: woman into savage; banner lines presented fantastic images of sexualized, brutal, man-eating Amazonian cannibals and sadists. Typically the last banner in such a series, (we can almost hear the breathless "thank god"), showed the Ape Woman...CAPTURED. Concurrent with the popularity of EEKA and ZOMA, real women were struggling to bend back the bars in cages of social constriction. A more lucid reflection of the backlash response to women redefining their own roles and identities could hardly be found, than in the banners that depicted Strange Girl acts. The Ape Girl shows and the polarities it encapsulated are not a thing of the past, and the pageant/dialogue about the commingled destinies of men and women and art and culture continues to unfold. We now find an appropriate flip-side view

 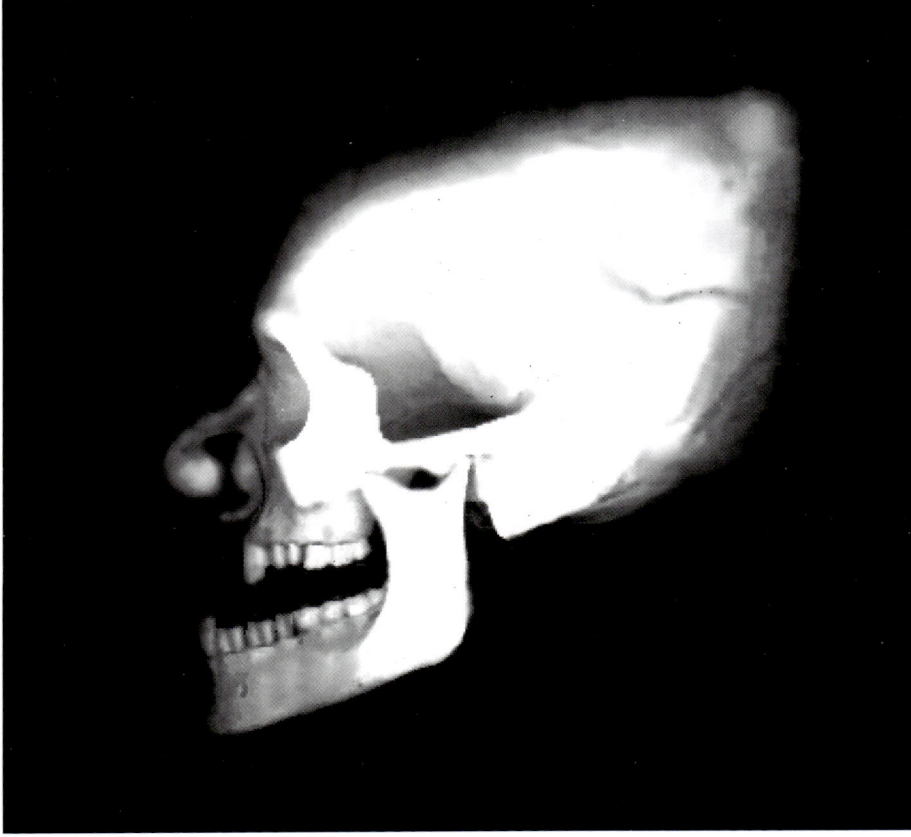

Fred G. Johnson, (detail), *Spring Carnival*

Randy Johnson, (installation detail), *Homo sapiens scurra bozus,* computer generated rear lit transparency

The clown persona was one of many circus and sideshow images painted by Fred G. Johnson, Chicago banner painter extraordinaire. His grandson, Randy J. Johnson, who grew up in the shadow of these images, extends the family tradition in his own explorations of the social clown and the clown inside.

in the activist "sideshows" of the Guerrilla Girls, who attempt to even the score, addressing gross inequities in depictions and manipulations of women in our culture.

American culture in general has changed drastically in the last six or seven decades, and sideshows no longer exist on the scale or in the form that they did when most banners featured in this book were painted.[2] As laws were enacted regulating aspects of the "freak" trade, shows disbanded or became more transient. Canvas sideshow banners were gradually supplanted by semi-trucks and trailers airbrushed with images of chicken-head-eaters, pickled punks, and the like inside—shows that could be down the road in a flash if the heat was on. The impulse to confront our post-modern equivalent of freaks, geeks, and strange girls, however, is alive and well, though the mediums of advertisement have become more ubiquitous, pervasive, and the gaze has turned slightly inward. The sideshow is everywhere— in the the supermarket, at home, in our bodies and our minds. Flip on Donahue, grab an *Enquirer*, view victims in the limelight, exposing their souls and tangled interior lives. Witness sensationalized reenactments of incest, rape, whatever, on television shows that offer selections from our pantheon of distorted social constructs, complemented by the corporate freak show of contemporary advertising. The current (soon to be dated) electronic banner line offers "Canings—Live from Singapore," "Wife Chops Off Husband's Penis (but he gets it back)," "O.J.—The Hottest Show in Court," and, in this political climate "The Death Network" is sure to follow, on T.V. or via the Internet.

This is not to suggest that the traditional sideshow banner should be viewed as an

Fred G. Johnson, (detail)

Karl Wirsum, *Digital Presense*, 1993, Acrylic on Wood, 48" x 35"
photo: William H. Bengtson, courtesy Phyllis Kind Gallery, private collection.

Fred G. Johnson created masterfully weird fantasy paintings of his own invention, occasionally adopting a vision of the future. This photograph was taken by Fred sometime in the 60's showing a detail of a work in progress — a banner for a house of mirrors. It shares aesthetic space with Karl Wirsum's visualization of "Digital Presence," a more contemporary view of the figure in the age of technology. The two artists met in the 70's at Johnson's studio at Chicago Tent and Awning.

anachronism, nor is it a sentimental yearning for the simpler days of "Laugh With Dolly" fat shows, in a time when gross obesity is decorously described as "pituitarily challenged." Our language is replete with so-called politically correct designations, but our collective conscience is lagging far behind. The public exposition of the darker aspects of being human, ALIVE, is a trajectory, and though the media has responded with a self-perpetuating onslaught of sensational, myopic hype, contemporary artists maintain the tradition forged by banner painters, exploring the visual and psychological depths of sideshow terrain.

Freaks, Geeks, and Strange Girls presents an anthology of perspectives on the history of the sideshow, accompanied by a line-up of outstanding images by artists of exceptional talent and ingenuity. Unlike most books that progress hierarchically (first there's an idea, then a plan, and then a clear path, plus writers, editors, and photographers who all know their tasks), this book evolved centrifugally—perhaps mirroring the sideshow phenomena itself—to the credit of all involved. A handful of "persons of greatness and strength" (and guts) decided that the sideshow banner was no longer to be an unrecognized genre of Art in America. One thing was for certain though, the sideshow banner was not to be presented as a relic, but as part of the continuum of searing reflections on culture that artists provide. So, instead of isolating banner artists and their paintings from this procession, we present here a short (and by no means comprehensive) banner line-up of works by a few contemporary artists with images by their sideshow counterparts, depicting the demons, inside and out.

Snapshot of Pinhead "On Stage" by Jack Cripe

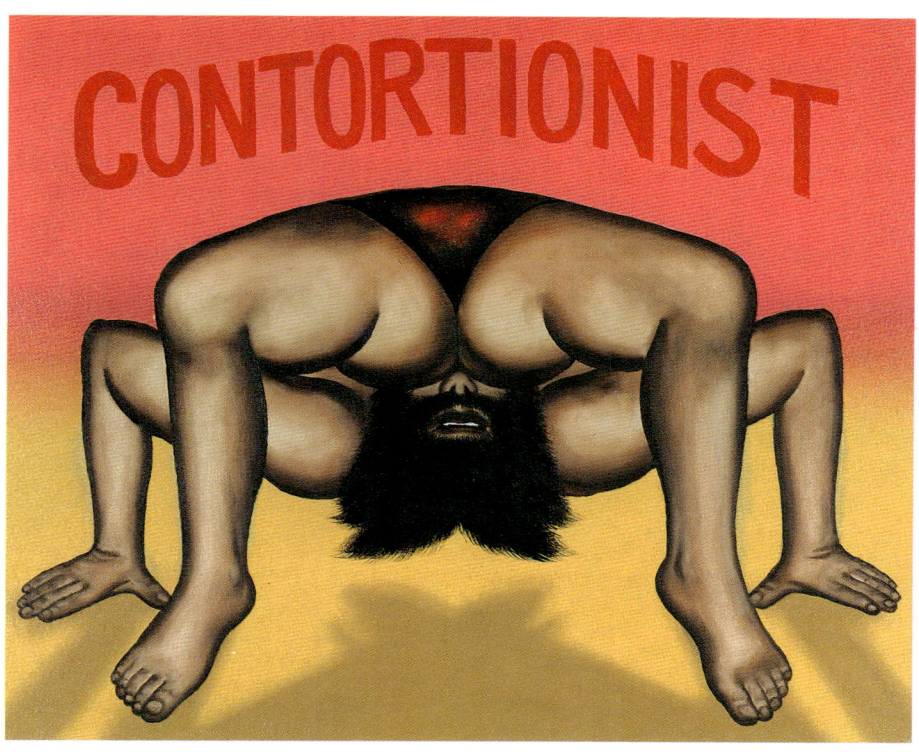

Roger Brown, *Alan Artner: Ironic Contortionist of Irony,* 1994, oil on canvas, 20" x 24", photo: William H. Bengtson, courtesy Phyllis Kind Gallery.

Some of the finest sideshow banners reveal the polorarized relationship between banner subjects, and social attitudes that assure them an afflicted, distorted identity, albeit with high entertainment value. Taking his cue from banner artists and infusing it with his own inimitable spin, Roger Brown pictorialized the sideshow of art criticism in his thinly veiled portrait of Chicago critic Alan Artner as Contortionist.

NOTES:

1- In addition to artists, dealers, and collectors, a few institutions (such as Circus World Museum in Baraboo, Wisconsin), have preserved sideshow banners and presented them to the public, primarily in the context of circus history.

2- Traditional sideshow genre and culture lives on in the the life and works of contemporary banner artist Johnny Meah, who has resisted the extinction of the sideshow, maintaining the traditional art form of the painted canvas banner while also performing many sideshow acts in venues around the country on a breakneck schedule. Meah's scintillating and incomparable perspectives on the subject are scattered throughout this book. Other traditional sideshows in existence today include Ward Hall and C. M. Christ Shows (traveling); Harvey Boswell's Palace of Wonders, North Carolina; Bobby Reynolds, Coney Island, New York; and Dick Zigland, also at Coney Island,, in the summertime.

A note about spellings in this book: many original writings, quotations, quoted captions, and banner titles were spelled intuitively, though not necessarily correctly. We felt that our corrections would change the character of original text in some cases and interjections of "(sic)" would be condescending flow-stoppers. So we left spelling alone.

THE TRUTH IS STRANGER THAN FICTION

Johnny Meah

Pictorial canvases — "banners" in the parlance of the portable amusement industry — have been around as long as accounts of these nomadic entertainment enterprises have been kept. Garish and often crude, these tanbark tapestries have brightened not only the tented establishments that they advertised but, in many cases, out-dazzled the very attractions they illustrated.

Since carnivals and circuses are kalidescopic in nature, bombarding all senses with a veritable meteor shower of distractions, it is indeed significant that any clearly defined images linger in the publics' mind, yet the scenes depicted on those huge billowing billboards do just that.

Were those who produced these advertisments merely hacks who cranked them out cookie-cutter fashion in some dingey loft or were they inspired artisans who pondered the effectivness of each brushstroke? Were any of them sufficiently familiar with the subjects that they pattently oversold to feel a wry sense of lighthearted larceny? Were there any among them who ever experienced the irony of being the subject of his own boisterous broadsides?

A blanket, "Yes.", to all of the above paradoxicly suggests a banner in itself; "The truth IS stranger than fiction"!

Most of us who have succumbed to the temptation of sideshow banners have, upon entering the tent, been predictably disappointed. Did you really expect Freddy the Frog Boy to be perched in a Disney-like swamp setting, sloshing his amphibian feet and peering at you through bulging green eyes? Well no, not really, but you didn't quite imagine him as a bored little gnome of a man in a dirty T-shirt either. "Known in his home-town of Ludiwici, Georgia as Freddy the Frog Boy", the sideshow's M.C. had said, doubtless provoking the thought in your mind that folks in Ludiwici, Georgia had very fertile imaginations.

Today, in a world nearly devoid of such quaint things as sideshows, we casually accept the canards pitched at us on television, knowing in our hearts that the washer that never needs a repairman usualy does and the exhaustive clinical studies done on Glitz or Glop rarely decrease your visits to the dentist.

Freddy the Frog Boy, you see, was just the Ipana of his day.

And what of those devious charlitans, those cunning crafters of dreams, chortling in glee with each new rainbow that they create for us to chase? Do we execute them with laughing gas? Bury them in a sand hill populated with battery-operated ants? Of course not! Like the banner painters, they provide us with the very vital ability to laugh at ourselves and our fears and foibles.

So come with us in our maintainence free automobile to a land of perfect smiles, instantly relieved headaches and little green men who await us, seated on their lilly pads, just around the corner.

The doors to the big show are now open!

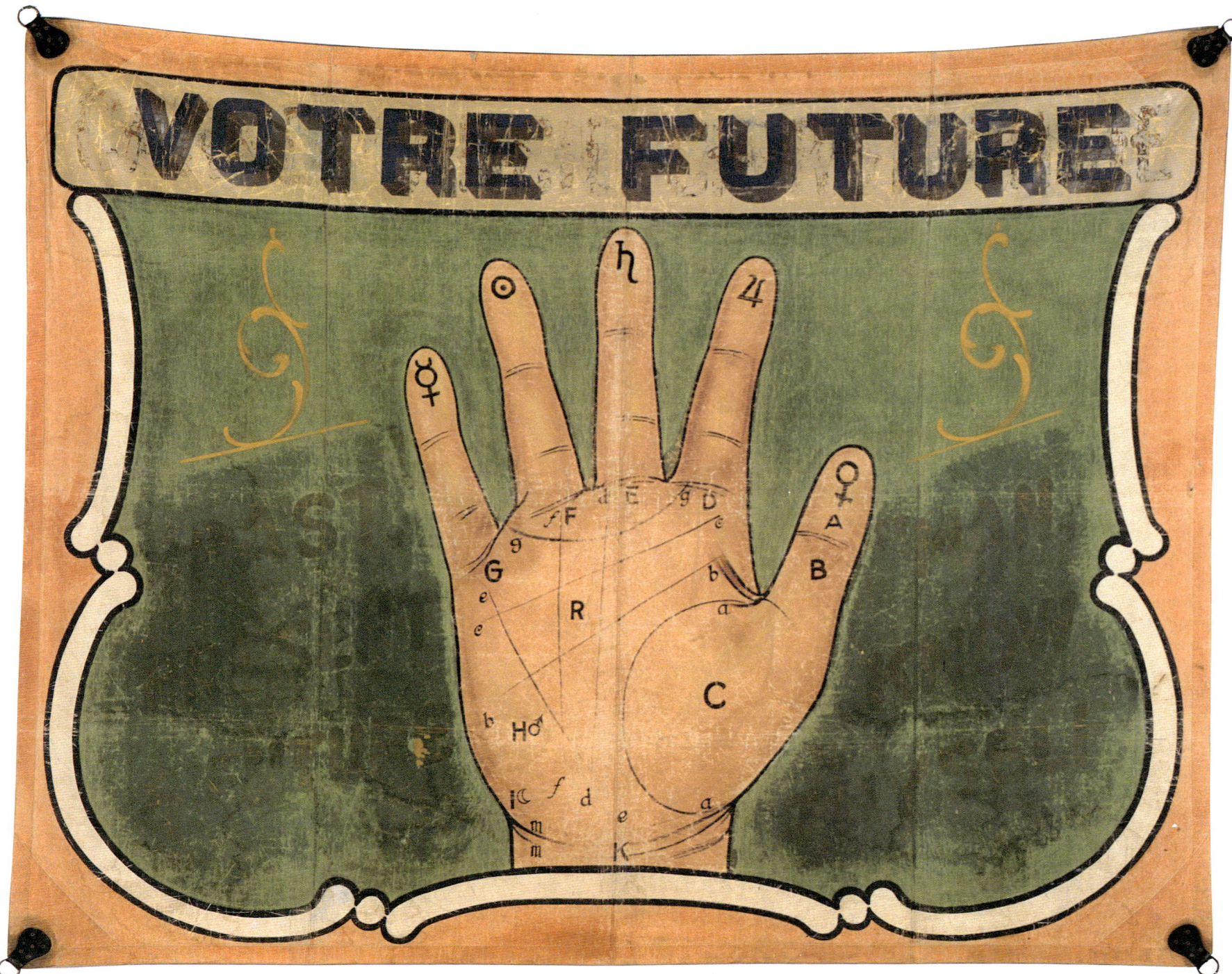

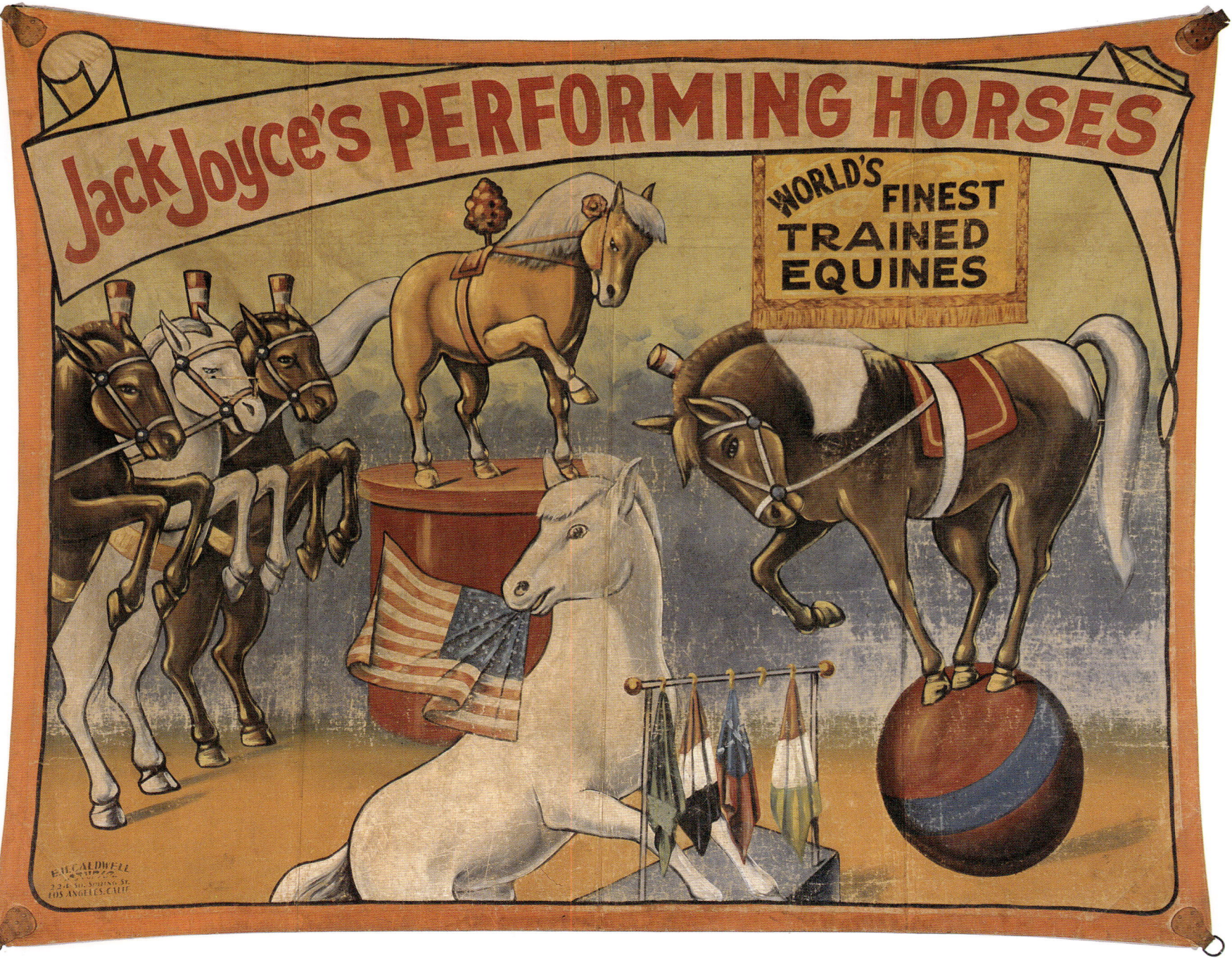

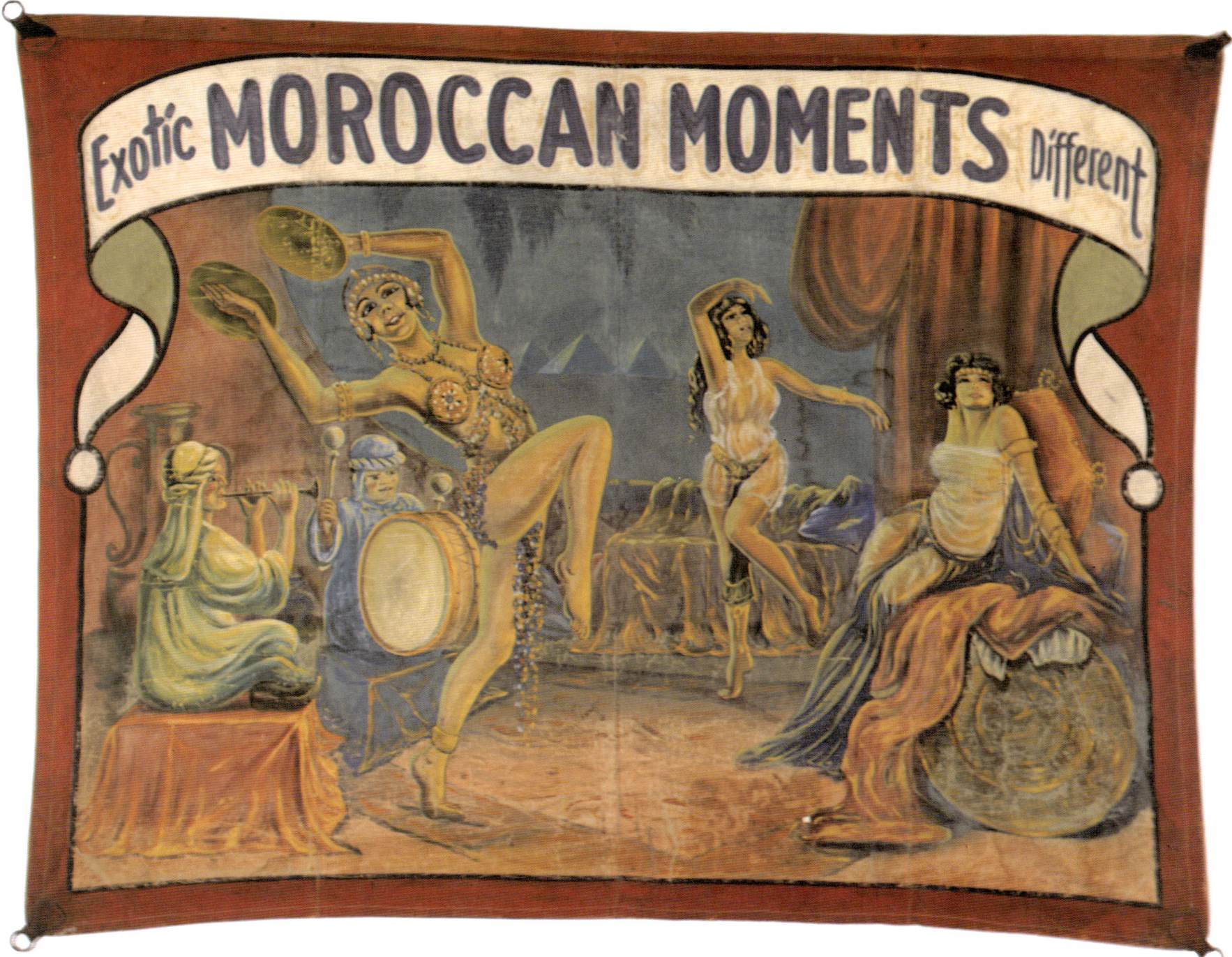

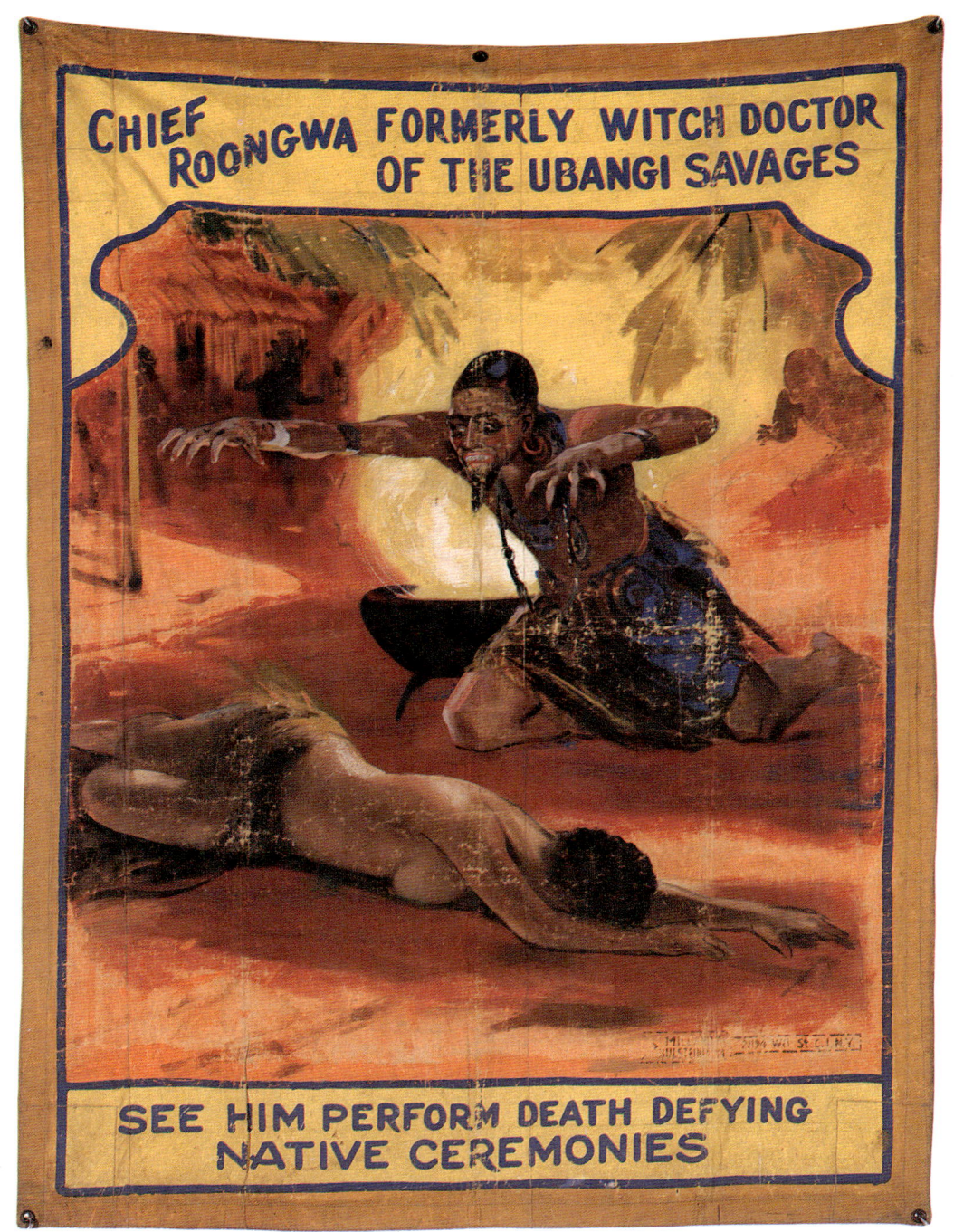

Alive and on the Inside
Historical Notes on Sideshow Paintings & Banners

John Polacsek

The eye catching and imaginative canvas illustrations of the sideshow have heralded every type of attraction that showmen could secure from the four corners of the globe. One of the earliest known sideshow banners featured an "African Bison" which was on display in Charleston, South Carolina in 1818. The bison was sixteen hands high, weighed fourteen to fifteen hundred pounds, and for one week, the *Charleston Courier* noted that "his likeness will be hung at the corner of Meeting and Ellery Street."

As early as the 1830s so-called "outside shows" became aligned with traveling circuses and menageries. To bring customers into their attractions, early showmen relied upon sight and sound to sell their novelty. Unlike circuses or menageries which used colorful posters, couriers, pamphlets, circulars, heralds, and newspaper ads to spread the word, the sideshows did not advertise using conventional media. Instead, they relied upon the attracting power of the main show, and flourished in lots nearby, even though some of the main shows advertised that "no sideshows of pygmy children, overgrown men, abortions, and monstrosities" were allowed to accompany them.

By the 1850's a relationship between the main shows and sideshows was established. A typical sideshow just off the show lot was described as follows:

The scene outside was vastly amusing - there was a half a dozen supplementary tents, containing most attractive, instructive and elevating exhibitions. One contained a French Giant, with a Prussian name and an English face, whose portrait outside occupied full 12 feet of canvas. Another bid from public sight the 'Skeleton Man' whose merits and perfections were not only depicted upon canvas, but were noisily heralded to an admiring crowd by a round, brandy-faced Johnny Bull. "Valk in, gen'lmen, the honly real, ginooine, skiliton man bin Hamerica. 'E vas born just as you see 'im delinivated hup on the canvass, with ha perfect face hand body, vith hall the bones fur legs hands harms, but no flesh hon 'em. Valk hin gen'lmen - honly vun dime. Vun dime, gen'lmen vill iadmit you to the greatest curiosity hin existence. Hif you neglect this the honly chance you vill hever ave, you vill regret it furhever. Vun dime, gen'lmen, valk hin." [1]

Sideshows relied upon a major illustration, an orator, and in some instances music to attract a crowd, though this combined stimuli was not always appreciated. When an eight-foot-two-inch tall giant was on exhibit in one Ohio town the local newspaper commented on the attraction:

Quite a crowd of boys hung around the door, evidently satisfied with looking at the mammoth picture at the entrance. The music was horrid hand organ which grated harshly on the ear, and our citizens were glad to have it cease.

By the early 1860's some sideshows came together under a manager who then purchased the privilege to exhibit in conjunction with a circus or menagerie. Joseph Cushing had the sideshow on the 1863 L.B. Lent Equescirriculum, one of the first railroad circuses. His show was conducted under a fifty-foot round top with every available spot on it covered with full length paintings.

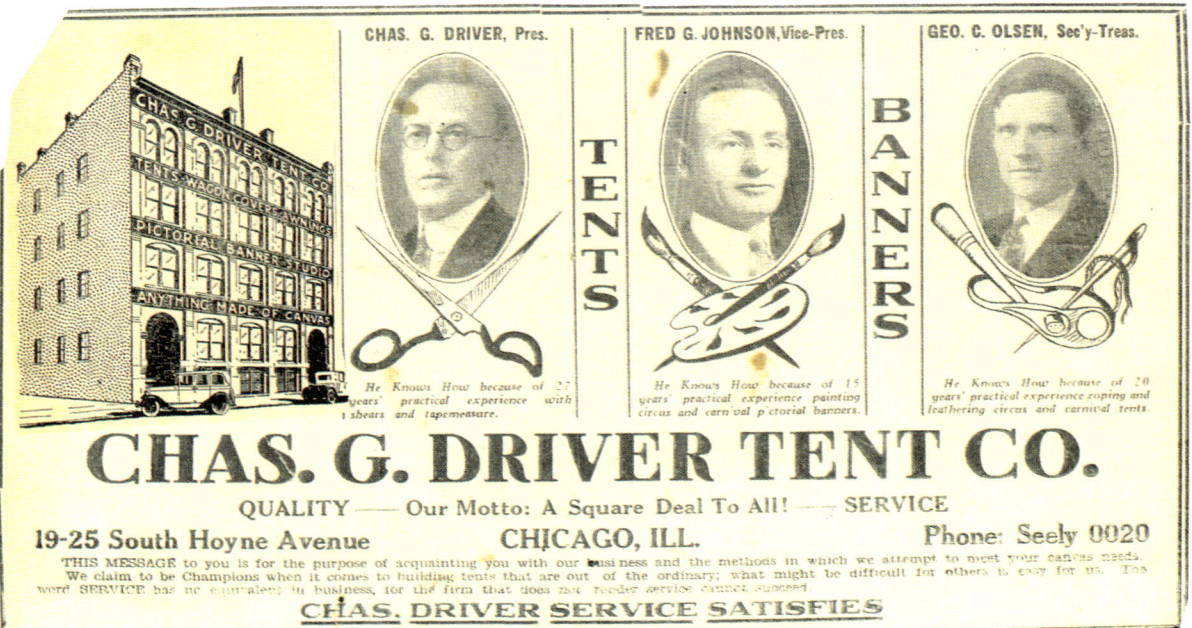

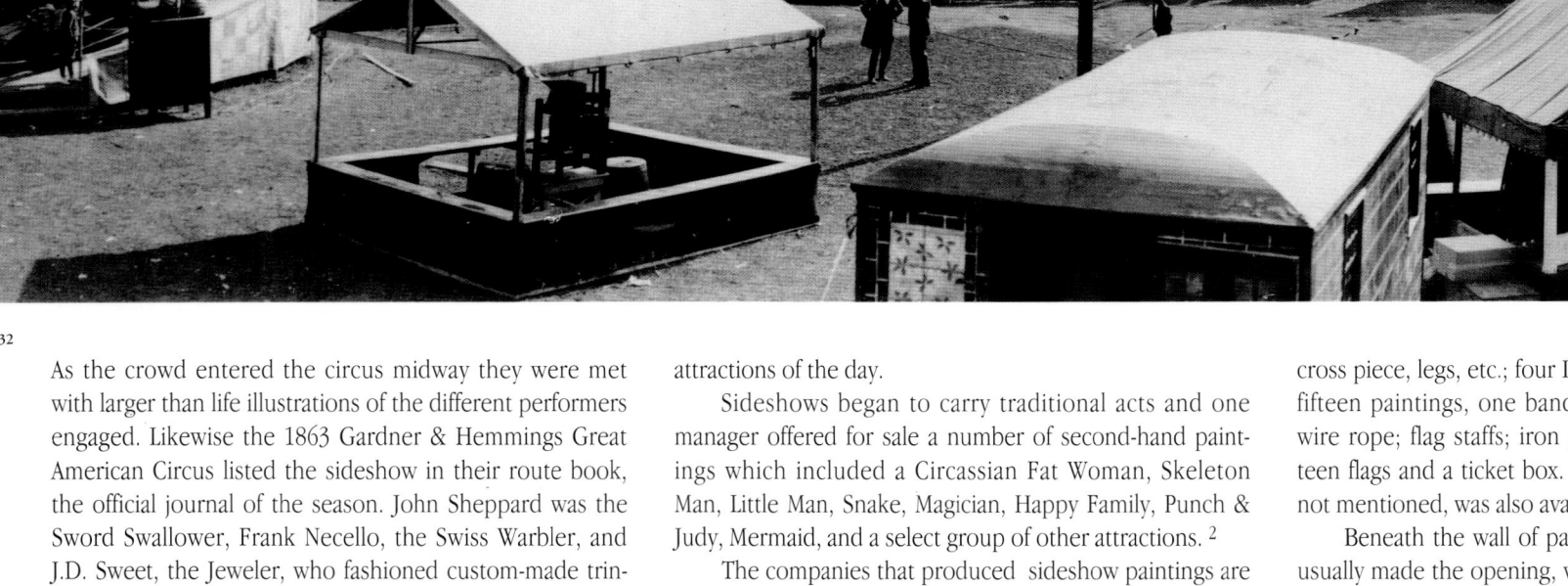

As the crowd entered the circus midway they were met with larger than life illustrations of the different performers engaged. Likewise the 1863 Gardner & Hemmings Great American Circus listed the sideshow in their route book, the official journal of the season. John Sheppard was the Sword Swallower, Frank Necello, the Swiss Warbler, and J.D. Sweet, the Jeweler, who fashioned custom-made trinkets for men and women. The whole was under the proprietorship of Henry Slaymaker, while Edward Dogget was the manager, assisted by M. Slaymaker.

Sideshow attractions in the 1870s began to note the artistic firms which provided them with paintings. In 1873 a sideshow consisting of a living alligator from five to six feet long, a collection of living snakes, and a nearly new canvas painting by BRUCE was offered for sale at $300.00. The firm of J. BRUCE, Show Painter from Williamsburg, New York was always prepared to do a limited number of first class paintings, as long as their terms of half cash in advance were met. Mr. Bruce advertised paintings of a bearded lady, a magician, and a lady snake charmer, the typical sideshow attractions of the day.

Sideshows began to carry traditional acts and one manager offered for sale a number of second-hand paintings which included a Circassian Fat Woman, Skeleton Man, Little Man, Snake, Magician, Happy Family, Punch & Judy, Mermaid, and a select group of other attractions. [2]

The companies that produced sideshow paintings are chronicled in the amusement world trade paper *The New York Clipper*. *The Clipper* noted in 1874 that the firm of JOHNSON & SMITH had left their Boston, MA address and it was presumed that they were no longer in business. Notes on the firm of TUCKER BROTHERS in New York City included the destruction of their old shop at 600 Broadway and the opening of their new quarters at no. 78 Walker Street, a few doors west of Broadway.

Many circuses owned their own sideshows, contracted performers for the season, and purchased sideshow paintings from established firms. In the 1888 auction of the Doris and Colvin Mammoth Show in St. Louis, MO, the sideshow property included the following: nine stages with cross piece, legs, etc.; four Inquisition cases; one Mermaid; fifteen paintings, one band stand; balancing pole; rope; wire rope; flag staffs; iron painting poles; tarpaulin; thirteen flags and a ticket box. A two-pole sideshow tent, size not mentioned, was also available.

Beneath the wall of paintings the sideshow manager usually made the opening, worked the crowd, and had the bands play a few numbers. Performers were brought out on the bally platform as a teaser, and the talker extolled their features—as presented on the paintings—claiming that everything was "alive and on the inside." The paintings were suspended from iron or wooden poles which were guyed out to stand up to a moderate breeze. They were aligned either in a straight line or slightly curved around the tent, with a break in the center for the customers to pass through. Some shows used double-decker paintings to flank the entry, to make the show appear larger than it really was, not unlike the "false front" architectural device used at the time.

Sideshow paintings could be purchased from a num-

firm of CLARENCE FAGG, since Stanton Tucker had joined that company. It was also stated that William T. Lee—for twenty-four-years America's greatest show painter—remained in charge of all work done by this firm. CHARLES WOLF & COMPANY Show Painters studio, located at No. 8 Second Street near the Bowery, surpassed the usual advertising come-ons such as "artistic" and "durable," stating instead "If you get any, get the best."

Circuses were the major market for sideshow paintings. Correspondence from the CLARENCE FAGG studio of Show Paintings & Pictorial Displays, Brooklyn, NY stated that the firm could not take on any new work due to the pending tenting season in March, 1902. They were extremely busy with show fronts for various sideshows, and being an honorable company, they did not overbook. However, if a streamer was requested it could be done quickly, as it consisted primarily of text, with very little pictorial work. As for paintings, "the field of assistance in this line is very very limited consequently we can do only a certain amount of work." [3] A month later the Fagg firm shipped one case containing a number of paintings to the Ringling Circus in Baraboo, WI, with a note about handling from Clarence Fagg:

I would suggest that when you receive them it would be best to have them unpacked at once and hung up or thrown over a tightly stretched rope, or let them lay in long smooth folds, the idea is not to crease them up too much when they are fresh.

At the turn of the century a new market for sideshow paintings appeared as the street carnival blossomed. Instead of being confined to one tent approximately forty-by-seventy-feet, the attractions of the carnival were spread out over several blocks. Each attraction found that it needed several paintings or canvas announcements to decorate their frontage.

Possibly because of the multiple text that was used on the street carnivals a new term was working its way into the sideshow vocabulary—banner. The term originally referred to a line of text which was painted on a flag or canvas. The term banner then evolved from narrative into graphic form, and referred to the painted canvas illustrations advertising sideshow acts. The resulting banners provided stimulus to the imagination through visual means, and no longer needed to be read, though text often clarified the exotic painted images.

Correspondence from the E.J. HAYDEN COMPANY Side Show Painters (established in 1894 and incorporated in 1906, Brooklyn, NY), indicates that they controlled a good part of the market, providing material for seven circuses and the Buffalo Bill Wild West Show in 1907. The Buffalo Bill Wild West account alone must have kept the HAYDEN firm busy, as it had twenty three different sideshow attractions, and a banner line featuring illustrations of Punch & Judy; Snake Charmer; Conjuror; Blue Man; Three-Legged Man; Moss Haired Lady; 2 Tattooed Men; Bearded Lady; Man with an Iron Skull; Japanese Jugglers; Comedy Sketch; Drum Major; Comedians; Physical Culture Girl; Elastic Skin & Giraffe Neck; Mind Reader; Scotch Piper & Polyphonist; Parisian Horse Lady; Fire Eater; Glass Blower; Musical Act; Song & Dance; and

ber of east coast firms in the 1890s. In New York City LAWRENCE W. SEAVEY of 138th Street claimed that his firm had been established in 1865. The studio of J.W. CRIDLAND offered sideshow paintings that were rich in color and had fine faces. TUCKER BROS. offered a number of paintings which were ten-by-twelve feet and eight-by-seventeen feet and included such subjects as Monks, Circassian Ladies, Demon Child, Double Children, Half Lady, Wild Man, and entrance paintings. The CHARLES M. WOLF & COMPANY offered sideshow paintings and museum displays. The firm of FRANK M. CHAMBERS advertised ten-by-twelve foot paintings for $15.00, eight-by ten-foot paintings for $12.00, and six-by-eight foot paintings for $10.00.

Philadelphia, PA was the home of the firm HAFNER BROTHERS who advertised that they were the largest show-painting studio in America, or so they claimed. The firm of HUMPHREYS offered bright colors and low prices, and they had some second hand paintings—trade-ins on new work—that were also inexpensive.

At the beginning of the tenting season in the spring, a number of shows wanted to start out with a fresh look. Such was the case with the Adam Forepaugh-Sells Brothers Circus in 1897. Their brand new sideshow had a two-hundred-sixteen foot front made up of eighteen double-deck banners painted by the TAYLOR company. The presentations consisted of McFarland's Man Eating Lion, Sultan, performed by Jennie Lee; Major Ray and wife, midgets; Colonel Cooper, giant; Chauncy Morlan and wife, fat people; George Karlavagn, tattooed man; Miss Clio, snake handler; John Carter, iron-skull man; Mlle. Jack, electric lady; Mlle. Corina, mind reader; Patsy Branigan, trained monkey; W.H. McFarland and wife, Mexican knife throwers; South Sea Island Joe and wife; La Fayette Harrington, magician and lecturer; and Shine, wild man.

The sideshow business is by nature itinerant and subject to change, and like other businesses, it was affected by illness and/or friction amongst personnel, the expiration of performers' contracts, and other fluctuations in its makeup. In 1897 W.H. Yearns, a magician and ventriloquist,

joined Colorado Charley's Circus and Wild West show, along with the musical duo of Leis & Campbell. The manager, Colonel F.W. Porter, went to Baltimore with four new double decker paintings for the sideshow. In the summer of 1897 Gus Lambrigger's Museum of Living Curiosities, Collection of Reptiles and Concert Company experienced a major face lift with new advertising material, new paintings, and new posters. They incorporated new acts, such as Major Charles Gantz, miniature man; Harry Jones, living skeleton; Mrs. Wallace, impalement act and juggling; Professor Sill A. Paris, comedian and musical moke; with F.W. Wallace giving the openings and lecturing.

In the late 1890s a number of New York sideshow painting firms expanded and became the main suppliers of graphic imagery to the bigger circuses. The A.W. MILLARD COMPANY announced a break from the TUCKER BROTHERS COMPANY and advertised that they were the creators of the brightest, best and most effective Paintings, Side Show Fronts, Museum Displays, or scenery. TUCKER BROTHER Show Paintings were reportedly made by the

Vocalist Eccentric.[4] What a line up for a quarter of a dollar!

During the 1920s the large canvas suppliers such as Chicago firms of DRIVER BROTHERS and NEUMAN TENT & AWNING provided banners to various shows as part of their tent and canvas needs, expanding the parameters of the sideshow banner world even further. Competition was keen between the two firms to keep their artists working.[5]

In December 1927 Mr. Edward Neumann (whose studio was located at 120 North Ann Street, Chicago) wrote a follow up letter to Mr. Peter Staunton, sideshow manager of the Hagenbeck-Wallace Circus of Peru, Indiana, attempting to solicit business for new banners. He was still able to quote the price of $48.00 for a twelve-by-twenty-foot double-decker banner, and for an additional $1.50, a rope could either be sewn or run through rings across the back. Neumann was in a position to start the banners for prompt delivery.

Mr. Staunton had already made contacts with a number of sideshow performers. One performer, Mr. Rex Karson, who did a novelty escape act, sent back his signed contract with a photo and $10.00 deposit for his banner. His money order was made payable to the Hagenbeck-Wallace Circus—a guarantee that he would be there in the spring when the show opened. After his money order and contract arrived, Mr. Karson's banner was ordered.

The DRIVER TENT COMPANY (19 to 25 South Hoyne Ave., Chicago) did indeed provide the Hagenbeck-Wallace Circus sideshow with twelve-by-twenty-foot banners for $48.50 each. The performers were J.E. Burton, Midget; Jessie Franks, Bag Puncher; Jolly Babe, Fat Woman; Mickey Mansion, Tattoo Man; Jimmy Logue, Juggler; The Klein Albino Family; Princess Aurora's Snakes; Madame Virginia, Fortune Teller; The Hassen Troupe, Mystic Hula Hula Dancers and Musicians; Professor Sarony; Punch & Judy; and an Impalement Act by Clemens. This array of carnival art was shipped in a two-week period and flew on the Hagenbeck-Wallace Circus midway when they opened under canvas in Cincinnati, Ohio, April 23.

Prior to the 1900s canvas paintings were considered to be in the class of the higher arts, but after the turn of the century, sideshow 'banners' began to appear, expanding the genre of painted canvas surfaces beyond the academic realm. Banner artwork became more illusionistic—fiction on canvas—rather than depictions of reality. Artists produced fanciful illusions of almost every subject, at the same time proclaiming that their attractions were ALIVE AND ON THE INSIDE...

The history of sideshow banners is complex, and this overview of sideshow paintings and the firms that produced them is by no means complete. There are many more firms and artists whose works need to be chronicled to enhance our understanding of this significant aspect of American culture.

NOTES:

1. Bucyrus Journal, Bucyrus, Ohio. May 28, 1858.

2. New York Clipper, New York. July 4, 1874.

3. Clarence Fagg to Al Conlon, March 11, 1902. Prening Collection.

4. Charles E. Griffin, Four Years in Europe with Buffalo Bill, (Albia, Iowa: Stage Publishing Co., 1908).

5. For additional information about Chicago Tent and Awning Company and sideshow banner history in Chicago see "The Cunning Crafters of Dreams" by Johnny Meah, and "Memorial to the Milestones" by Glen C. Davies in this book.

GLASS BLOWERS

38

ONLY 3 LEGGED FOOTBALL PLAYER
IN THE WORLD!
ALIVE
MILLARD & BULSTERBAUM
2894 W8 St Coney Island N.Y

40

41

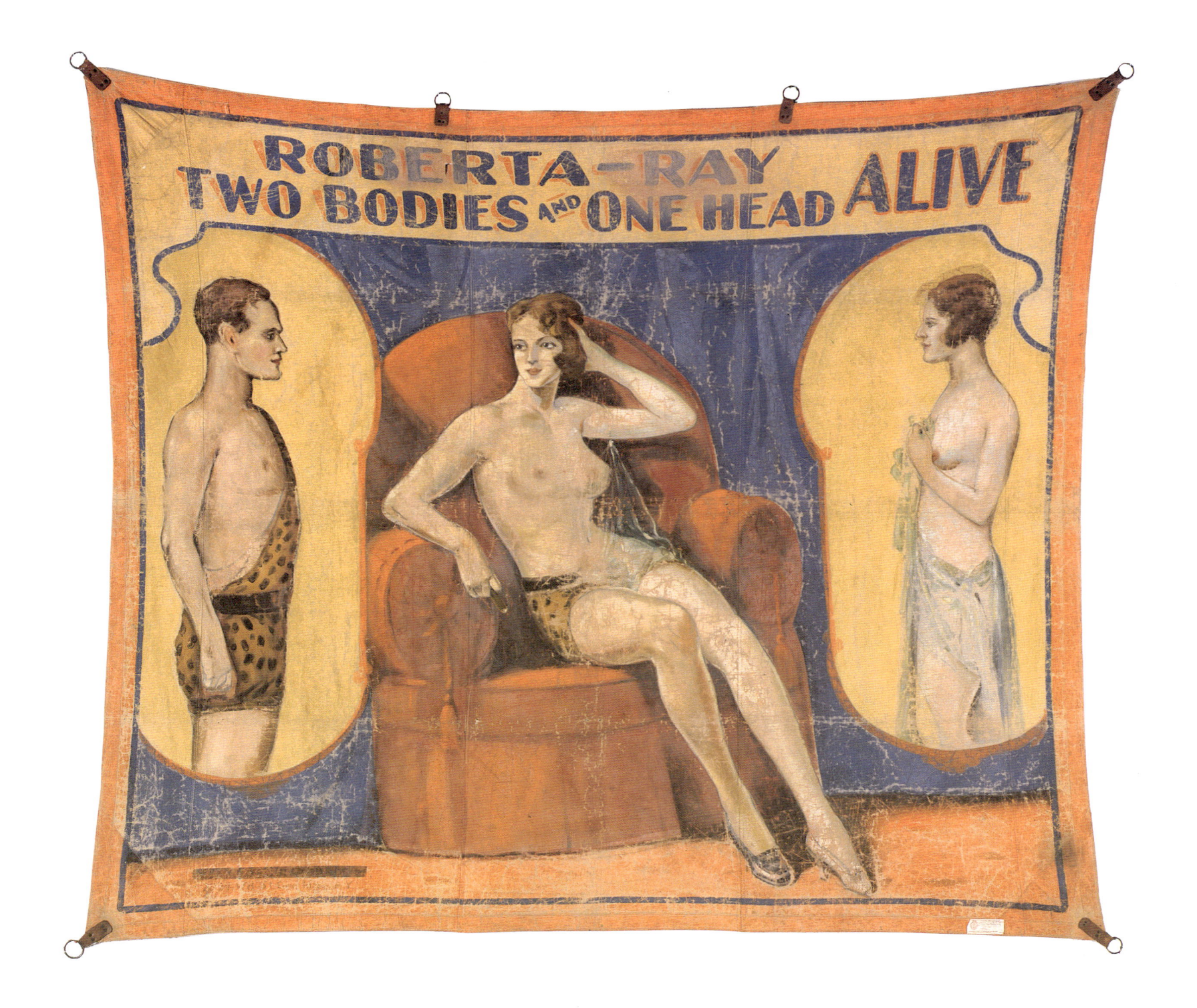

42

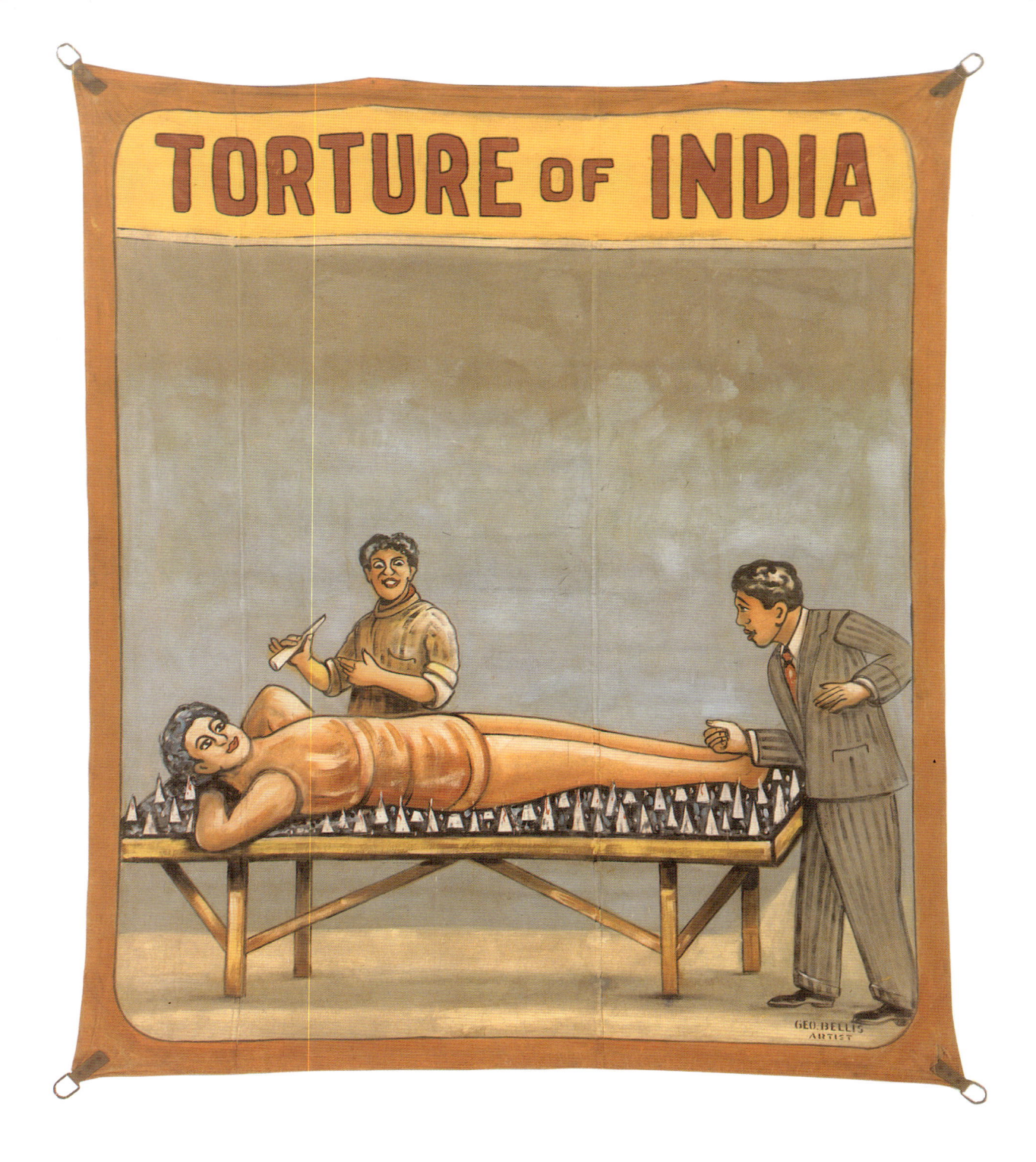

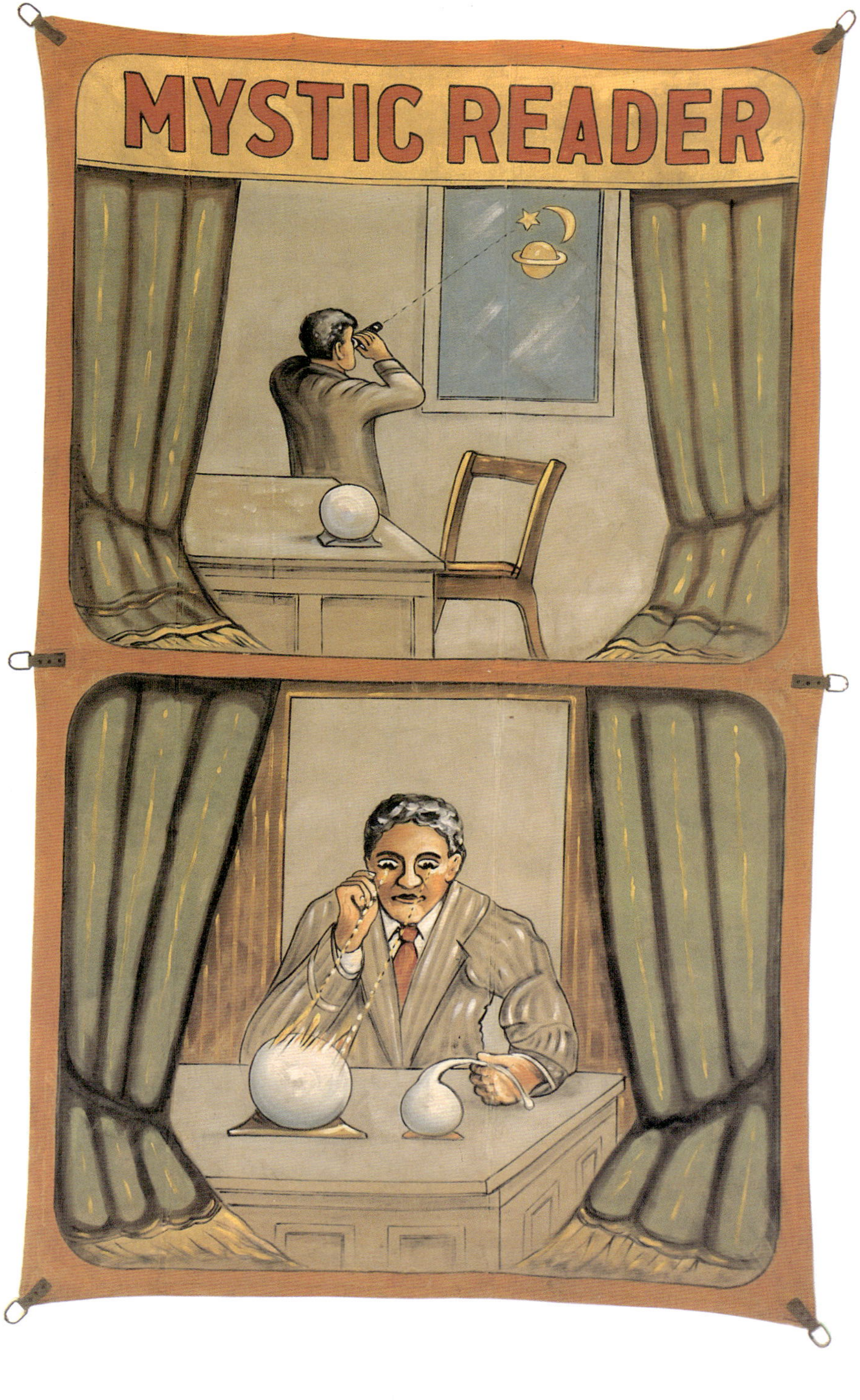
MYSTIC READER

44

45

46

Cunning Crafters of Dreams

— Johnny Meah

1.

There have been many banner painters over the years. Despite the fact that a good portion of them were reasonably proficient artists, few were outstanding and even fewer could be classified as unique. Fred Johnson and Snap Wyatt were unique. Danny Cassella, although somewhat obscure due to lack of national exposure, (his work was almost exclusively for New York's Coney Island), was also unique.

Each of these artists had a distinctive style. My favorite was Cassella. His work bordered fine art, with subtley graduated wet blends and minimal hard lining. Next was Johnson, who managed to create an aura of weirdness approaching the ominous with curious color combinations and lavish brushstrokes. Wyatt's strongest suite was speed. He created tons of banners over the years using a bold cartoonical style. Although lacking Cassella's muted blends or Johnson's eye-catching composition, they were still unique in their own brash way.

Interestingly enough, my awareness of these three men came in the same order that I've just described them. Even more interesting, my least favorite artisticly, Wyatt, was directly responsible for my own early emergance as a banner painter.

It wasn't as though I'd never seen pictorial banners before. Connecticut in the 40's hosted many traveling circuses and carnivals, all of which displayed these colorful advertisments. That June night in New Britain, Conn., however, was the first time I ever saw them in a way that would eventualy guide the direction my life would take.

I not only saw them, I drank them in huge gulps, savored them as though I was satisfying a hunger that I was hitherto unaware of. The banners

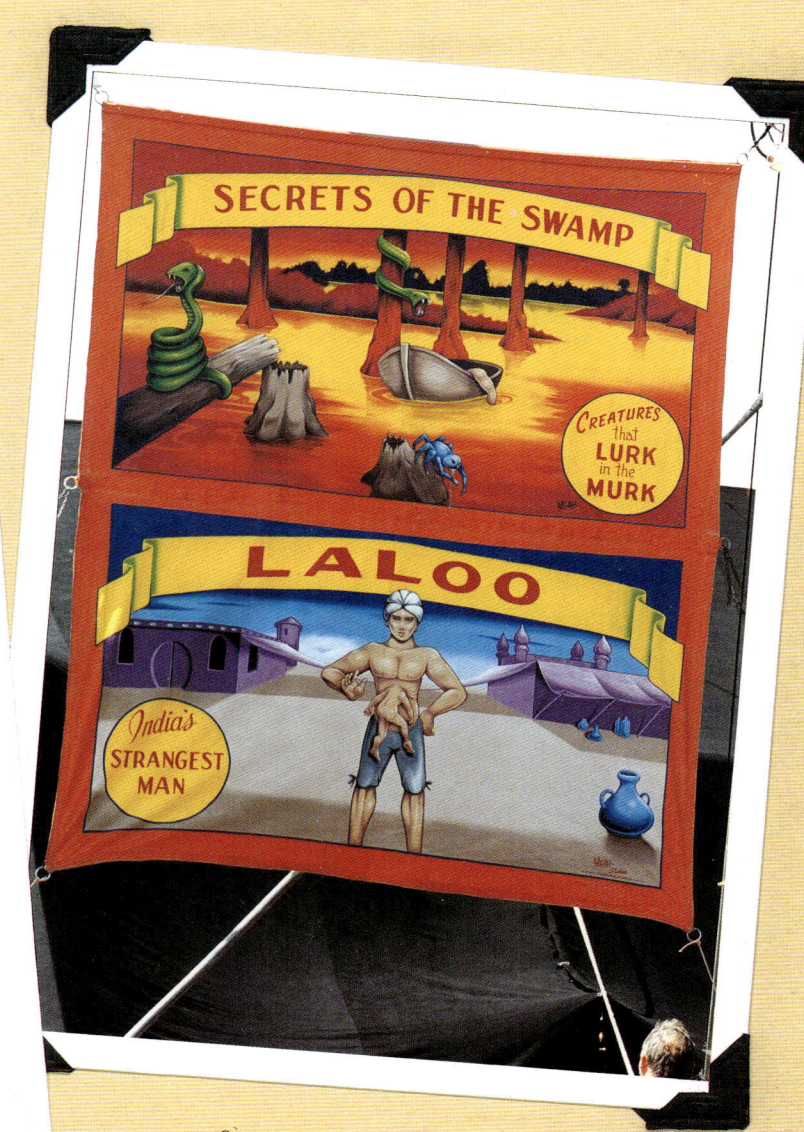

One of nine banners painted by Johnny Meah for the C.M. Christ and Ward Hall Show, Georgia State Fair, Georgia, 1994

②

WERE PAINTED BY FRED JOHNSON. HIS NAME APPEARED OVER A STENCIL IN THE LOWER RIGHT CORNER PROCLAIMING THAT THEY WERE MADE BY THE O. HENRY TENT AND AWNING CO. OF CHICAGO, ILLINOIS. THEY HUNG IN FRONT OF WHITEY SUTTON'S SIDESHOW, TOURING THAT YEAR WITH THE JAMES E. STRATES SHOWS, AN ENORMOUS RAILROAD CARNIVAL.

EARLIER THAT YEAR I HAD BECOME AWARE OF DANNY CASSELLA VIA AN ARTICLE WRITTEN ABOUT HIM IN THE NEW YORK HERALD TRIBUNE. TITLED, "HE GLAMORIZES THE FREAKS AT CONEY", THE STORY WAS ACCOMPANIED BY A PHOTO OF A BANNER DEPICTING, "BOBBY THE BOY WITH THE REVOLVING HEAD", ACTUALLY A MAN NAMED LAURELLO WHO HAD THE ABILITY TO DISLOCATE VARIOUS VERTEBRA AND TURN HIS HEAD AROUND FACING BACKWARD. (TO ADD A FOOTNOTE OF SIDESHOW TRIVIA, IN THE TITLING OF BANNERS, MEN WERE ALWAYS "BOYS" AND WOMEN WERE ALWAYS "GIRLS" REGARDLESS OF THEIR ACTUAL AGE. ONE ATTRACTION, A MAN WHO HAD PECULIAR LITTLE ARMS AND LEGS AND, AT AGE FIFTY, WORKED AS "THE FROG BOY", WAS REGRESSED TO INFANCY BY ARTISTS CASHING IN ON THE THOLIDOMIDE PANIC AND RE-TITLED "THE WONDER DRUG BABY").

CASSELLA WAS PROBABLY THE LAST NOTE-WORTHY ARTIST EMPLOYED BY MILLARD AND BLUSTERBAUM, A PICTORIAL STUDIO THAT SERVICED, AMONG OTHER CLIENTS, THE SIDESHOW OPERATORS OF CONEY ISLAND. A NUMBER OF ARTISTS PASSED THROUGH THE MILLARD AND BLUSTERBAUM ART MILL, INCLUDING JOHNSON AND WYATT. BESIDES PORTRAYING PINHEADS AND PENGUIN BOYS, THE TALENTED HANDS OF THAT COMPANY ALL TOOK TURNS AT RENDERING THE GIANT MUSTARD AND PICKLE RELISH FESTOONED HOTDOGS OF "NATHAN'S FAMOUS", A CONEY LEGEND THAT STILL ENDURES.

AS CLOSELY AS I CAN RECALL, SNAP WYATT, OR MY AWARENESS OF HIS WORK, CAME A YEAR OR TWO BEYOND THE CASSELLA/JOHNSON EXPERIENCE. MUCH LIKE THE OTHER TWO INDIVIDUALS, THAT AWARENESS WAS THE RESULT OF

Top: Popeye banner by Johnny Meah, Photo: Krannert Art Museum
Bottom: Popeye at Riverview Amusement Park, Photo: Tom Palazzolo

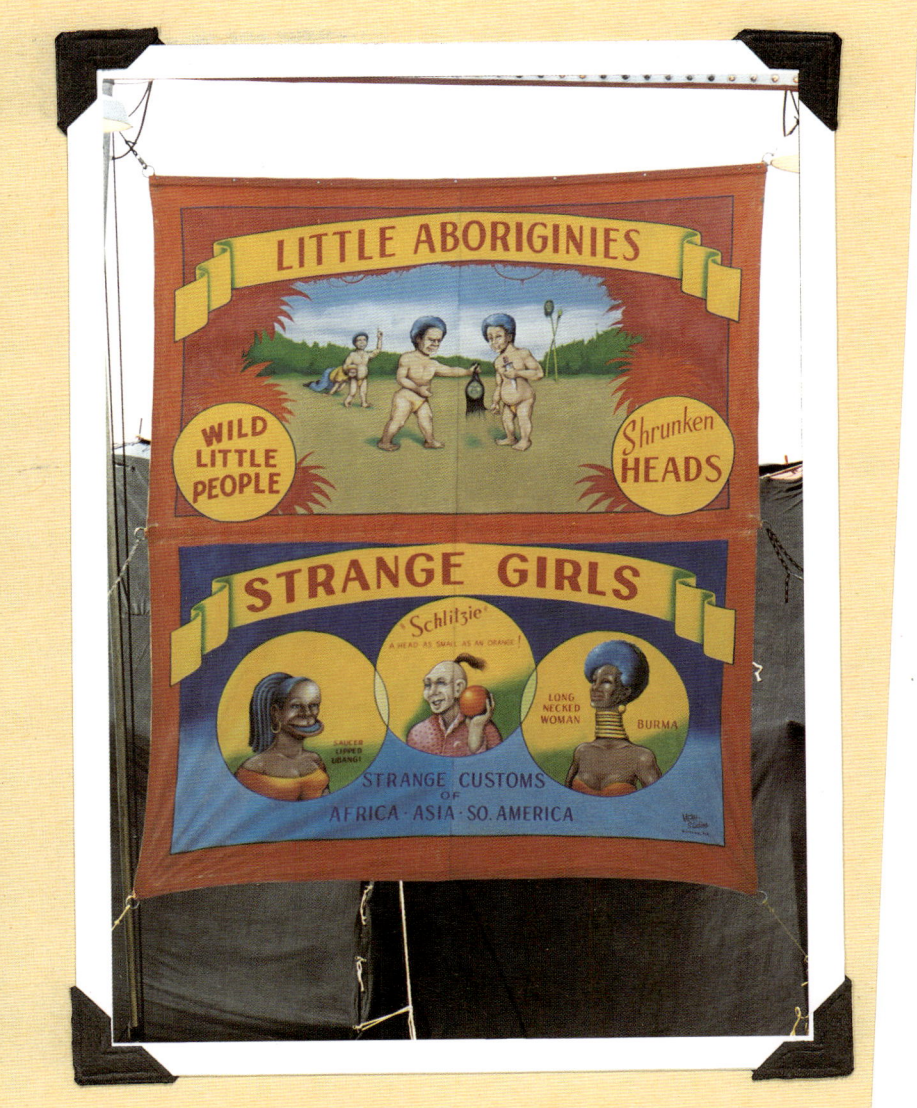

C.M. Christ and Ward Hall Show,
Georgia State Fair, Georgia, 1994

(3.)

FIRST SEEING HIS WORK ON VARIOUS SHOW BANNERLINES. (AS ANOTHER QUICK SIDE TRIP, WYATT'S FIRST NAME WAS DAVID, THE NICKNAME, "SNAP," CAME FROM SIGN SHOP VENACULAR. WHEN A HUNGRY SIGN PAINTER HITS THE HIGHWAY GRABBING WHATEVER WORK IS AVAILABLE IT'S KNOWN AS "SNAPPING SIGNS". EVIDENTLY WYATT DID ENOUGH ITINERATE WORK TO EARN HIM THE TITLE THAT WOULD, FOR MOST OF HIS LIFE, REPLACE THE NAME ON HIS BIRTH CERTIFICATE.)

IN 1956 I WAS, FOR A BRIEF PERIOD OF TIME, PERFORMING WITH LEOLA'S SIDESHOW ON THE ROSS MANNING SHOWS CARNIVAL. "LEOLA," (ACTUALY HOMER TRACY, A FEMALE IMPERSONATOR WHO WORKED AS "LEO-LEOLA, HALF MAN, HALF WOMAN") WAS A "SUITCASE OPERATOR" WHO MANAGED THE CARNIVAL-OWNED SIDESHOW. EACH YEAR THE CARNIVAL OWNER WOULD BUY A NEW SET OF BANNERS, A RATHER MINOR EXPENDITURE IN THOSE DAYS. APPARENTLY CHICKENS WERE PRETTY SCARCE IN THE MANNING CAMP THAT YEAR, SO WHEN LEOLA DISCOVERED THAT, BESIDE MY REPITOIRE OF ACTS, I PAINTED, SHE SET ME TO TOUCHING UP THE PREVIOUS YEAR'S BANNERS. THEY WERE WYATT PIECES AND I APPROACHED THE PROJECT WITH THE MIXTURE OF REVERANCE AND TREPIDATION ONE MIGHT EXPECT FROM AN ART RESTORER AT THE LOUVE. MY OWN ARTWORK WAS STILL IN IT'S FORMATIVE STAGES AND MOST OF MY PAINTING AT THAT POINT WAS SIGN LETTERING. LEOLA, HOWEVER, EXPRESSED GREAT DELIGHT WITH THE WORK — DUE LARGELY, I SUSPECT, TO THE FACT THAT IT COST HER NOTHING. THERE WERE ELEVEN BANNERS IN ALL AND WHEN COMPLETED SHE ASKED ME IF I'D DESIGN A SET OF "FAT SHOW" BANNERS FOR A SECOND, SMALLER SHOW THAT WOULD FEATURE — WHAT ELSE — A FAT MAN.

ALTHOUGH THE THOUGHT OF PAINTING A BANNER OF MY OWN SCARED THE DAYLIGHTS OUT OF ME, DRAWING THEM WAS AN EASY ASIGNMENT. I TURNED OUT WHAT WAS TO BE MY VERY FIRST SET OF SCALE DRAWINGS FOR BANNERS IN AN AFTERNOON AND PRESENTED THEM TO LEOLA WHO WAS — ONCE AGAIN — BOTH DELIGHTED AND FINANCIALLY UNENCUMBERED.

④

Leola told me that she was sending the drawings to Snap Wyatt to be transformed into banners. I personally regarded this as submitting my humble scratchings to God for his approval. I seem to recall that, for a fleeting moment, I had an urge to say, "Why don't you let ME paint them?", but the words never quite made it out of my mouth, attributable to my common sense winning a quick one-rounder with my ego.

The following week a letter came from Wyatt accepting the banner order and heaping praise on the artist who'd done the drawings. I was hooked. The Grand Poobah of Painted Peculiarities had praised my work!

Shortly after receiving Snap Wyatt's letter I left Leola's show and joined a small circus where I remained to the close of that season. Although I was unaware of it, the new fat show banners never made it to Leola's hands; for that matter, the fat man never showed up either. In the spring of 1957 I rejoined Leola in Kingstree, South Carolina, where the Manning show was wintering in a tobacco warehouse. According to Leola, the banners that Wyatt had painted the previous year languished on some Railroad Express platform for lack of payment and were, subsequently, returned to Wyatt who peddled them to another operator. "What a shame," I told Leola, "I would have liked to have seen my drawings produced as banners." "Ah, but you will," the sideshow operator replied, "you're going to paint me new ones," at which point Leola produced a set of raw canvas blanks! So began my career as a banner painter. Come to think of it, I didn't get paid that time either.

The Great Johnny Meah
Georgia State Fair, Perry, Georgia 1994

51

Left: Fred G. Johnsonm painting top half of a clown front in his Chicago studio
Right: Photo of House of Mirrors at the 1970 Illinois State Fair, Springfield

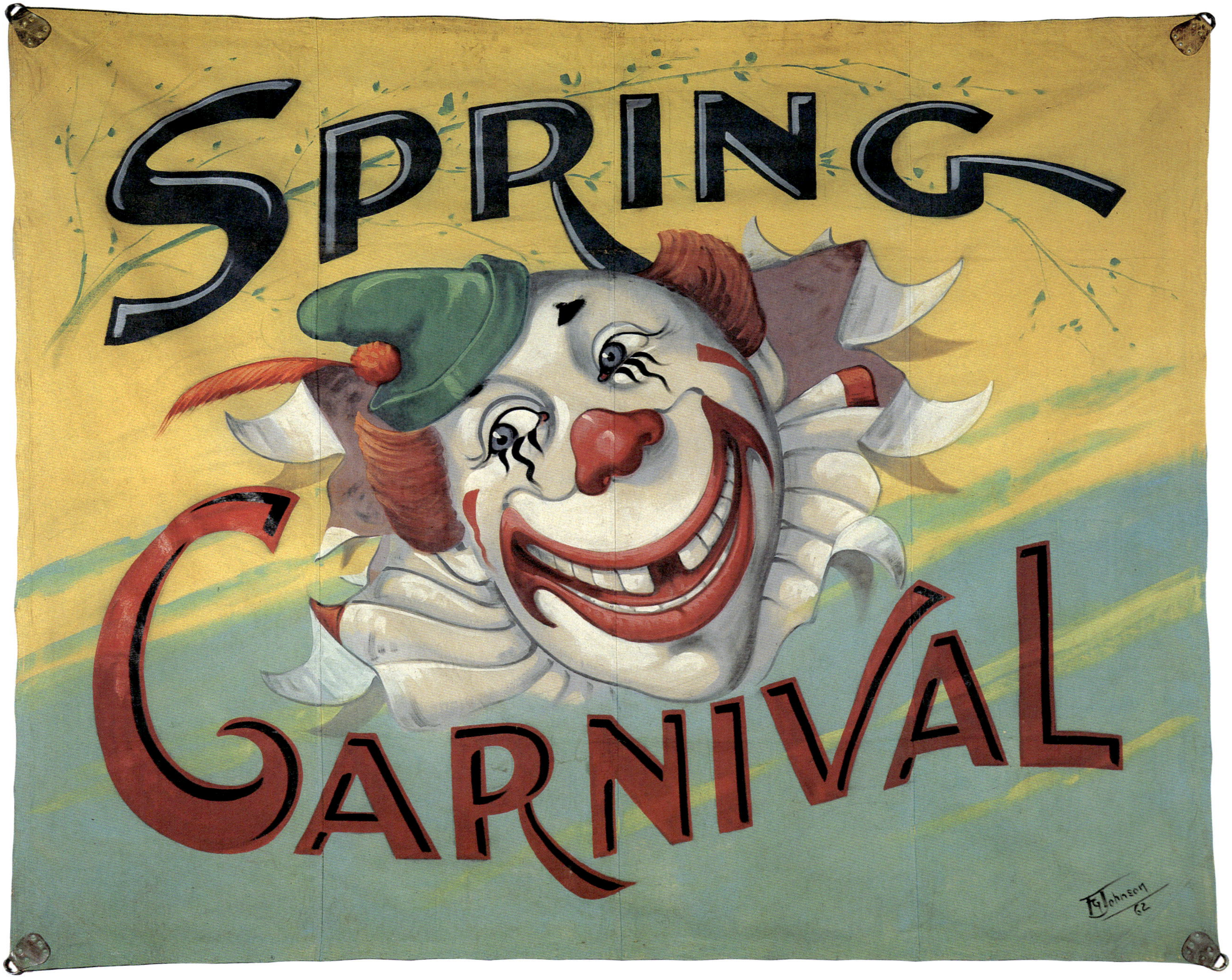
SPRING
CARNIVAL

54

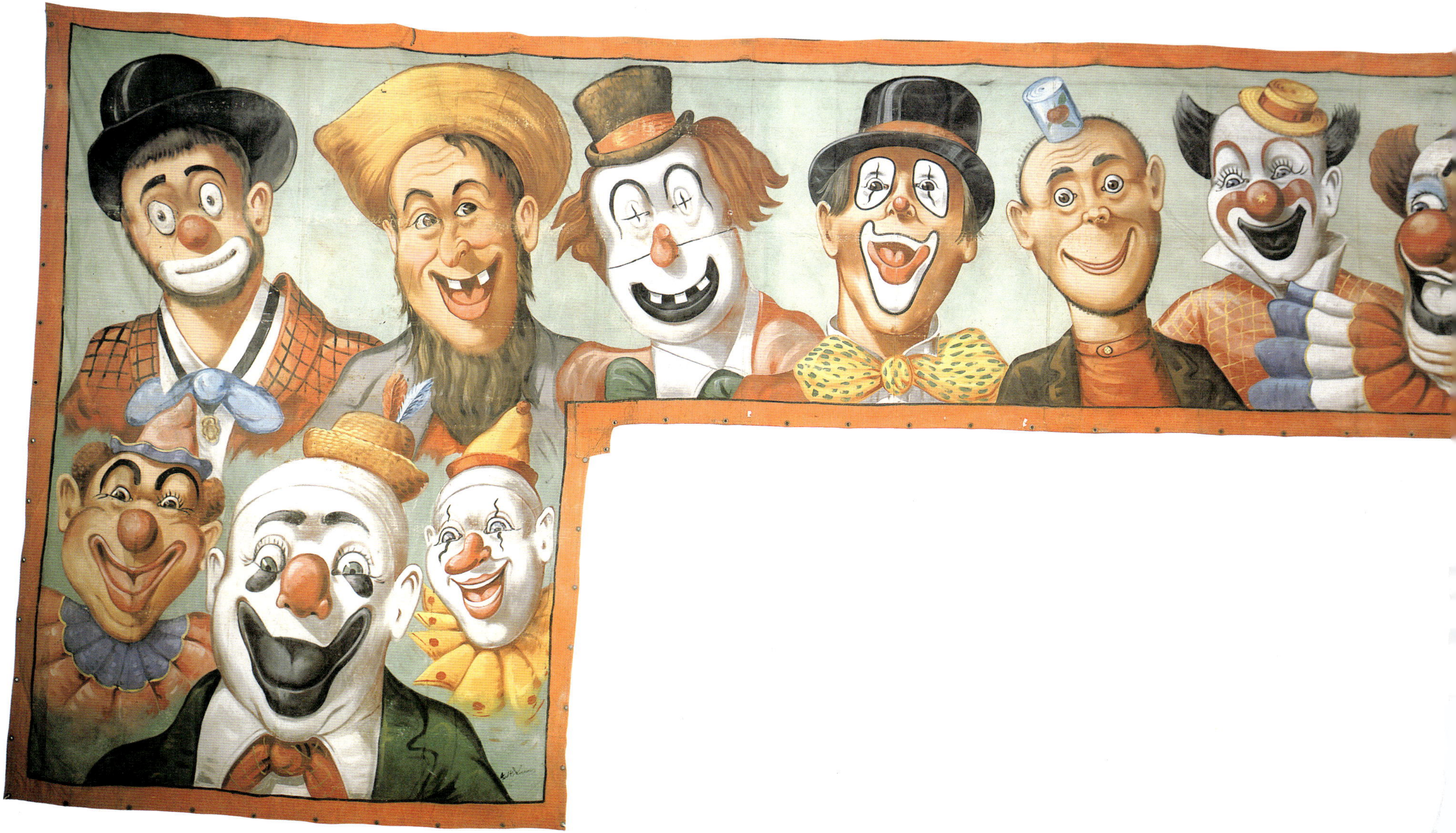

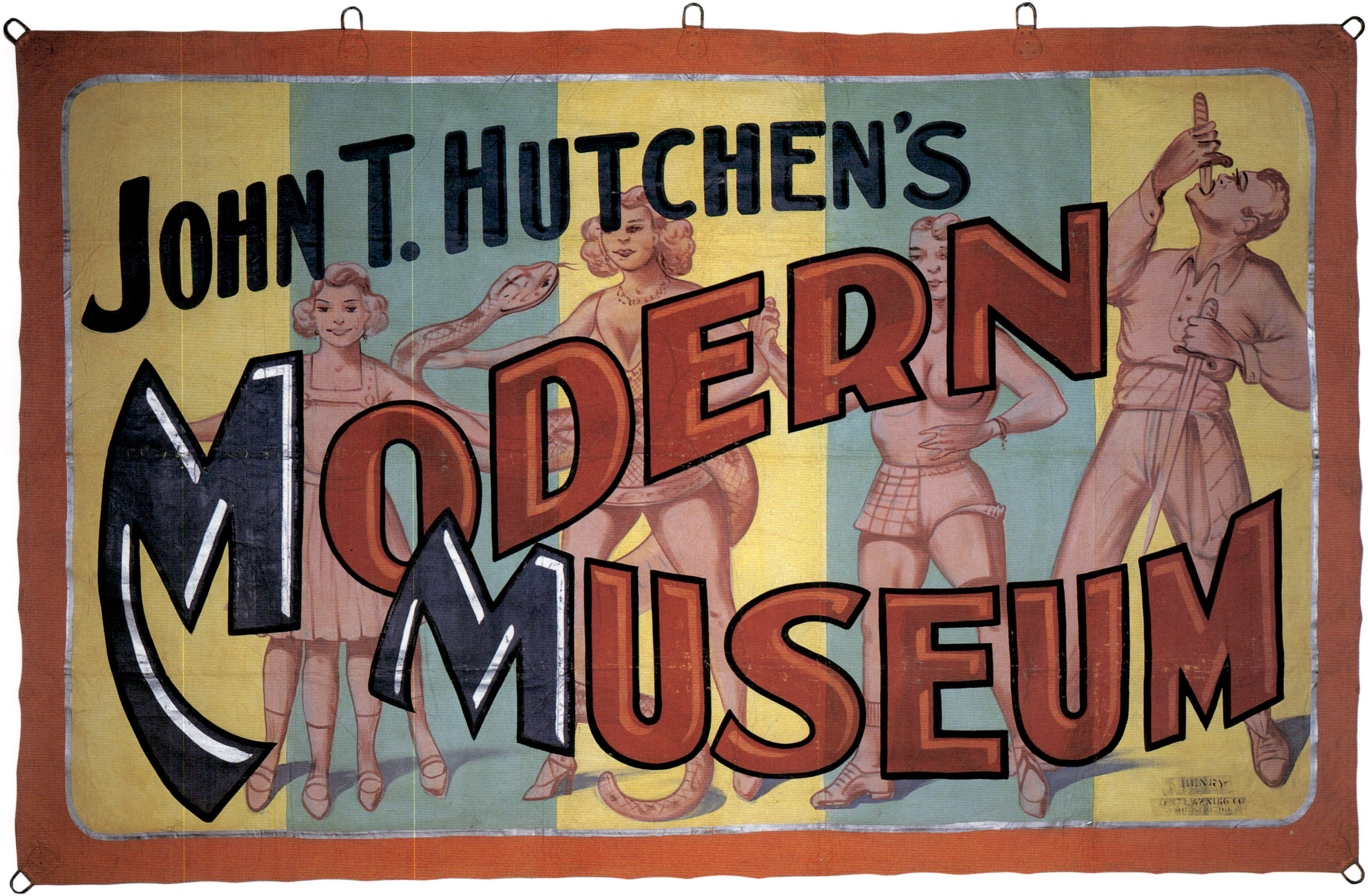
JOHN T. HUTCHEN'S
MODERN
MUSEUM

MYSTERY BOY
ROBERTO RUSSO
O. HENRY TENT & AWNING Co.
CHICAGO. 45 - ILL.

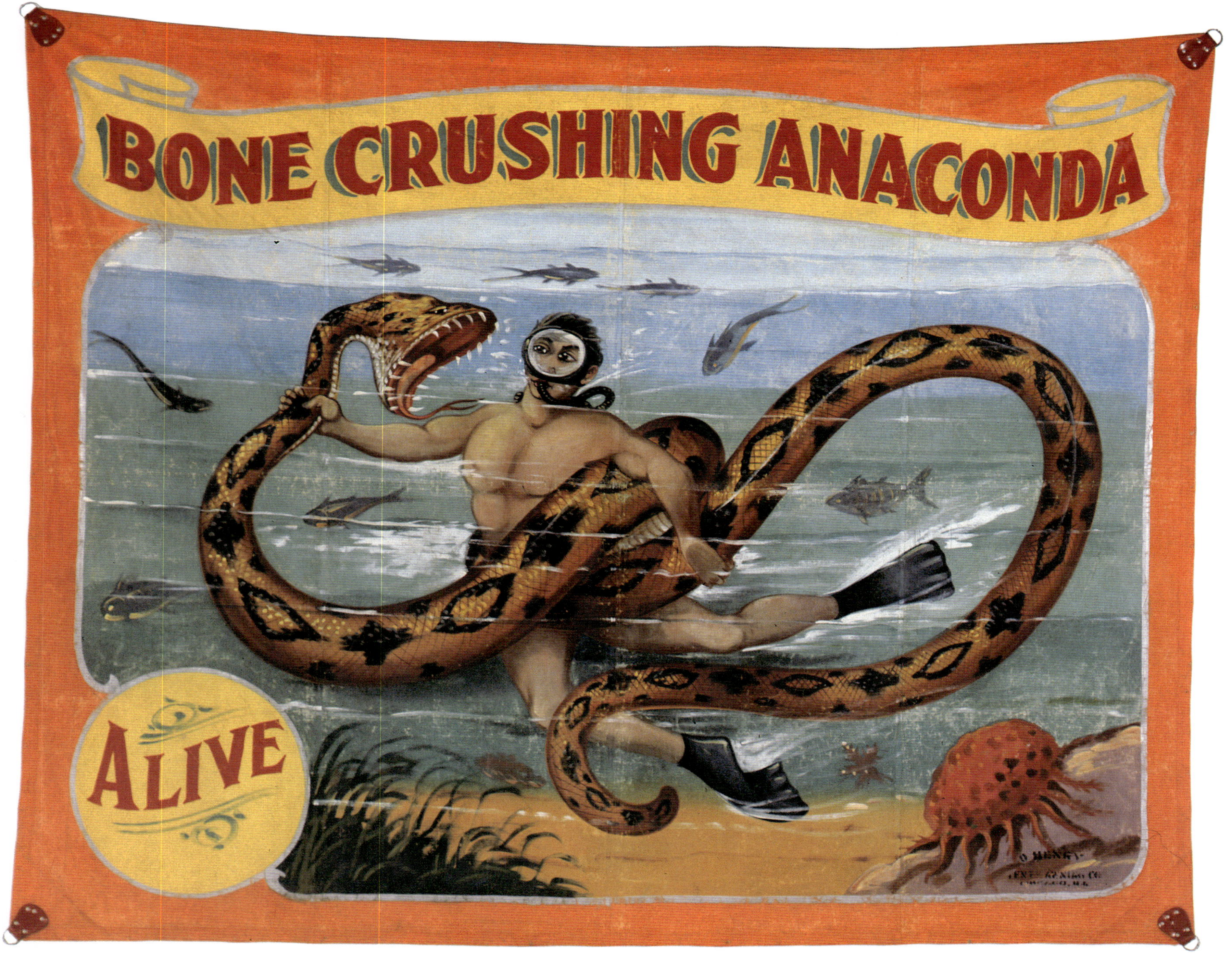
BONE CRUSHING ANACONDA
ALIVE

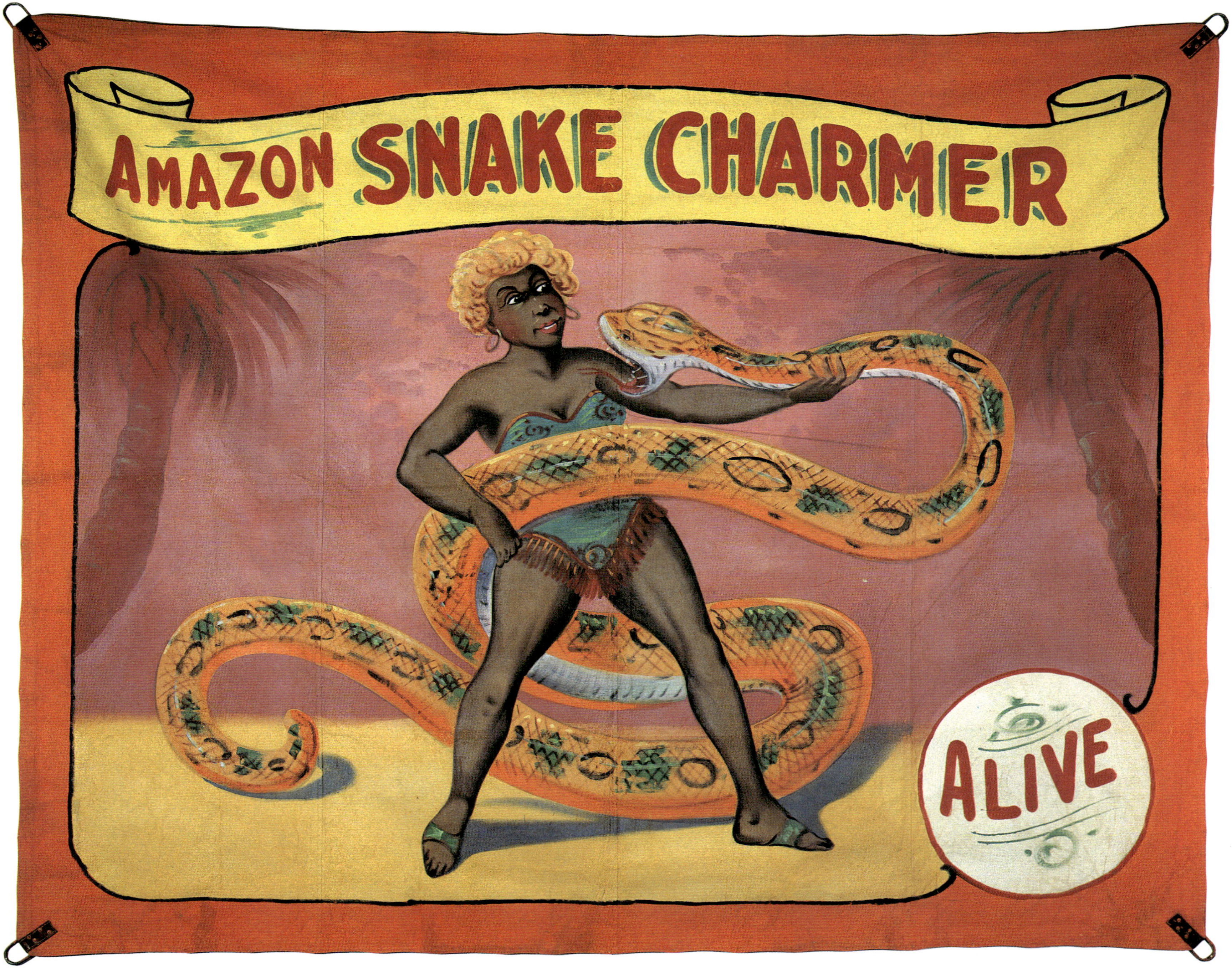
AMAZON SNAKE CHARMER
ALIVE

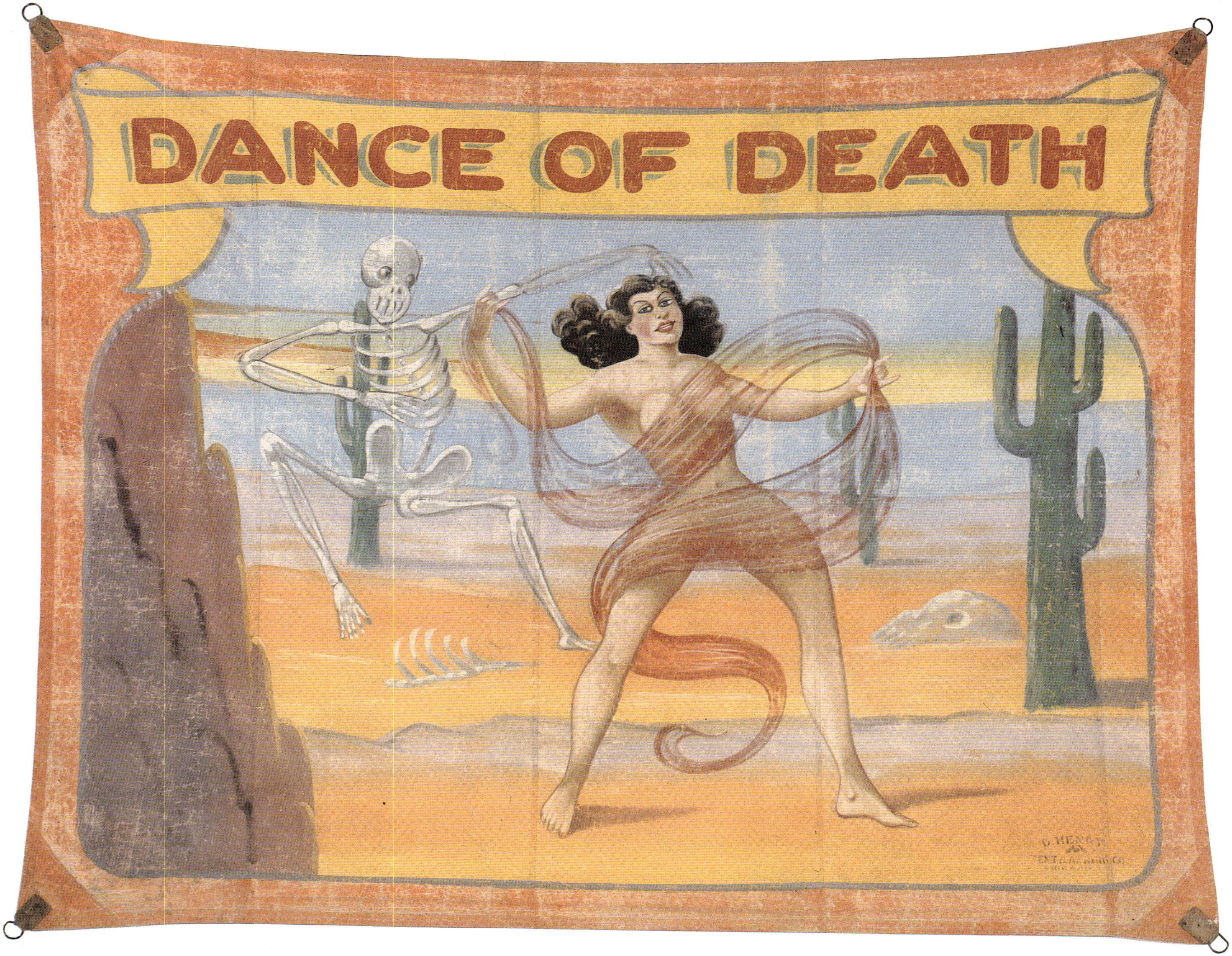
DANCE OF DEATH
O. HENRY

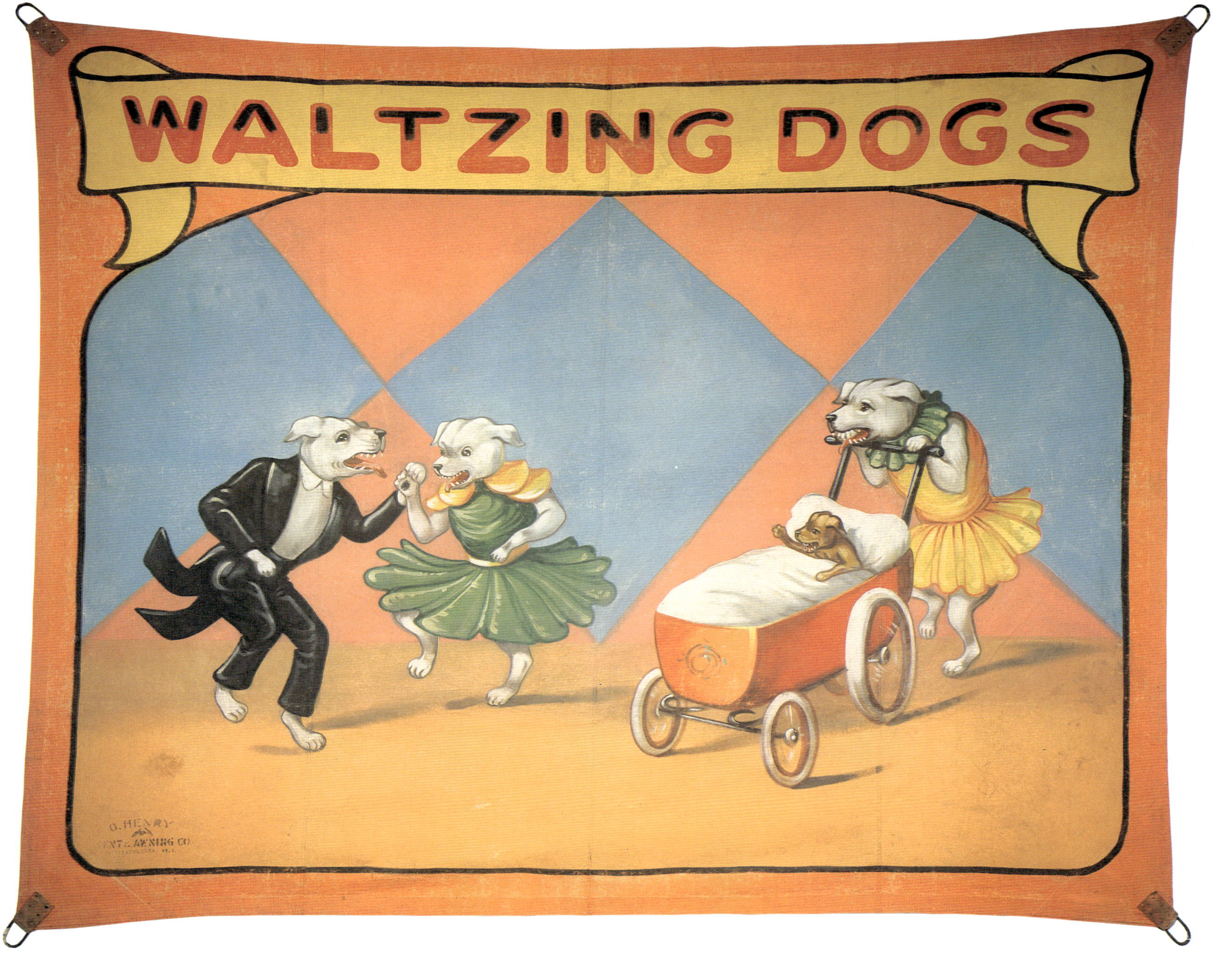
WALTZING DOGS
O. HENRY

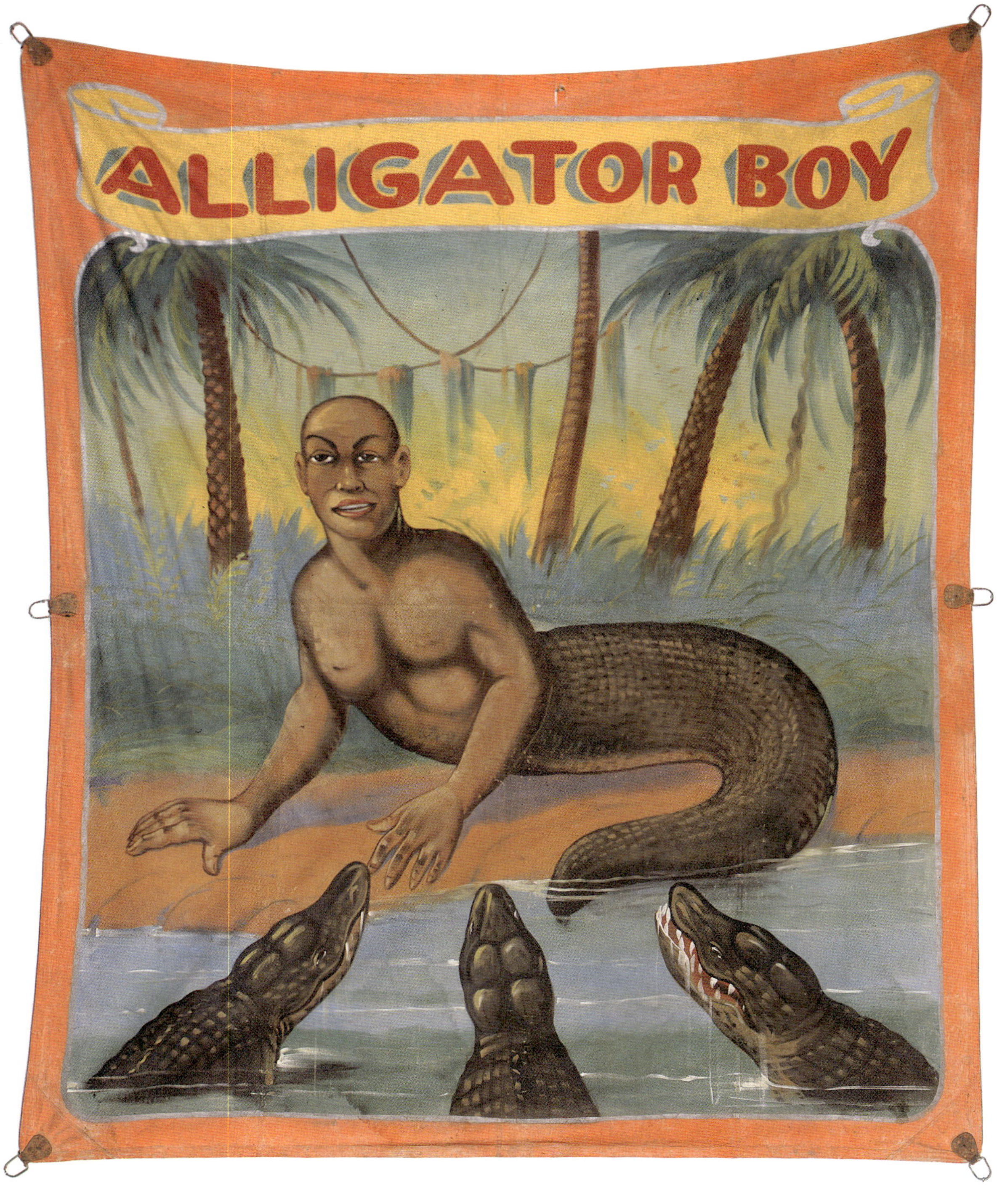
ALLIGATOR BOY

MEMORIAL to the MILESTONES

Glen C. Davies

The influences of flash, flim-flam, and fantasy were deeply rooted in my suburban Chicago upbringing in the 1950s. My father, Paul Davies, was a commercial artist and entrepreneur whose love of opera, comedy, costumes, and makeup inspired my eventual obsession with theatrics, monsters and the macabre. Some of my first memories involved our family visits to museums and my father's morbid enthusiasm for all things sensational or grotesque. While doing freelance work for a Chicago novelty company, he designed packaging and illustrations for such classic gag items as "Phoney Hypo" and "Whoops," the imitation vomit. Further encouraged by film, television and a steady diet of reading satire, comic books, and monster magazines, I was primed for anything shocking, exaggerated or unusual.

Each summer my family made its pilgrimage to Riverview Park, Chicago's now defunct amusement mecca. Although I loved the rides, my fondest recollections center around the old Riverview sideshow. There was an intangible aura of societal taboo and mystery that pervaded this venerable "institution of the odd." The appeal for me seemed rooted in my heart. I perceived that the sideshow personnel not only revealed their vulnerabilities and unusual physical attributes, but did so openly, with bravado and a sense of humor. I would watch in awe as the "show talker" executed a masterful rendition of the "blue plate special," a crowd-puller, audience participation gimmick guaranteed to "turn the tip." Inside I had my first glimpses of the Alligator Skinned Girl, Human Pincushion, and Rubber Skinned Man.

Crawfish Boy was featured as the "blow-off," an extra attraction requiring a silver coin and direct exit to the midway. Crawfish Boy was born with a crippling skeletal deformity that curved his bones and stunted his physical development. The Alligator Girl was born with ichthyosis, a medical condition that left all of her skin covered in leather-like scales. With few options available for these people other than a life behind closed doors or institutionalization, the circus or carnival sideshow offered a fraternity of fellow outsiders. This carnival community provided protection and control over their lives and destinies.

Tacked to the plywood walls of this Palace of Wonders were the first banners I had the pleasure of viewing. Snap Wyatt was the banner artist. I was stunned by the fantastic color and obviously exaggerated content in his art work. As a fledgling artist, I remember thinking that here might be a line of work that could combine two of my greatest interests: the world of art and the world of the carnival. This exposure left an indelible impression on me and helped to solidify my link between fine art and showmanship.

When I grew older I began to see a link that artists forged between the real and the imaginary. Banners were a strange fusion between these worlds. On one hand they advertised a real (usually), living (often), attraction, but the context of the painted canvas facade took a giant step toward a kind of spiritual, almost regal world of fantasy. The combination of sideshow reality and overstated banner content created a mixture that made the experience complete and meaningful to me.

Main Entrance to Riverview Park, Roscoe and Western, Chicago

By the time I began attending the School of the Art Institute of Chicago in 1968, I was an affirmed sideshow devotee. This interest was developed by teachers such as Ray Yoshida and Mary McCarty who encouraged the use of unique Chicago institutions as inspirational art resources. The Field Museum of Natural History, Oriental Institute, Chinatown, and Maxwell Street Market figured significantly as great spots to draw from and experience life. South State Street, with its burlesque theatres, penny arcades, and flop houses was only a couple of blocks from the school and offered a world of unique characters and cheap thrills.

Chicago in the late 60s was a dream come true for me—a strange melange of appropriated funk and kitsch—a literal monster mash of phlegm, armpit hair and gross distortion. Timing was right for me to experience some great surrealist shows and Red Grooms' "City of Chicago." Karl Wirsum's paintings about Chicago blues musicians really inspired me with their use of bright primary colors and large figurative distortion. Roger Brown was beginning to do paintings containing strong social messages that read almost like signage. Ed Paschke's acid-colored art work was filled with human oddities, tattoos, and transvestites. These visual elements, combined with the almost carnival-like atmosphere of the School of the Art Institute, made this period of my life a vivid learning experience and helped to fuse the growing relationship between carnival show painting and the so-called "high" art world in my own artwork.

During the summer of 1971 I took short term employment with Century 21 Shows working as a ticket taker and errand boy at the Iowa State Fair. The "back end" of this big carnival featured an impressive array of sideshows and pit shows including everything from freak animals and the Swamp Creature to Giant Rats "Straight from the Sewers of Paris," and the Jayne Mansfield Death Car.

Pit shows were typically viewed from above by climbing stairs and filing past a plywood enclosure or small room visible only to the paying patron. The Swamp Creature pit show was a variation on the old geek show where a man or woman billed as a missing link or drug-crazed victim cavorted with and ate portions of live frogs and snakes. The giant rats were usually nutria—large Central American rodents "sold" almost solely by the banner or show front artist's exaggerated depictions of a gruesome (though nonexistent) blood bath within.

I took tickets at one of two stylish "Girl" shows. These venues typically featured burlesque-style entertainment complete with comedy routines and souvenir sales. One show, Cabaret, featured "Brandy Alexander the Cajun Queen" and "Sacharine Sweeter than Sugar." I worked for Miss Roxanne's Black Lace Revue featuring "Naughty Nikke."

Along with these shows, the M.C. pitched sets of novelty items guaranteed to be unique and daring. These included the Little Frenchman's Joke Book, a humorous 12 inch ruler call "The Peter Meter," and a pair of novelty, miniature dice that the buyer was instructed to soak for 10 minutes in a warm salt water solution, then hold both together, and look through while rotating. You were promised images of Brigitte Bardot wearing only a smile and her boyfriend wearing a guitar in various adult poses, all for 75¢. Of course by the time you got ahold of hot salt water, the show was long gone.

It was at this time that I was introduced to the famous showpainter "Duke" Ash. Show front painting is a legitimate off-shoot of banner painting that combines the subject and flash of banners with the blended scenic styles prevalent in hand painted movie marquees of the 1930s, 40s, and 50s. I was impressed with his snow-white jump suit complete with the name "Duke" embroidered in red on the pocket and his flamboyant personality as he chatted with the exotic dancers and other show personnel. For me, Duke came to represent a whole new world that was out there for me to experience. He was an insider, a show personality full of interesting stories and painting information.

Slides taken by Glen C. Davies of Captain Harvy Boswell's Palace of Wonders and The Moody Freak Animal Show at Fort Bragg Army Base, North Carolina, 1974

In the summer of 1972 I had my first opportunity to travel and paint with Carson & Barnes 5-Ring Circus. I was working there for a day helping to put up the big top for a free ticket when the lot-boss overheard me saying I was an art student. He told me that they were looking for someone who could paint "a giant jungle rat, eating a guy's leg off." After considering the prospect for a moment, I assumed I could probably do the job and volunteered. He hired me and I was promptly elevated to a higher strata in the circus hierarchy—show artist. I shared the back of a truck crammed with juggling equipment and a one year old chimpanzee named Cookie. Each morning we made the jump to a new town, set up the big top and performed two shows. This schedule was repeated 30 times in a month, throughout which I painted several midway attractions. One night I even had the privilege of being introduced by the ringmaster to a sellout crowd as "the world's greatest show painter," a dubious honor in a world where everything is the biggest or greatest. My one month stint was a cathartic experience that strengthened my resolve to follow in the footsteps of the great banner painters and show front artists.

It was during a painting job for Dell & Travers Carnival in 1973 that I had my chance to learn more about banners, particularly the work of Fred G. Johnson. I was hired to repaint an old "Himalayas" ride and ended up hanging around Captain Harvey L. Boswell's Palace of Wonders, a mobile museum filled with shrunken heads, Pygmy blowguns, pickled punks and the mummified body of a 1930s gangster named "Gold Tooth Jimmy."

The banners for this venue were unbelievably beautiful. They created an aura of mystery and almost religious intensity that literally swept people off the midway and inside the tent in great numbers. Each was an absolute masterpiece of Fred G. Johnson, a Chicago banner painter from the old school. Painted at the height of his form, they depicted such things as "Strange Births" surrounded by astonished doctors and nurses, "Crime Doesn't Pay" with its double high depiction of Gold Tooth Jimmy being gunned down and carried away to the morgue (with a side note stating that doctors and morticians would be admitted free), and "The Last Mile," portraying a selection of capital punishments through the ages. This huge show offered something for everyone by combining curiosity, education, sensationalism, and hype. Along with the Palace of Wonders stood Al Moody's freak animal show, featuring one of the largest banner lines available. Six rows of five by seven foot banners stacked three high were divided by a huge marquee banner depicting a two-faced cow. Banners from both shows were the work of Fred Johnson and I decided then that I would try to visit his studio when I returned home to Chicago.

Chicago artist Karl Wirsum and I paid a visit to Johnson's studio at the O'Henry Tent & Awning Company in the summer of 1974. We were ushered through the main sewing room where a huge big top was being pieced together. We found Fred Johnson upstairs in a dingy loft. He seemed agile and wiry for a man of 82. He had recently completed a set of snake show banners, folded and ready to ship, and was now working at lettering a set of awnings. We were shown the huge banner boards where the raw canvas was tacked up. These panels were pitched slightly forward to keep paint drips off the surface of the works in progress. The rolling table that he used was piled high with the paints he mixed himself from white lead paste, color ground in oil, Japan driers, and benzene. His technique was perfected over a great span of years and to Fred, who was paid "by the piece," speed was essential.

Johnson's copy materials consisted of books, magazines, farm journals, and children's book illustrations, as well as photographs and information sent by clients describing specific banner subjects. Letters were everywhere requesting banners or suggesting banner line or bullet text. The bullet is a round circle of color or white paint usually positioned in the corner of a banner. This area was reserved for descriptive text, a secondary title or the ever popular word "ALIVE." An ample supply of templates were used to lend uniformity to banner tops, borders and other repeated shapes and graphics.

At his studio and in subsequent visits to his home, Fred Johnson opened my eyes to the link between banner artists and the great tide of immigrant master craftsmen who came to America during the golden era of architectural and amusement embellishment. I was introduced to a neighbor of Fred's who produced ornamental plaster decorations for Chicago's theatres and other amusement spots. Fred had been apprenticed to several shops and banner painters in his younger days and in the help he provided for me, this tradition was continued in some small way.

Soon after this visit I began to incorporate banner formats and materials in some of my serious art pieces. Like sideshow banners, I wanted my personal expressions to suggest the link between everyday experience and the exploration of some metaphorical, imagined realm. Using subjects like the "Tower of Babel" or "Adam and Eve," I explored the idea of personal mythology. I featured a set of banners in my first one person show in 1974 entitled "The Museum of Mystery." These quasi-religious banners were displayed along with an antique fraternal lodge coffin and several painted and sculpted "Mystery Boxes."

I worked for a billboard company in 1975 and honed my mural painting skills over the next few years working off and on painting signs, show fronts, discos, and massage parlors.

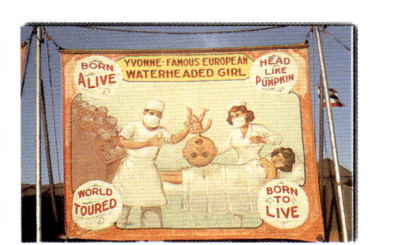

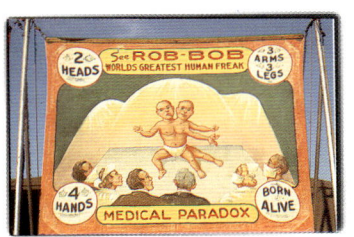

Around this same time I was seeking out information on banner painting techniques and began corresponding with Snap Wyatt, another legendary banner painter. Like Fred Johnson, Wyatt was schooled in the old traditions where banner studios competed for clients and painting techniques. His recipes for mixing paint and applying it to canvas were a closely guarded secret. He responded to my request for information by placing a $600 price tag on his signature formulas for painting banners. Needless to say, I declined his offer.

In the early 1980s I began winter quarters work for various shows in the south. During a visit to Florida in 1983 I had the pleasure of visiting banner painter Johnny Meah at the winter lot of sideshow entrepreneur Ward Hall in Gibsonton. To this day, he is one of the few banner artists who still paints in the traditional style of oil paint on a slightly wetted canvas. In our world of the modern theme park and sanitized "family" entertainment, Johnny Meah is an anachronism. Along with Ward Hall and a few others, he has managed to usher the world of sideshows and banners into the modern limelight. He has mesmerized and electrified audiences with his deeds and words in shows for the Smithsonian Institution as well as in lecture/demonstrations for contemporary art galleries and lecture halls. After years of experience as a sideshow talker, Meah can banter in a relaxed and jovial manner while pounding a spike up his nose or preparing to swallow a neon sword. Taking mostly the banner painting jobs that interest him and working otherwise as a clown and sideshow performer, Meah continues to create some of the best banners available with his characteristic original imagery, bright color, fluid blending, and comic word play.

While producing a series of small banners for escape artist Andy Dallas during the 1980s, I once more began to use banner themes and subjects in my studio paintings. Certain painting ideas became "banner subjects." I treated them differently, setting these paintings aside for a loose canvas format. My more self-consciously preachy or latently moralistic themes seemed better suited for this treatment. Inbred in the format and spirit of banner painting these subjects have continued to influence much of my art throughout the last decade. There is something about the loose canvas and industrial strength hardware that demands a certain kind of attention when being viewed. Unlike stretched and framed paintings, the banner context relaxes the boundaries implied by the high art format, and lends my chosen moral dramas the freedom to be played out in the visual realm of a less strictly disciplined arena: that of the sideshow.

Like warning signs, my banner-related art work cautions viewers to stop, examine the situation, assess the wonders and dangers that surround us, then proceed with caution and reflection. In my 1993 painting "Communication Breakdown" the monumental figure that confronts the viewer is constructed of visual metaphors that suggest ways that our abilities to communicate are sidetracked, causing confusion. The head is really two heads—one listens but doesn't speak, the other speaks without listening. The whole figure is like a puppet without strings or a pencil that can't draw. These images are designed to present information in a nonverbal manner, to communicate with visual dialogue.

Banners provide sideshows a context that invites skepticism, curiosity, and religious or moral questioning while encouraging a willingness on the part of the viewer to be "taken in" and sold a bill of goods. It is the ephemeral nature of the banner and its manner of display that side steps the "fine art" stigma and allows us to be drawn into a different mystery.

Today, the sideshow has become a shadow of its former self, replaced by tabloid journalism, magazine format news shows, and "Geraldo." A resurgent interest in sideshows and banner art has kept the door open for a mini-revival. Interest in tattoo art, self-mutilation, and body piercing have all been observed as growing trends. Also contributing to this trend is the recent popularity of MTV, exotic rock music stage shows, and performance art. The imagery of banner art continues to exert its influence, fueled by interest in outsider art, comic books, and pulp journalism.

There is a grand, gaudy, and sad quality in banners now, that suggests a slightly tarnished elegance, a fall from grace. Harkening back to an earlier time, these brightly colored exaggerations were a diversion from the humdrum routine of daily toil. Avenues of painted canvas created eye-popping facades, rife with scientific misinformation, updated folklore, and a veneer of sophisticated urbanity. Walking into the canvas cathedral awakened primeval yearnings and, for a small fee, the freedom to indulge our curiosity and sate our appetite for the exotic, the strange, and the unknown.

Glen C. Davies, Communication Breakdown, 1993, courtesy Phyllis Kind Gallery

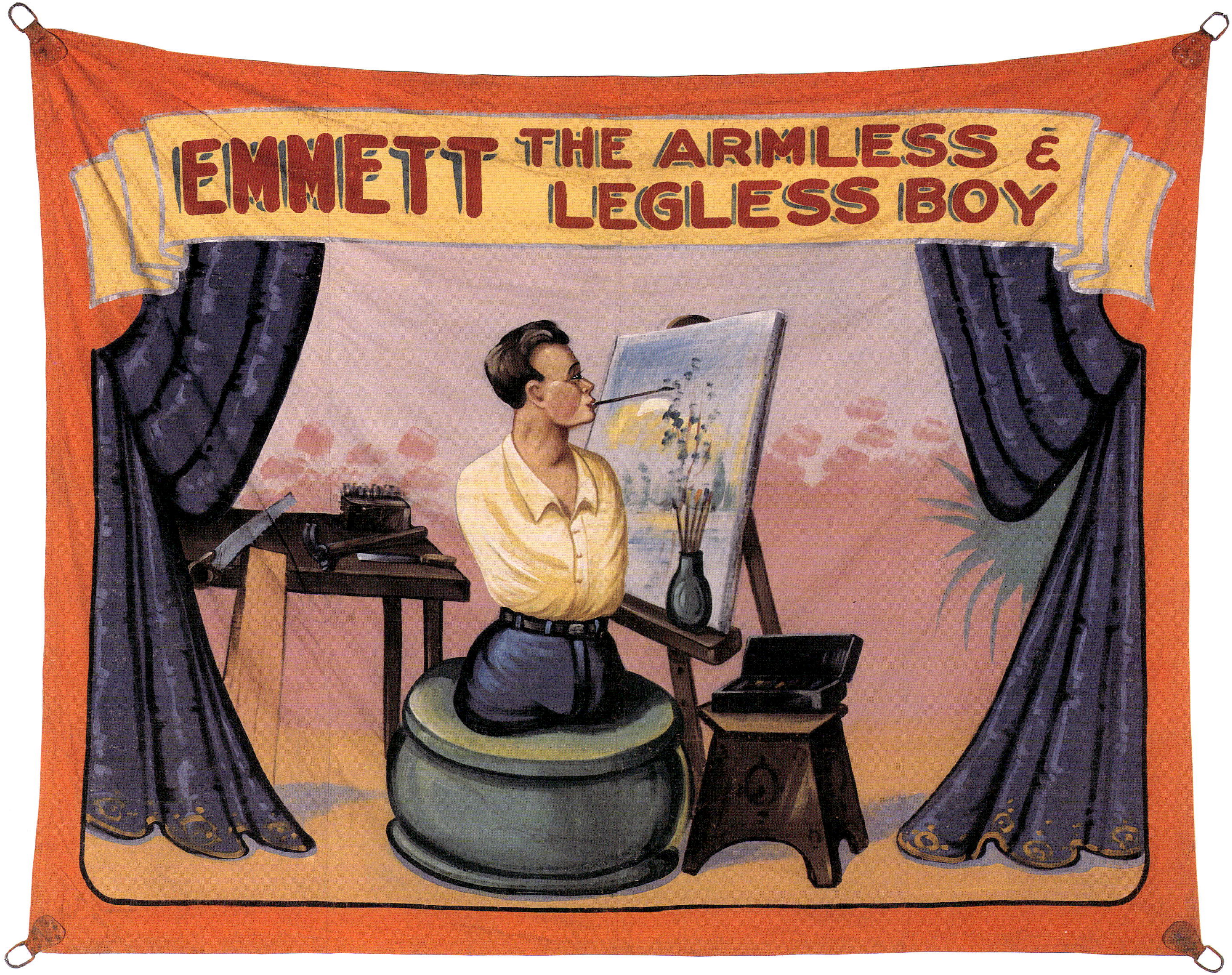
EMMETT THE ARMLESS &
LEGLESS BOY

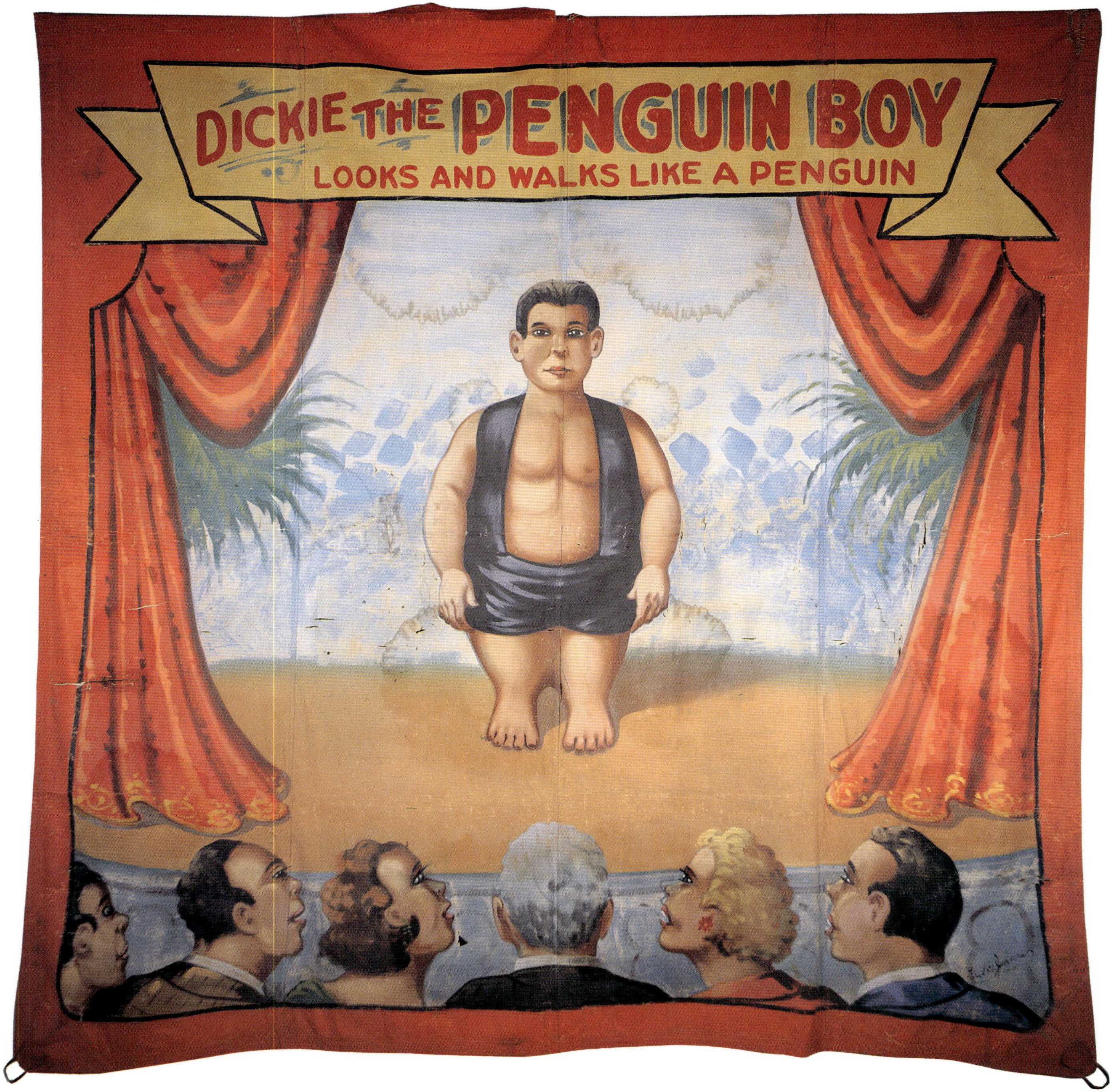
DICKIE THE PENGUIN BOY
LOOKS AND WALKS LIKE A PENGUIN

69

70

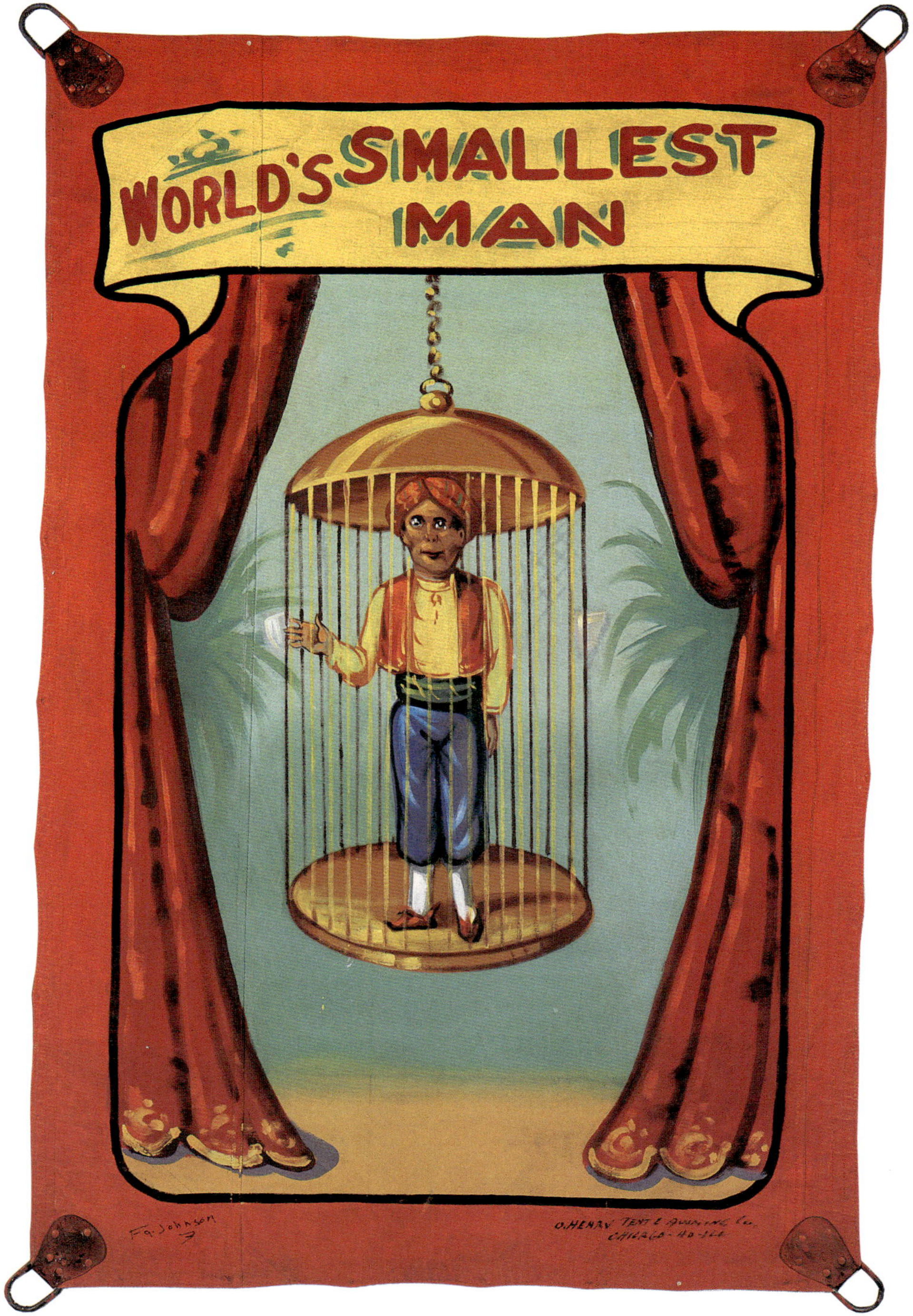
WORLD'S SMALLEST MAN
Fq Johnson

72

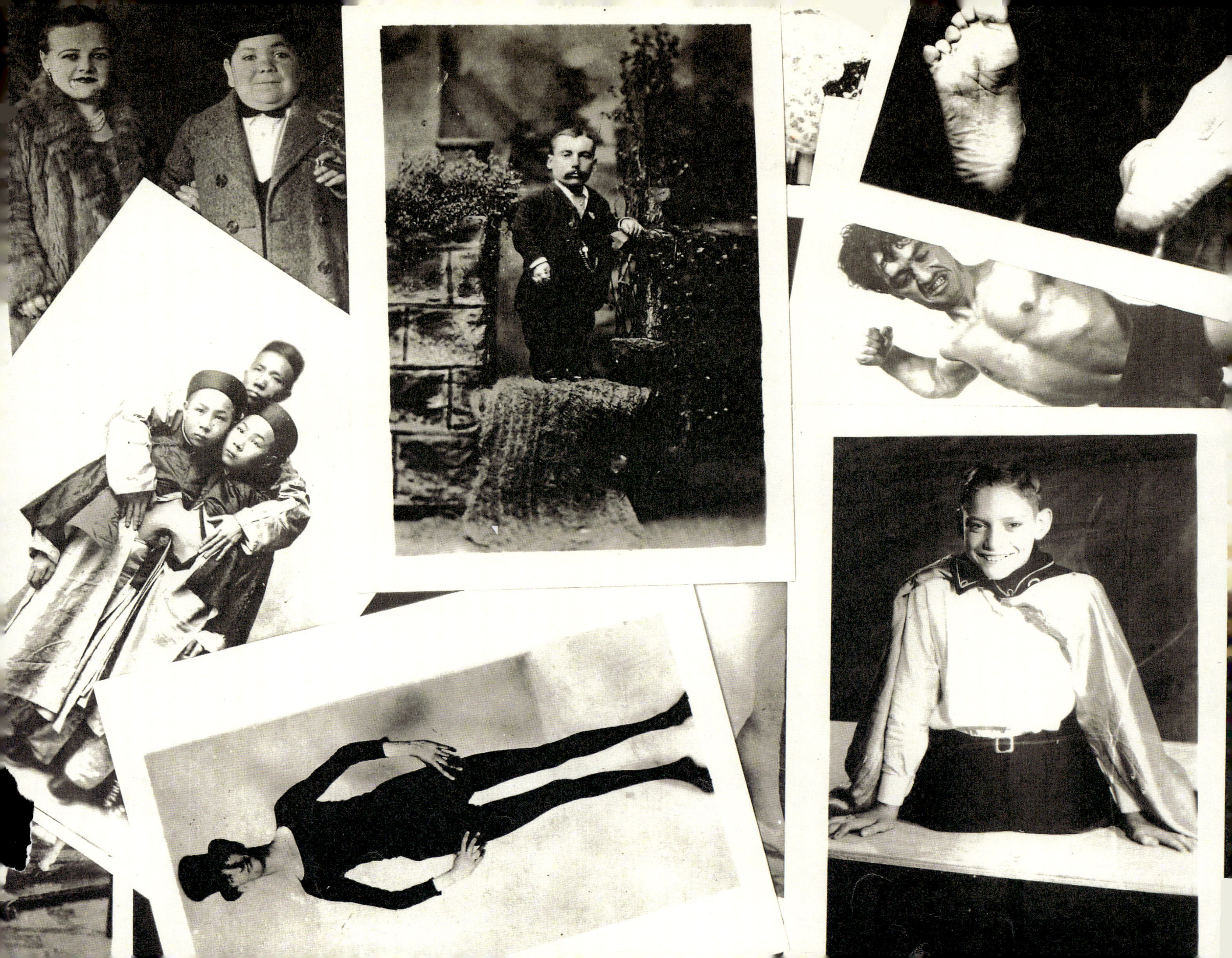

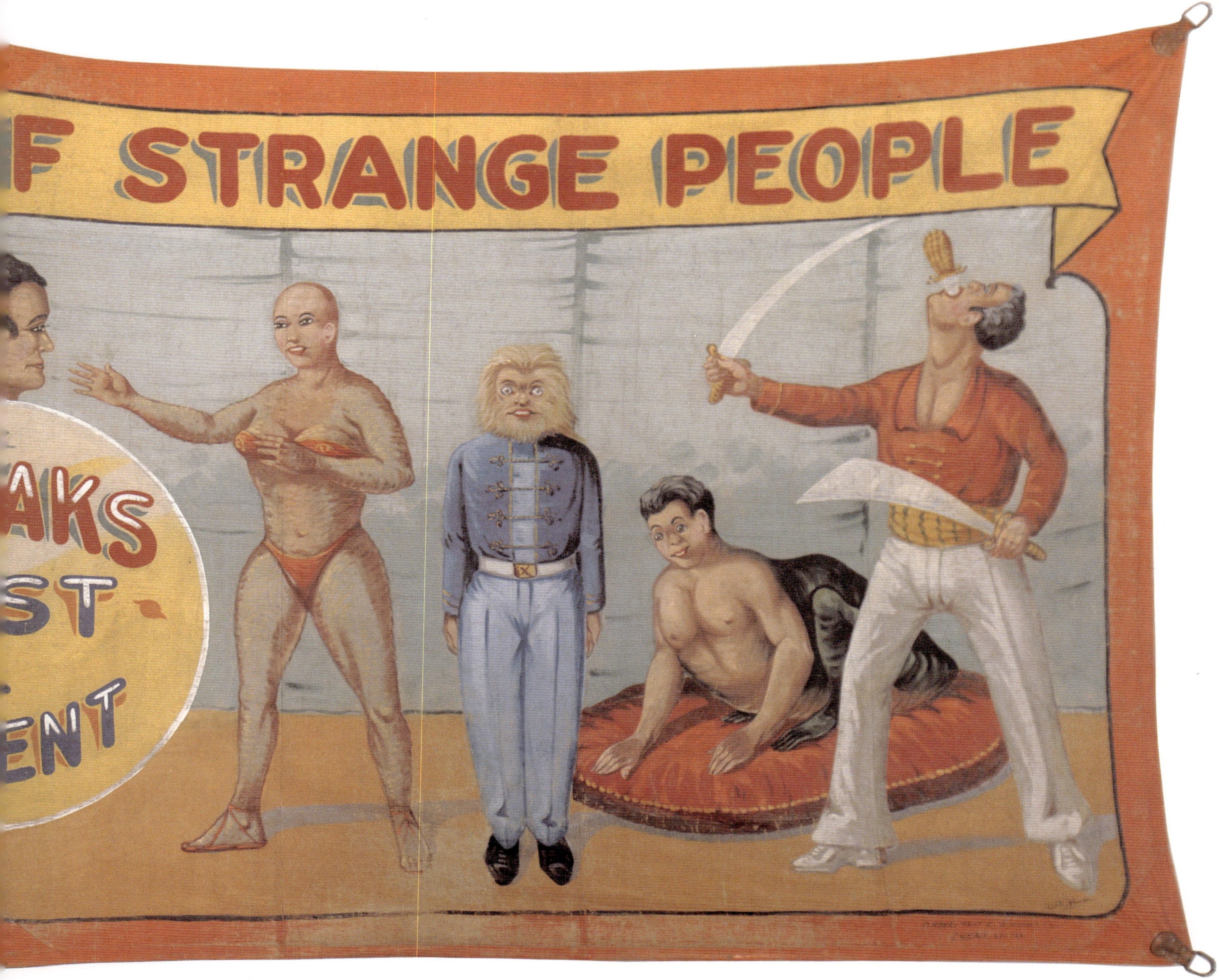
F STRANGE PEOPLE
AKS
ST
ENT

THE ROYAL FAMILY

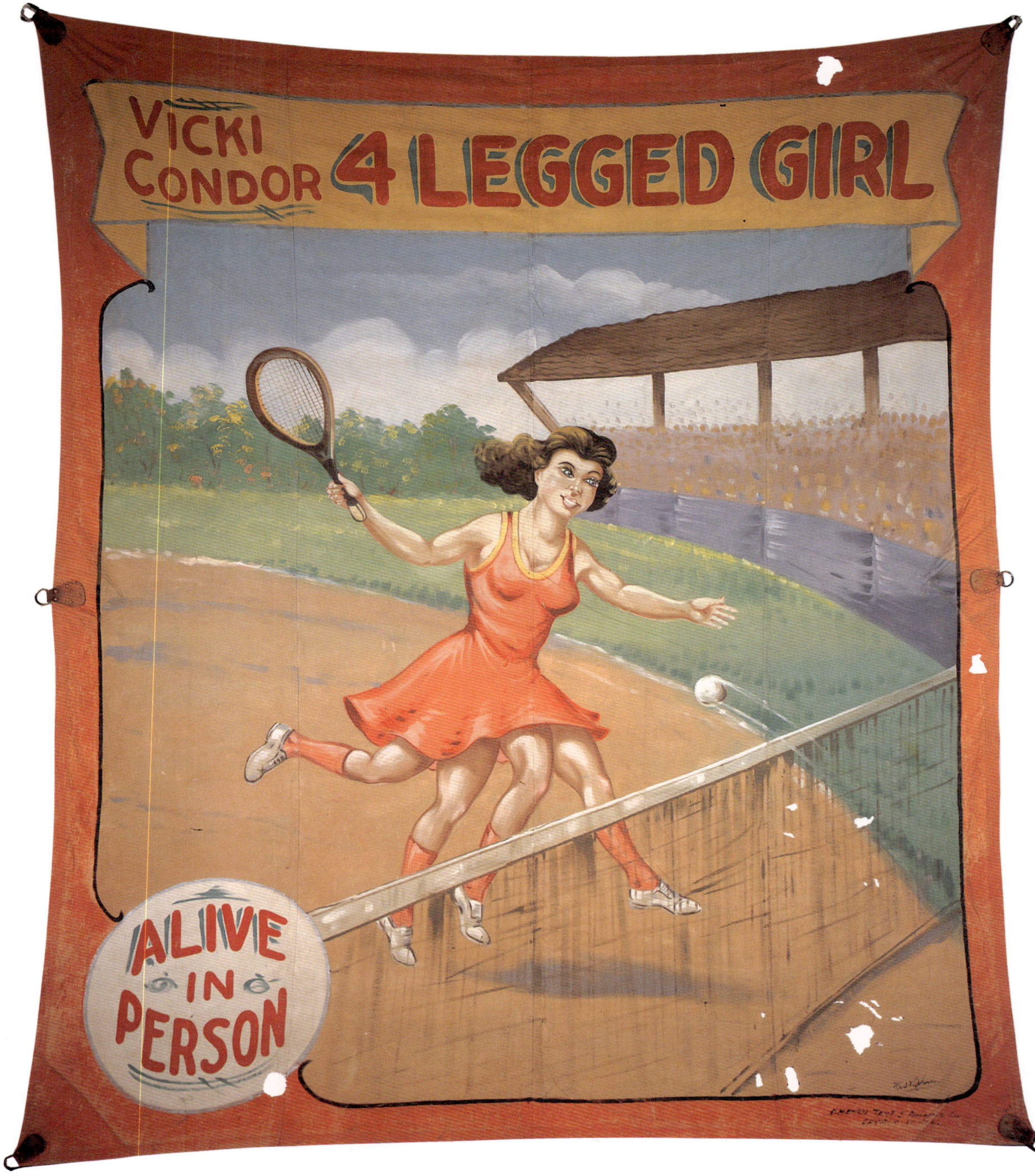
VICKI CONDOR
4 LEGGED GIRL
ALIVE IN PERSON

77

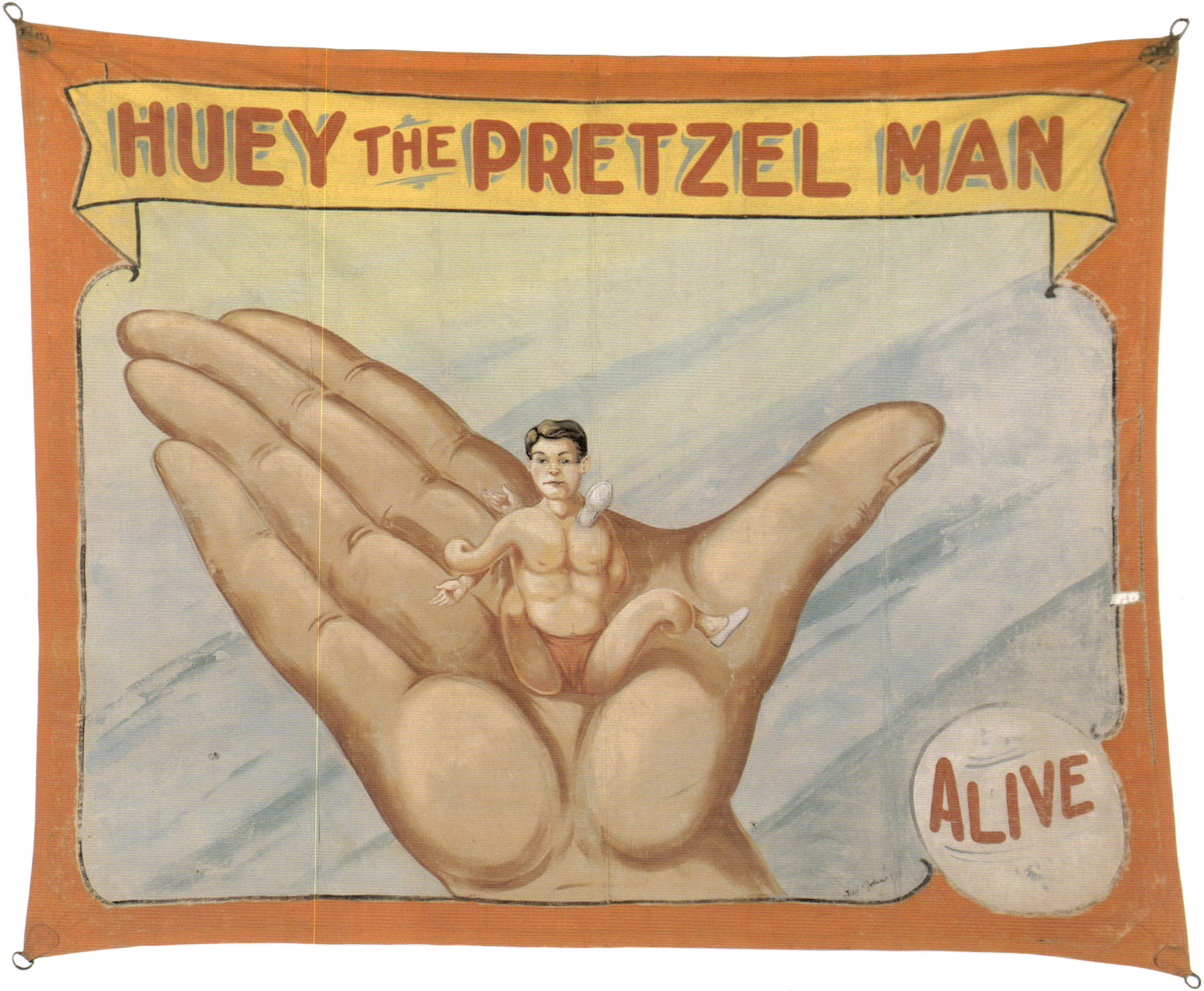
HUEY THE PRETZEL MAN
ALIVE

WORLD'S SMALLEST MOTHER
J. SIGLER
TAMPA
ALIVE
World's Smallest Woman
SMALLER THAN A 3 YEAR OLD CHILD

TINIEST ENTERTAINERS

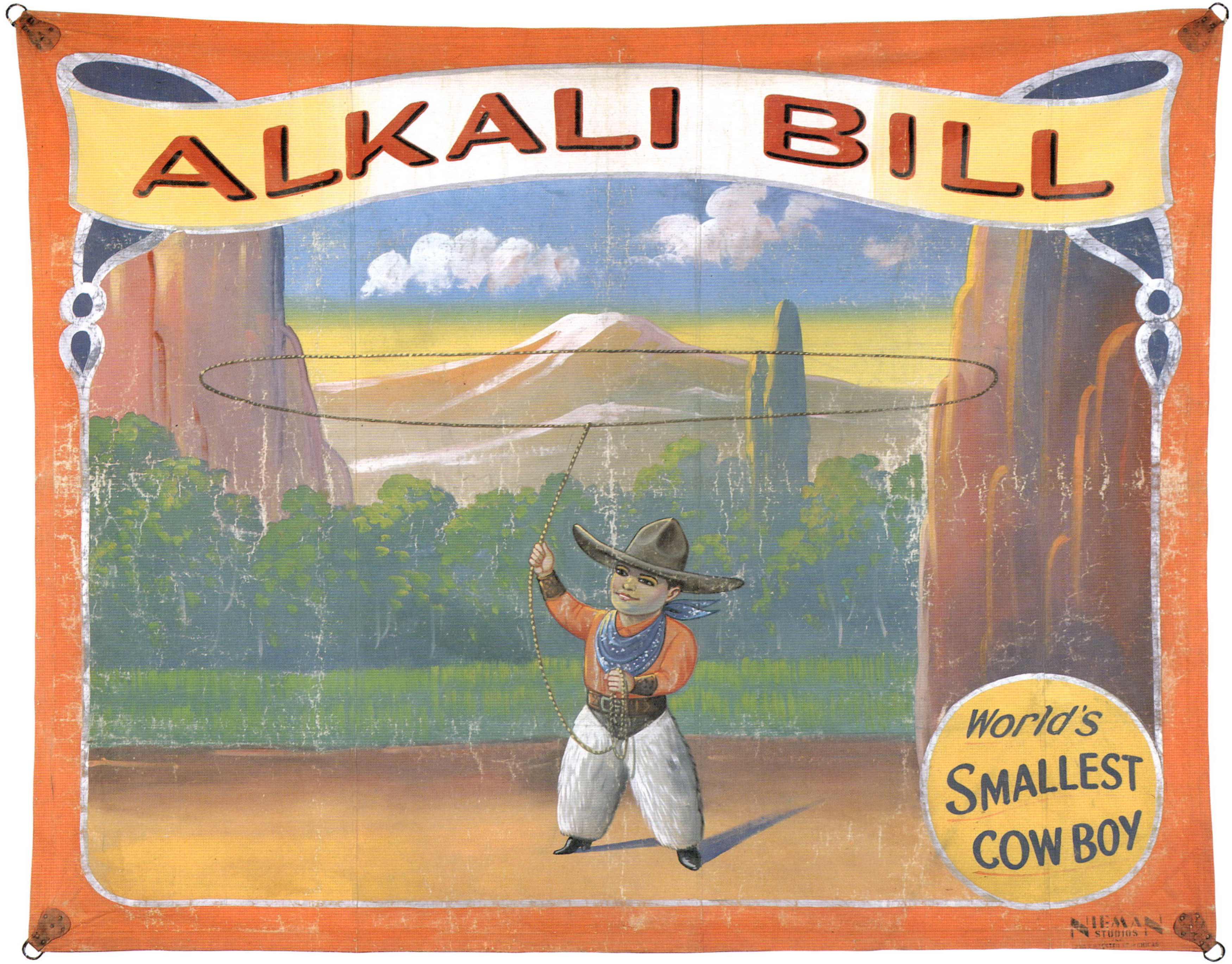
ALKALI BILL
World's
SMALLEST
COW BOY
NIEMAN
STUDIOS

82

83

84

BULKIEST-JOLLIEST MUSEUM
ON EARTH
MAGIC of the MOVING MARVELS
HOW
HUGE
CIRCUSES

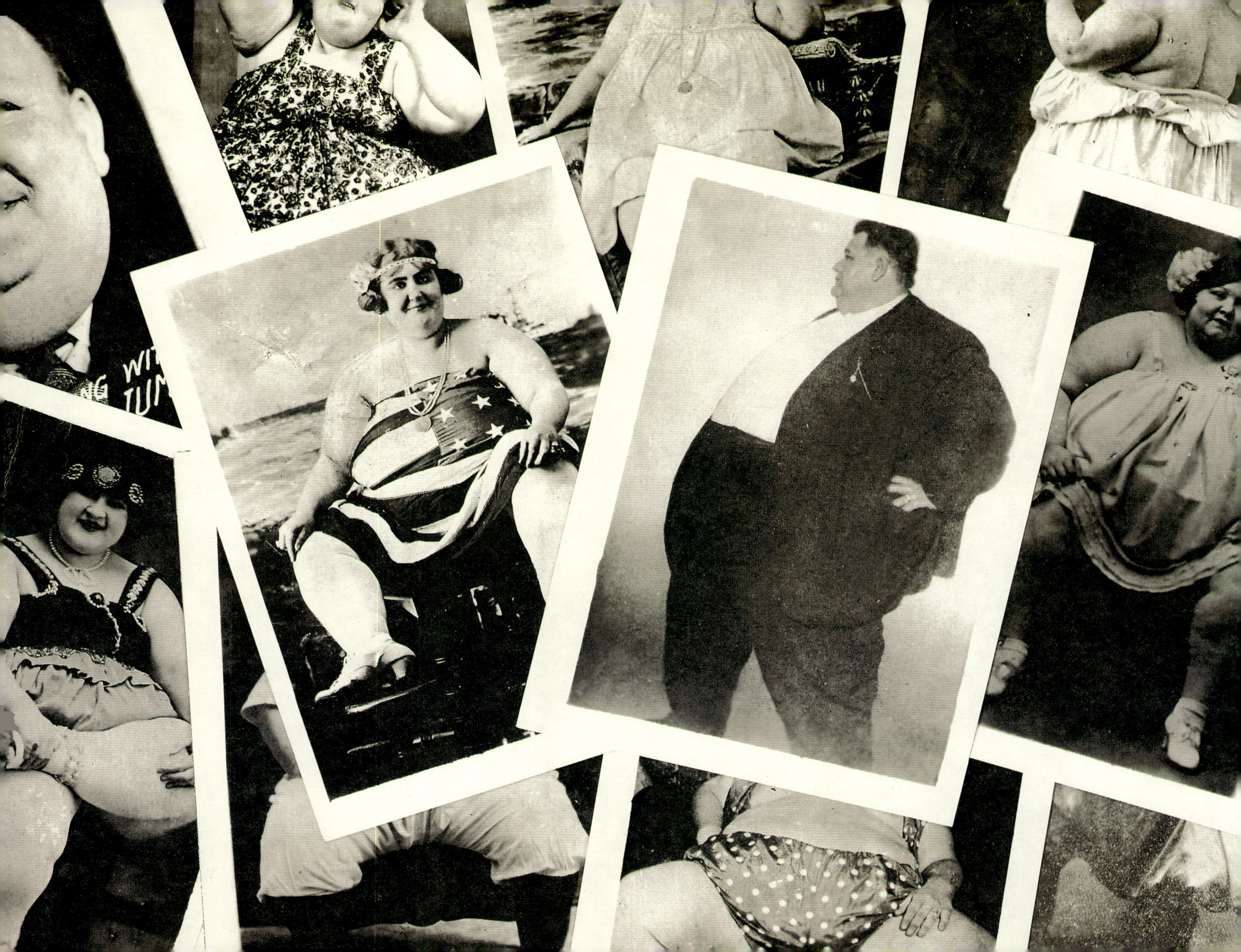

LARGER THAN LIFE
POSITIVELY FAT

Jim Secreto

"Step right up!" "Hurry, hurry, your last chance to see!" is the call of the midway. The Talkie stands above the sawdust, calling out to the crowd, pleading with us for a moment of our time as our attention is drawn to the continuous chatter. We stop and are struck by the oversized colorful canvases, the banner line, the calling card of the show.

These strong visuals created on canvas were used as attention-getters, to lure the audience closer to the action taking place on the platform. Banner painters used imagery and symbols to instantly evoke a response from their audience. The banner artist is and has been the story teller of the midway.

Paralleling the exaggerated size and visual effect of the sideshow banner on the outside was one of the more common attractions on the inside – the enormously obese FAT MAN or WOMAN, waiting to be ogled by crowds of ordinary-sized observers. This attraction has been rendered by a number of banner painters throughout the history of FAT sideshows. The stylistic variations of Al DeCura, Snap Wyatt, and Fred G. Johnson, who all painted banners advertising "FAT" people, elucidate the artistic originality inherent in banner painting – a field where artists share common subjects. DeCura, Wyatt, and Johnson all use symbols and scale as strong design elements to convey the amazing size of the subject to the viewer. The key element in their banners, in all banners, is color – a sense of flash.

One of the early examples of a "Fat Show" banner, painted in 1930 by Brooklyn artist Al DeCura, is a five by seven foot canvas featuring "Giant Baby." This piece was probably used by a local carnival or fair. The overall simplicity and primitiveness of this piece has a strong folk art quality. DeCura's flattened space typifies the work of 19th century folk painting, where subject and background often blend together. Lack of shading and tonal variation characterizes his "folk" style. The muted coloring of his limited palette creates a monochromatic effect, as compared to the more colorful, traditional banner line. The artist's whimsical interpretation of scroll work, lacking overall detail, helps to enhance the simplicity of the painting. By careful selection of contrasting words, such as "Giant/Baby" and "Ten Years Old/390 lbs." the artist is toying with the audience. In his direct and simple approach to a subject of great enormity, Al DeCura has created a banner of strong visual power that employs the naive style associated with 19th century folk painting.

In David "Snap" Wyatt's presentation of the same subject, entitled "Oh My! But She Is Fat/Positively Alive," a graphically strong image is delivered in the format that became the standard or traditional style for banners. The overwhelming size of this sideshow advertisement – ten feet by ten feet – was intended to render the crowd spellbound. The central figure, a charming bathing beauty, measures about eight feet from head to toe. Considered to be one of the best banner painters ever, Wyatt successfully achieved a strong sense of "flash" in this interpretation of the "fat lady."

Juxtaposition of such images as a woman wearing the tiniest of bikinis holding the hand of her small male companion, as well as the treatment of the distant landscape, draws the viewer into a heightened sense of scale and proportion. The dramatic feeling of this banner is set up by the use of such words as "Oh My!" and "Positively!" and the audience is left with no doubt that the act is ALIVE. The masterful painting skills of Snap Wyatt come into play in his use of color and shading. By painting a thick black line around this cartoon-like caricature, the artist is able to pull his subject out from the background; this device allows him to blend many different tonal ranges to create his robust figure. Little detail is used in a vast amount of space and the overall effect is skillful and convincing.

The key ingredient in Fred G. Johnson's banner is color – known as FLASH. His career spanned more than four decades with the O. Henry Tent and Awning Company (Chicago, IL), and his name is one of the most recognized among banner artists. Two of his banners depicting FAT sideshows illustrate the control Johnson had over his colorful palette. In his 1962 banner "Laugh With Dolly" the explosion of one dominant color – RED – creates an iridescent effect. He craftily highlighted the skin tone around the exaggerated subject with a magenta hue. This emphasis offsets the massive use of red in Dolly's bathing suit. The secondary figures standing on the beach bask in a reddish glow. Even the palm

88

89

trees in the distance have touches of red from an unseen light source. Johnson's teasing placement of red in the open mouths of the attacking sea creatures leads the viewer to the "alive" bullet in the right hand corner and suggest the gory result if Dolly should veer too close.

In an untitled "Fat Show" banner by Johnson the artist has reached back into time, engaging the painting style of the master banner painters of the turn of the century. With his selection of colors such as emerald green, sapphire blue, and ruby red, this banner has a jewel-like quality and trompe l'oeil appearance. Using compositional devices such as a chair and curtain, the artist created the illusion of a stage-like space. Johnson's skillful manipulation of classic painting techniques applied to a format commonly associated with folk or popular art blurred the distinctions separating so-called "fine art" from its more mundane relatives.

The banner line played on society's fascination with the bizarre. By widely distorting the truth, these outside advertisements turned passion for the unusual into profit. The thrill-seekers enticed by the artistry of these banner painters were often disappointed by the reality of the actual sideshow. The paintings of this small group of artisans opened a window onto a world unknown to the common people. The illusions created by these outside canvases brought entertainment to the masses with a FLASH!

In viewing circus and sideshow banners we experience a glorification of the ordinary or normal at the expense of the weird and grotesque, of obese people and other strangers. It is an upside-down world – a place of fear. "There, but for the grace of God, go I" comes to our lips and penetrates our consciousness. Now we can retreat to our bungalows, flats, or apartments, safely having escaped the abnormal and welcome our place in the solid scheme of things. The nightmare is over.

Notes On Fat People by Johnny Meah

Much like the basic food group there is a "basic human oddity" group. There are, in order of their popularity, Little People (Midget and Dwarfs), Fat People, and Giants. The aforementioned are not grotesque, they're just shorter, taller or wider than you and I, making them seemingly more acceptable to gawk at.

Midgets are perceived as being "cute" and have populated children's stories for centuries. They are also smaller than we are so we feel safe around them. Giants, much like the Wee Folk, are favorites of fiction writers, often portrayed as heroic characters—saving the day by virtue of their strength and awesome massiveness. They occupy the number three slot due to their relative scarceness. Mother Nature produces them on a limited edition basis.

Then there are Fat People. Many centuries ago a word crafter picked up his quill and scribed the words "jolly" and "fat" next to each other. In my opinion this writer never spent much time around Fat People; however, these two words have enjoyed the longest marriage ever recorded. Primarily, the "Jolly Dolly" myth is the reason that Fat People are the second in line on the "Most Looked At" list.

Carnivals and circuses abounded with Fat Men, Fat Women and even Fat Families. They oozed and undulated behind banners that bore slogans like "A Ton Of Fun" or "A Mountain Of Mirth." Another bullet would proclaim the individual's weight, in some cases exaggerated by as much as two hundred pounds. (There were only two Fat People that I worked with that lived up to their advertised weight—Martin Levey and Robert Earl Hughes, both over 1,000 pounds.)

Although I readily acknowledge Fat People as a popular attraction, I've never regarded them in the same way I regard Midgets and Giants. A Midget, Dwarf or Giant has a course charted for them at birth by their pituitary gland. Most professional Fat People, (mind you, I say most), are self-made freaks who have literally eaten their way into the spotlight. I've worked with at least twenty sideshow Fat People and, with the possible exception of one, never knew any of them to suffer from any type of glandular disorder. This is not to say they weren't overweight to start with, but, in most cases, a problem correctable by proper diet and exercise. These people aspired to super corpulence to enable them to exhibit themselves. One man freely admitted to drinking copious quantities of sugar water in an effort to become "The Fattest Man In The World." Another man, tiring of the "Fat-For-A-Fee" business, returned to his original occupation as a musician and dropped to a relatively normal weight of two hundred and fifty pounds.

Although I'm obviously not enchanted by the people themselves, I do enjoy painting "fat banners." They are, of course, outrageously cartoonish in all respects. Because of their exaggerated girth they usually preclude any detailed background—there's no room left for it! I have, however, done several sets of "situation" banners for fat shows, each banner depicting the person in a different setting, i.e., "Big Bertha At The Beach," "Big Bertha Goes Shopping," etc.

91

92

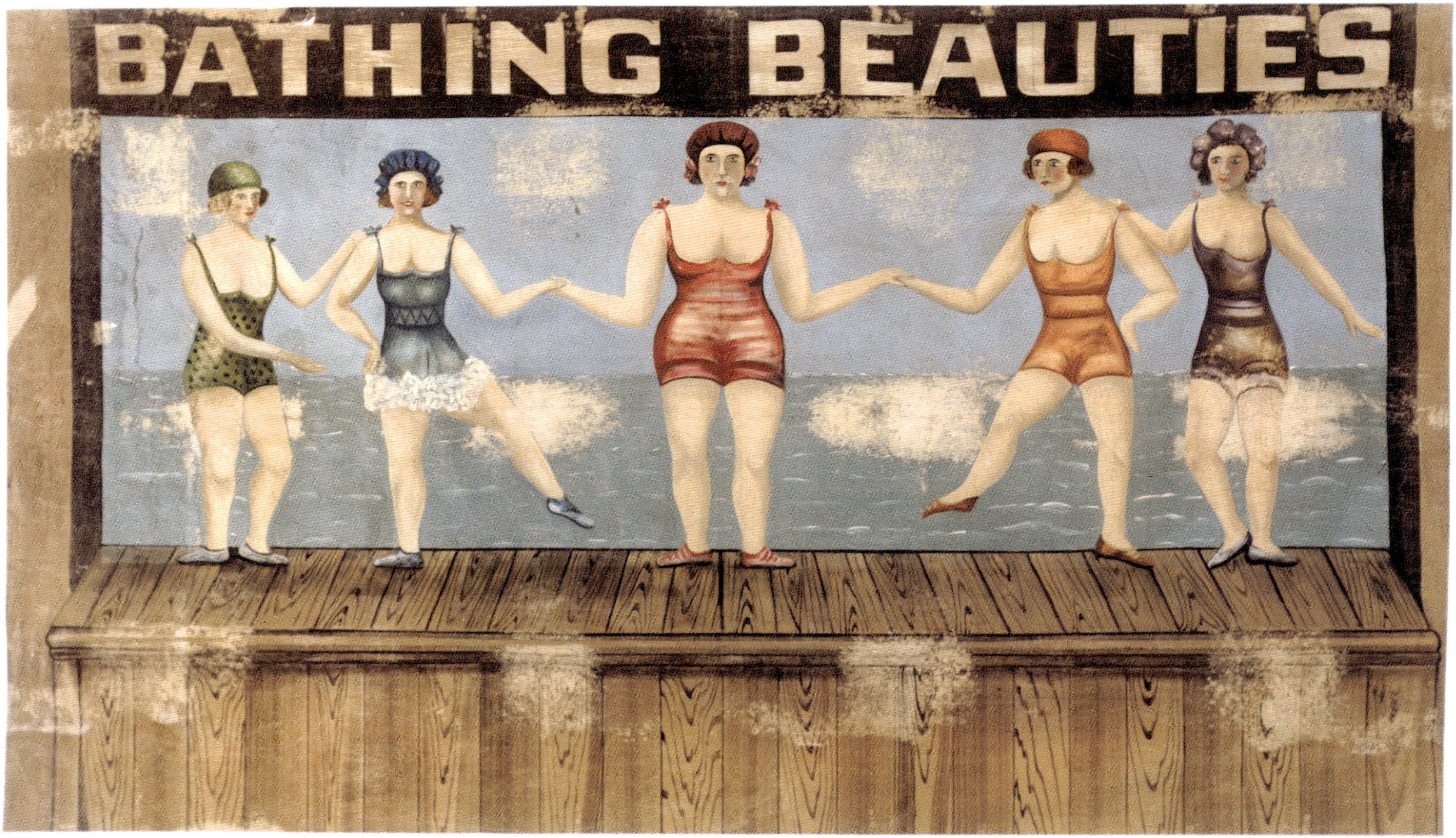
BATHING BEAUTIES

MAIN CIRCUS

FREAKS PAST & PRESENT

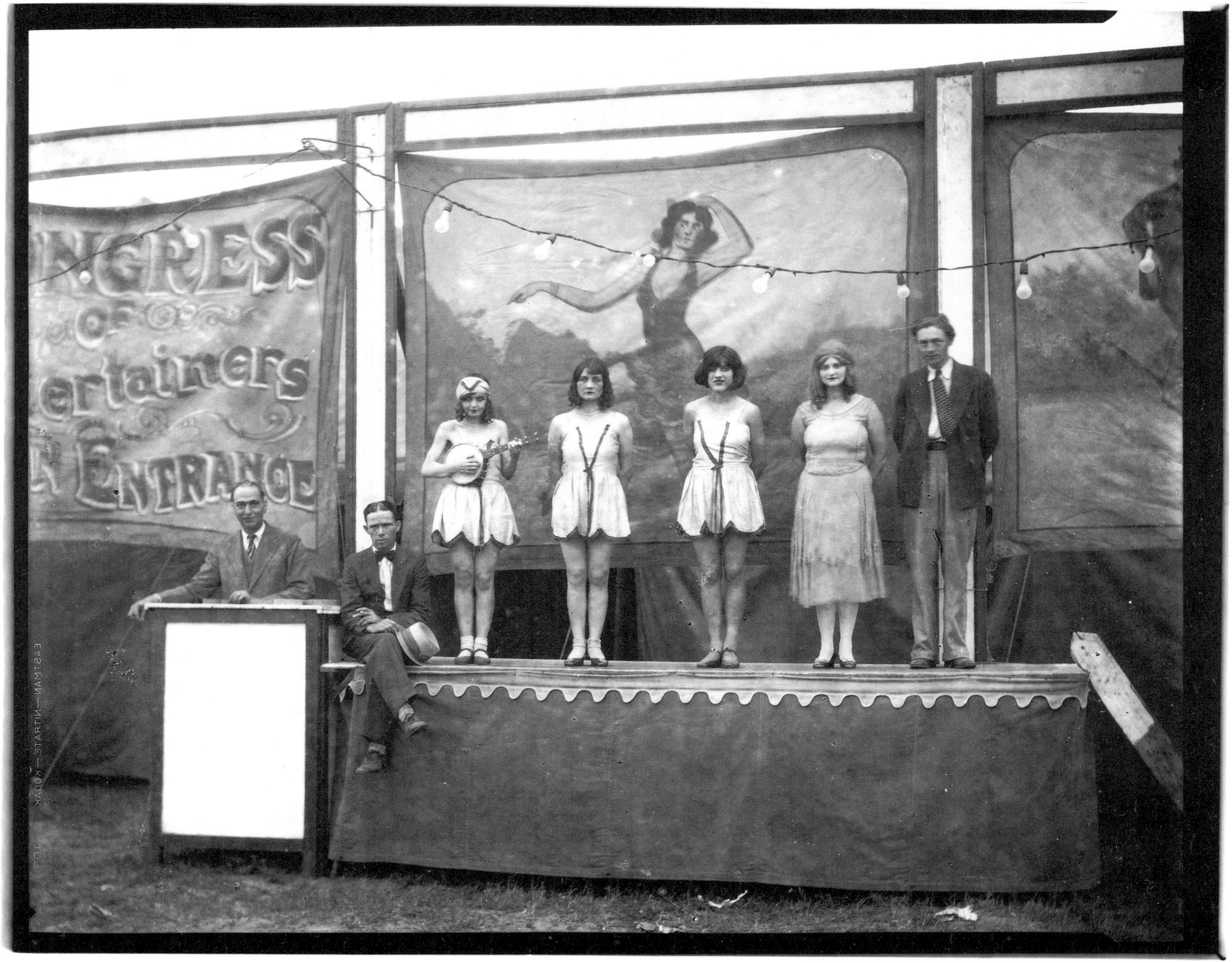
NGRESS
OF
ertainers
ENTRANCE

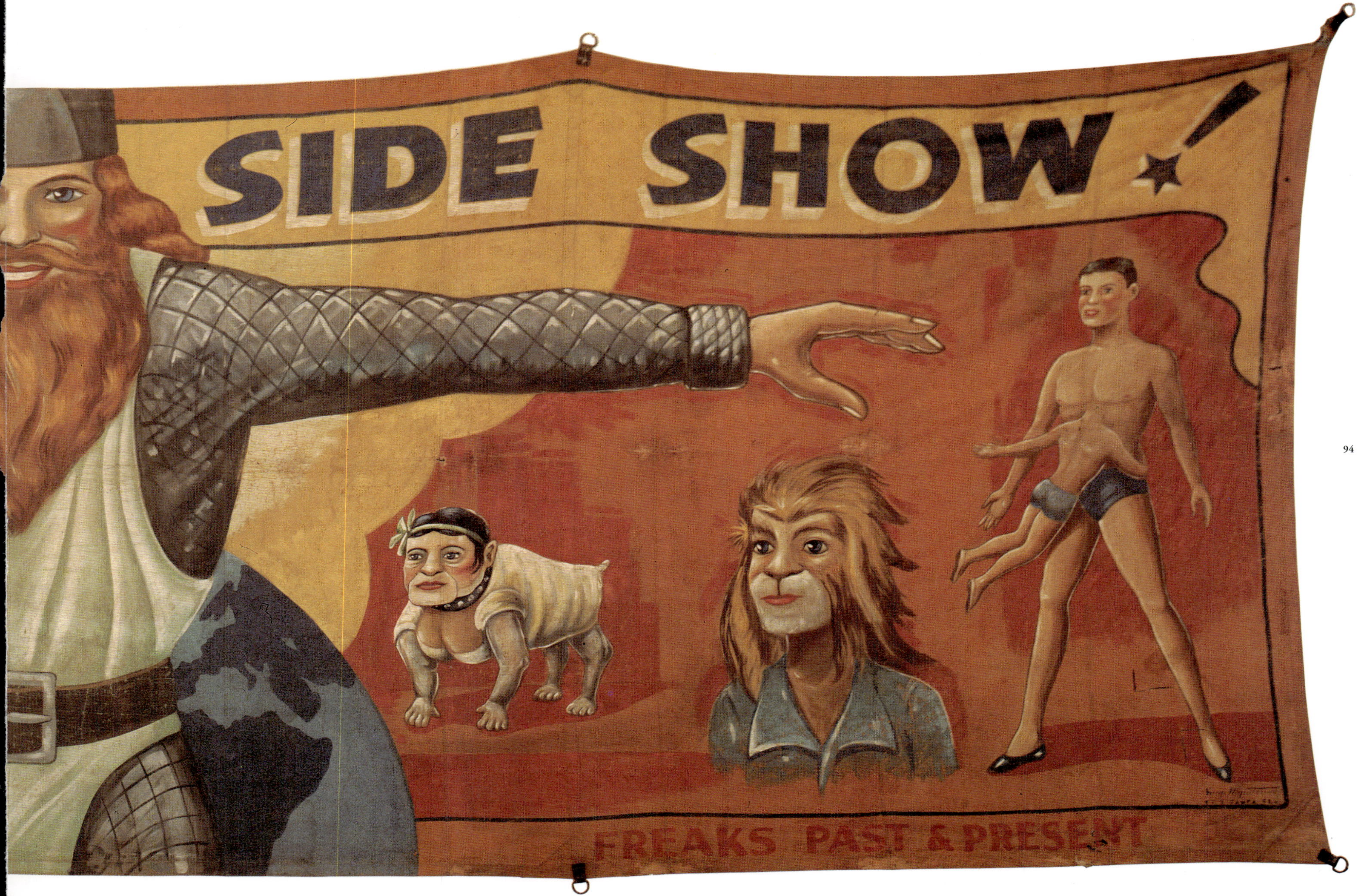
SIDE SHOW!
FREAKS PAST & PRESENT

97

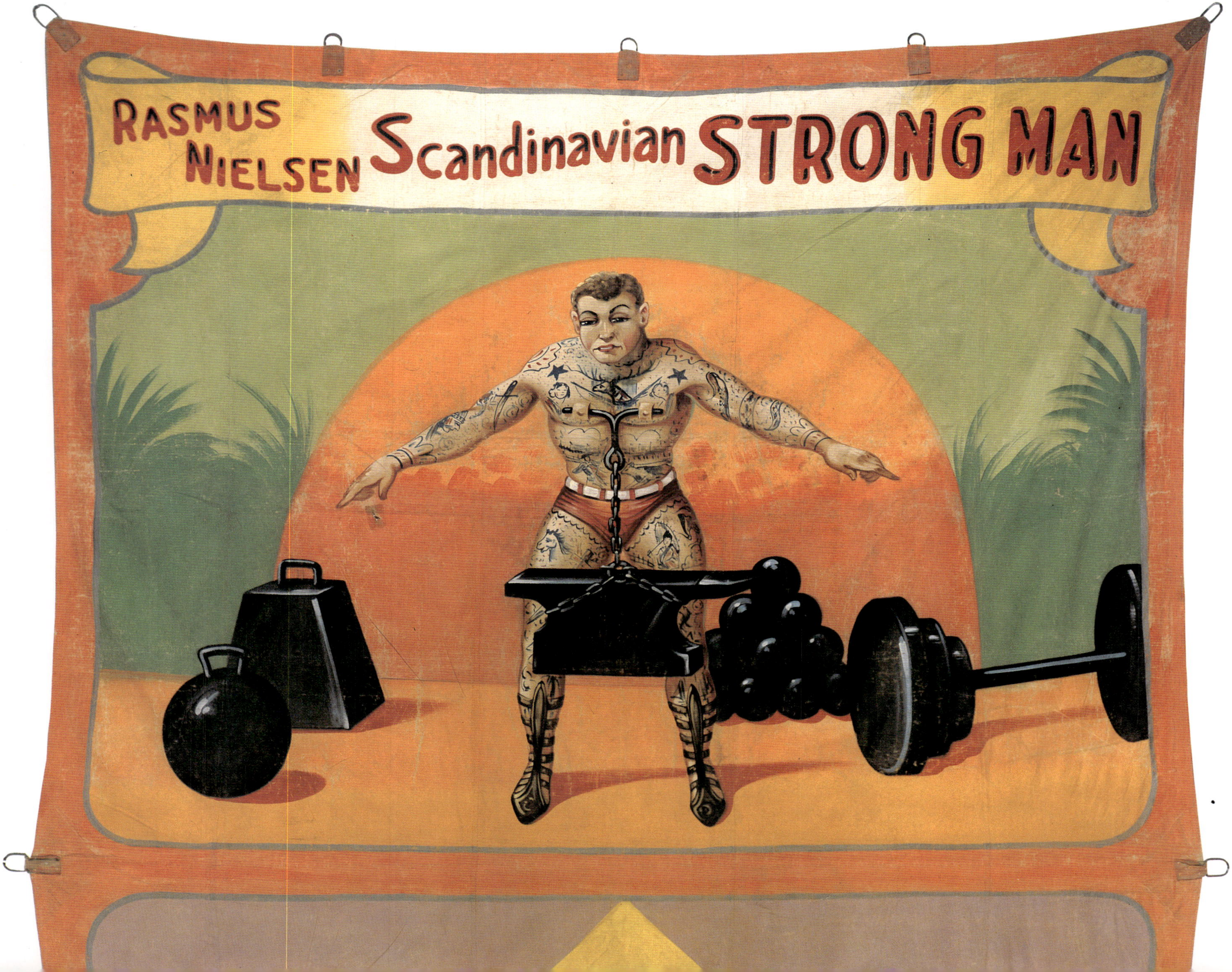
RASMUS
NIELSEN
Scandinavian
STRONG MAN

LIFTS AN ANVIL BY HIS BREASTS

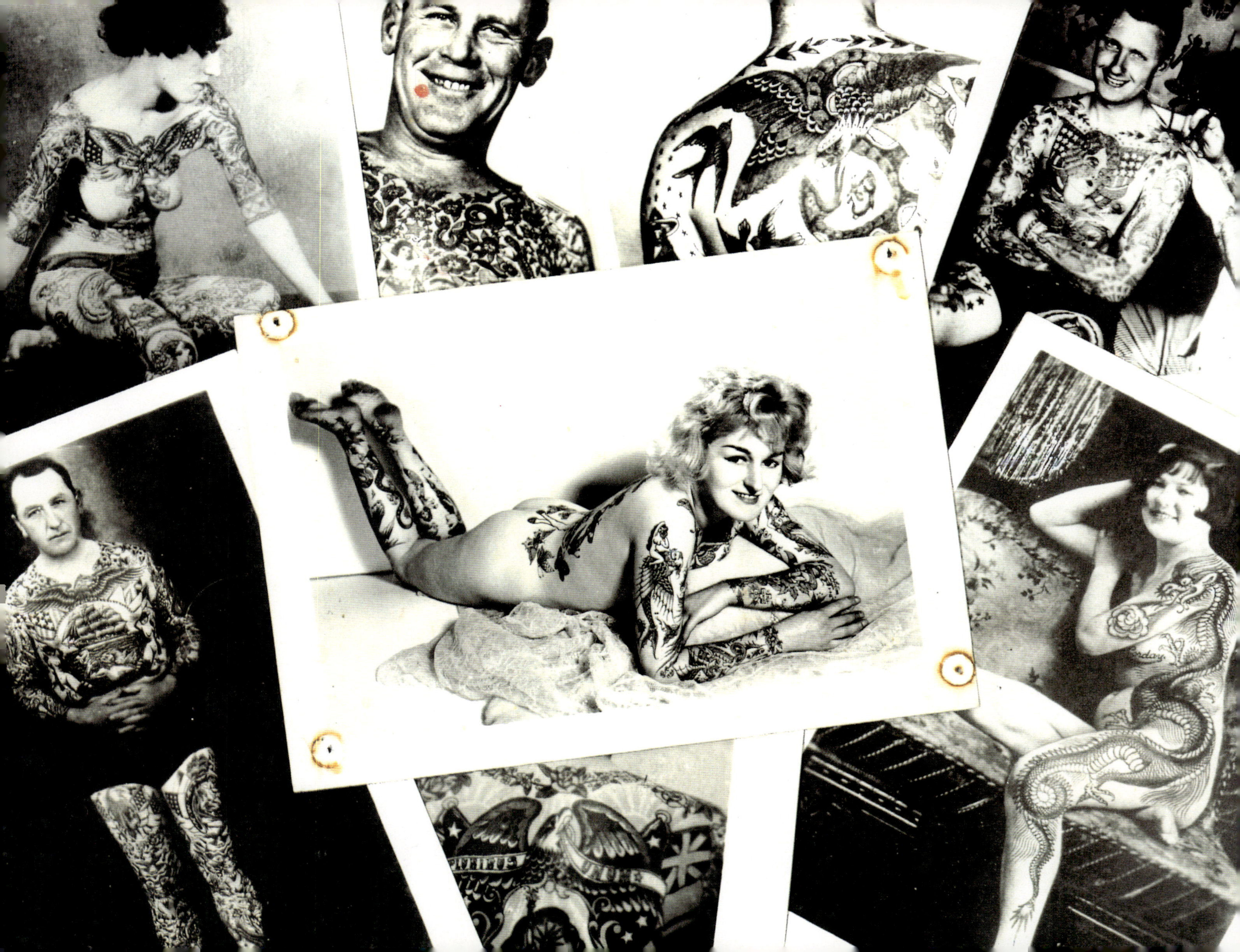

TOTALLY TATTOOED
SELF-MADE FREAKS of the CIRCUS and SIDESHOW

Steve Gilbert

The popularity of tattooing during the latter part of the nineteenth and the first half of the twentieth century owed much to the circus. When circuses prospered, tattooing prospered. When circuses went bankrupt, tattooed people and tattoo artists were out of work.

For over 70 years every major circus employed several completely tattooed people. Some were exhibited in sideshows; others performed traditional circus acts such as juggling and sword swallowing. Rival circuses competed with each other for the services of the most elaborately tattooed showpeople and paid them handsome salaries. Many of the old-time tattoo artists made most of their money while traveling with circuses during the spring and summer, returning to their shops and homes in the winter. The circus served as a showcase where tattoo artists could attract customers by exhibiting their work to a paying public. The only record we have of the great early tattoo masterpieces has come down to us in the form of photos and posters which were used for circus publicity.

The love affair between tattooing and the circus began in 1804 when the Russian explorer Georg H. von Langsdorff visited the Marquesas. There he found Jean Baptiste Cabri, a French deserter who had lived for many years among the natives. During this time Cabri had been extensively tattooed and had married a Marquesan woman who bore him several children.

Cabri returned with Langsdorff to Russia where he enjoyed a brief but successful theatrical career in Moscow and St. Petersberg. Langsdorff reports that "although he has by degrees become reconciled to European customs, he still thinks with delight of the men whom he formerly killed and exchanged for swine, or perhaps ate." Cabri told such extravagant tales of his adventures among the savages that, according to Langsdorff, " anyone who heard him relate them would be disposed to think himself listening to a second Munchhausen."

After working for a year as a swimming instructor in the Marine Academy at Cronstadt Cabri resumed his theatrical career and toured Europe, where he was examined by distinguished physicians and exhibited to royalty. But within a few years his career went into decline. During the last years of his life he was forced to compete with trained dogs and other popular amusements in country fairs. In 1812 he died, poor and forgotten, in his birthplace, Valenciennes.

The first tattooed English showman was John Rutherford. In 1828 an account of his amazing adventures among the Maoris of New Zealand appeared in the popular press. It was reported that he had been captured and held prisoner for ten years. Shortly after his capture he was forcibly tattooed by two priests who performed the four-hour ceremony in the presence of the entire tribe. During the process he lost consciousness and had to spend several weeks convalescing.

After his recovery he was adopted into the tribe, promoted to the rank of chief, and treated with great respect. The Maori tribesmen offered him over 60 girls from whom he was told he might choose as many brides as he liked. He prudently chose only two, both of whom were daughters of the ruling chief. During his years with the Maoris he participated in warfare, head-hunting, and other traditional tribal amusements.

In 1826 Rutherford was rescued by an American brig which took him to Hawaii, where he made good use of his time on shore by marrying yet another native princess. After a year in Hawaii he made his way back to England, where, according to his biographer, he "maintained himself by accompanying a traveling caravan of wonders, showing his tattooing, and telling something of his extraordinary adventures." The story of these

Charlie Wagner Tattooing His Wife Maude

adventures was printed and distributed at his performances. In 1830 extracts from his journals were published in *The New Zealanders* by George L. Craik.

Rutherford's detractors claimed that his story was largely fictitious. But although he might have embellished his adventures for public consumption, there is no doubt that the tattooing was authentic Maori work, and that he knew from firsthand experience a great deal about the lives and customs of the Maoris.

After 1830 Rutherford dropped out of sight. It was Craik's opinion that he had returned to live with his Maori tribe in New Zealand.

The great nineteenth century showman Phineas T. Barnum is credited with organizing the first group exhibitions of unusual individuals who were, in his words, "mysterious deviations from nature's usual course." They were exhibited in Barnum's American Museum, which opened in 1841. It soon became one of the largest and most profitable attractions in New York.

Patrons of Barnum's American Museum were treated to a hodgepodge of edifying exhibits and entertainments such as exotic animals, scientific lectures, magic shows, melodramas and human curiosities, among whom were such novelties as Siamese twins, dwarves, bearded ladies, albinos, gypsies, fat people, skinny people and cannibals. Some were real, some were fakes, and all were introduced with preposterous stories about their exotic origins and adventures.

One of the original human oddities at Barnum's American Museum was James F. O'Connel, who enjoyed the honor of being the first tattooed man ever exhibited in the United States. He entertained his audience with tall tales of exotic adventures like those told by Cabri and Rutherford. According to his story, savages on a South Sea island captured him and forced him to submit to tattooing at the hands of a series of voluptuous virgins. He discovered to his great distress that island custom obliged him to marry the last of the maidens who had tattooed him. She was, of course, a princess.

When O'Connel made his debut in the American Museum there were no professional tattoo artists in the United States. Museum patrons, most of whom had never

Rasmus Nielsen – Scandinavian Strong Man

seen tattooing before, were suitably impressed. After a few years O'Connel left Barnum's American Museum to travel with rural circuses and carnivals. Little is known of his later life. His last recorded circus appearance was in 1851.

In 1869 the circus was revolutionized when the east and west coasts of the United States were connected by rail for the first time. Traditional circuses had moved in horse-drawn wagons over unpaved roads, advancing slowly from one small town to the next. In contrast, train travel made it possible to move large numbers of people and animals, together with heavy equipment, between major cities in a few days. As a result, profits increased dramatically. The circus entered an era of growth and prosperity which resulted in employment opportunities for many tattooed people and tattoo artists.

In 1871 Barnum joined with two established circuses to form the largest circus in the world: P.T. Barnum's Great Traveling Exposition. It included a museum, a menagerie, and over 30 human curiosities. There was no tattooed man in Barnum's original traveling circus, but the position was filled two years later when Barnum discovered an elaborately tattooed Greek named Constantine.

Constantine's curriculum vitae sounded remarkably like an amalgam of Cabri's and Rutherford's: he claimed that he had been married to a native princess, taken prisoner, suffered torture by tattooing, and escaped to travel throughout Asia and Africa, where he had one incredible adventure after another! He was, by his own admission, "the greatest rascal and thief in the world, and always much admired by the ladies."

As the skeptical circus-goer might have guessed, this was something of an exaggeration. Constantine was a Greek who had spent some years in Burma, where he had himself tattooed with the intention of going into show business. His success was due not to his fanciful stories, but to the fact that he was more elaborately and artistically tattooed than his rivals.

His tattooing consisted of 388 symmetrically arranged and closely interwoven images that covered his entire body, including his face, eyelids, ears and penis. The designs, according to his publicity, consisted of "crowned sphinxes, dragons, serpents, monkeys, elephants, leopards, tigers, eagles, storks, swans, peacocks, owls, fishes, salamanders, men and women, fruit, leaves, and flowers, most of them quite small but exceptionally exact in their details." There was even oriental writing between his fingers! The artistry and craftsmanship of Constantine's designs far surpassed anything that had been seen up to that time.

In 1887 a talented young artist named Charles Wagner saw Constantine in New York City. Wagner was so impressed that he decided on the spot to learn tattooing. He had the good fortune to be accepted as an apprentice by New York's leading tattoo artist, James O'Reilly, who was at the time trying out his new invention: the electric tattooing machine, which he perfected and patented in 1891.

O'Reilly attracted thousands of customers, including many circus people. He enjoyed a period of prosperity during the early years of the twentieth century but his work deteriorated when he became involved in protracted lawsuits over patent rights to the electric machine. He died in 1908.

After O'Reilly's death Wagner took over his studio. For more than 40 years he was the best-known tattooer in America and tattooed over 50 completely covered circus attractions. His fame was due to a keen talent for media exposure and highly visible situation in New York City. Ironically, Wagner's skills were far outpaced during this period by many artists who avoided the spotlight and viewed his public antics with distain.

One of the most famous early examples of the art of the electric needle was "La Belle Irene," who was tattooed by both O'Reilly and Wagner. She made her London debut in 1890, claiming to be the first completely tattooed woman ever exhibited in a circus. Her decorations included an artistic assortment of flowers, birds, hearts, cupids, scrolls and sentimental inscriptions borrowed from the ornamental commercial art of the day. Londoners were asked to believe that she had acquired her embellishments

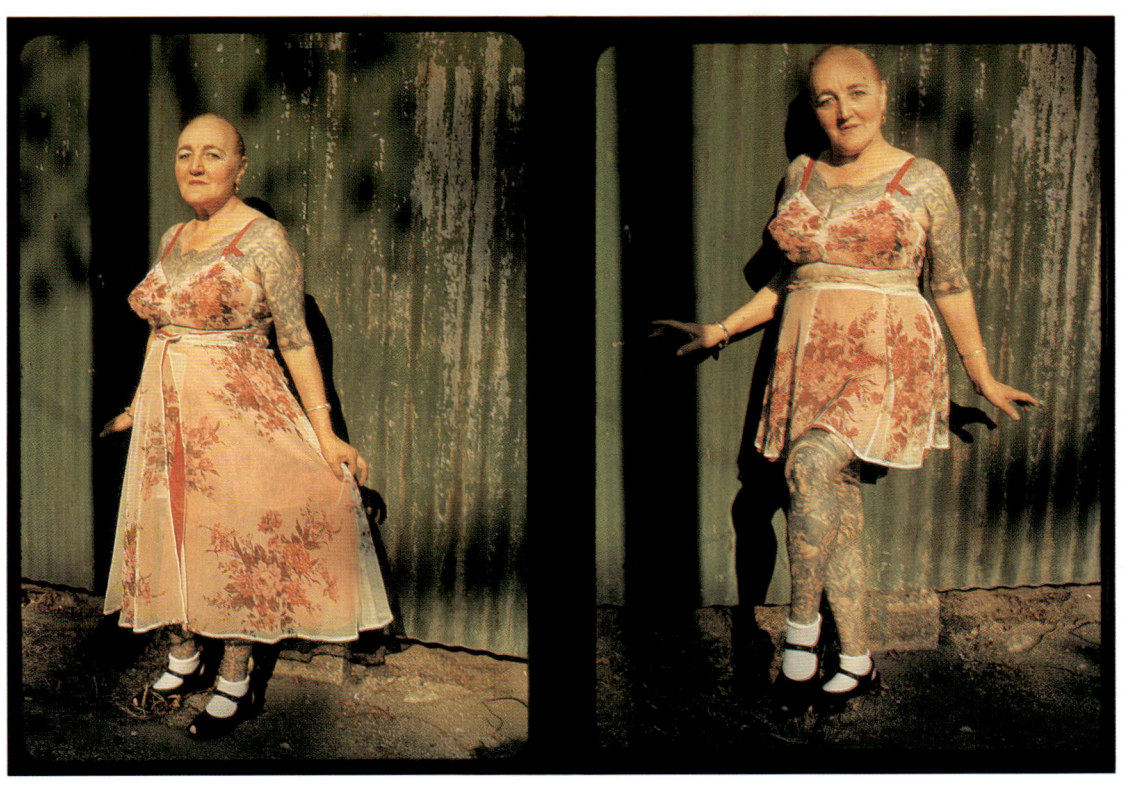

Originally Jean Furella had a "long, luxuriant, dark, silky beard," affording her a career in show business, while thwarting her romantic life. Sword swallower and confidant Alec Linton suggested that Jean transform herself from one of the few authentic bearded ladies in existence, into a totally tattooed woman, then considered to be a "greater rarity." Jean followed her friend's advice, having her beard removed and her body illustrated, resulting in a fulfilling career as "Tatoo Queen" at Chicago's Riverview Park, and a happy marriage to longtime admirer John Carson. She was photographed and filmed at Riverview by Chicago artist Tom Palazzolo.

in a strange and savage land (Texas) as a protection against the unwelcome advances of the natives.

La Belle Irene soon had competition in the form of Emma de Burgh, who was the most famous of O'Reilly's early masterpieces. Mrs. de Burgh was decorated with patriotic and religious motifs, including a rendition of *The Last Supper* on her back. She and her tattooed husband, Frank, enjoyed a successful tour of England and the continent in 1893, but she rapidly ate up her earnings with the result that her girth increased while her popularity diminished. The pre-Raphaelite painter Sir Edward Burne-Jones, who had admired her on her first European tour, saw her again several years later. He reported that "she had grown very stout in the meanwhile, and when I looked at the last supper all the apostles wore broad grins."

During the last decade of the nineteenth century the circus enjoyed an unprecedented period of growth and prosperity. Giant circuses such as Barnum and Bailey, Cole Brothers and Ringling Brothers traveled from coast to coast putting on shows in all the major U.S. cities. In addition, more than a hundred smaller circuses and carnivals crisscrossed the country, playing shorter engagements in rural areas. As the circus prospered, the demand for tattooed people increased.

The designs favored by circus people were for the most part patriotic and religious. Images of the American flag, the American eagle and the Statue of Liberty were perennial favorites. Also frequently seen were themes such as Christ's head in a crown of thorns, the Crucifix, the Madonna and Child and the Last Supper. These were often accompanied by scrolls and banners bearing mottoes such as "Love One Another" or "Jesus Saves." Perhaps such themes were an effort to deny the pagan origins of tattooing in order to make it more acceptable in the eyes of the predominantly rural and conservative circus patrons.

The competition became intense as circus owners competed with each other to come up with ever more extravagant tattooed novelties. Soon there were tattooed sword swallowers, fire eaters, jugglers, mind readers, dwarves, strong men, fat ladies, wrestlers, knife throwers and even circus animals.

It is estimated that by 1920 several hundred completely tattooed people were employed in circuses and sideshows. Some earned as much as two hundred dollars a week (a very considerable sum in those days). The prospect of being able to travel with a circus while earning such a salary must have seemed attractive to many an adventurous soul who would otherwise have been confined to a menial job in a rural community.

The most famous tattooed man of this period was Horace Ridler. Unlike his rivals, he came from a conservative upper-middle-class British family and was educated at one of the best private prep schools. Instead of continuing on to university with his classmates however, he decided on a career in the army. He saw combat as a commissioned officer during World War I and was decorated for heroism. At the end of the war he was honorably discharged with the rank of Major. It was then that his troubles began in earnest, for he had squandered his inheritance. After drifting aimlessly around Europe for several years he came to the realization that there was no peacetime employment in which he could use the skills that had made him a successful soldier.

There was only one occupation that interested him: the circus. Some of his happiest childhood days had been spent with his father's groom, Joe Green, who had once been a successful clown and acrobat. Green's stories of his travels and adventures with the circus had fascinated Ridler as a child. As an adult, Ridler longed to recapture that elusive magic.

What could he do in a circus? He was an accomplished horseman, but not as skillful as professional bareback riders and acrobats. He had a number of tattoos. He might acquire more so that he could exhibit himself as a tattooed man. But there were so many tattooed men! How could he do something different? He hit on an original scheme.

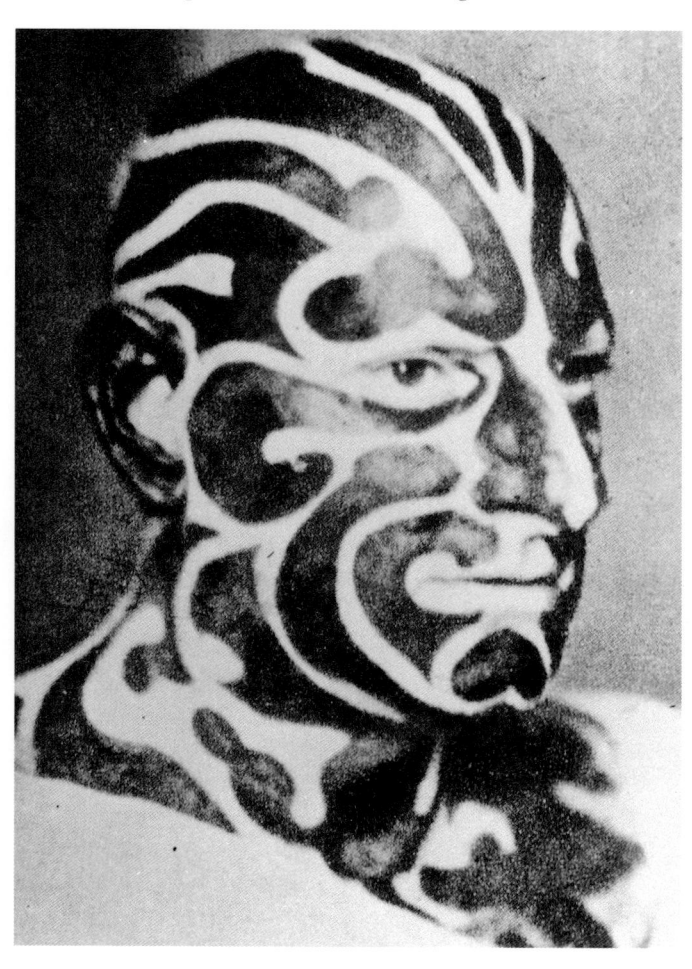

The Great Omi

In 1927 he asked London's leading tattoo artist, George Burchett, to tattoo him all over, including his face, with inch-wide zebra stripes. Burchett at first refused on the grounds that if he did so, Ridler would become a social outcast fit for no work except the uncertain employment he might find as a sideshow freak. But Ridler had already thought of all this. He insisted. Burchett finally agreed.

Burchett worked on him three times a week for over a year. The tattooing resulted in infections and other complications which made it necessary on several occasions for Burchett to interrupt the work schedule so that Ridler could take a few weeks to recover. Burchett considered it one of the most difficult assignments of his career.

When the tattooing was complete Ridler enhanced his appearance by having his teeth filed down to sharp points. He had his nose pierced so he could insert an ivory tusk in it and had his ear lobes pierced and stretched until the holes were more than an inch in diameter. At the end of this ordeal, Major Horace Ridler had been transformed into The Great Omi, one of the most succesful freaks in the history of the circus. He never again used his real name in public.

During this transformation, Omi was fortunate enough to have the support and encouragement of his loyal wife. Burchett wrote, "I have the greatest admiration for these two people. Their devotion to each other was one of the great experiences of my long life, during which I have met many brave and unusual people."

Accompanied and introduced by Mrs. Ridler, who took the stage name "Omette," Omi was a great success in circuses and music halls throughout Europe. Audiences gasped in amazement when he appeared in his jewel-studded costume to tell them how he had been captured by savages in New Guinea and (guess what?) forcibly tattooed!

In 1938 he joined Ripley's Believe It Or Not Show in the U.S. Later he appeared at the Ripley's Odditorium and at Madison Square Garden in New York City. After his success in New York he toured the U.S. with the Ringling Brothers' Barnum and Bailey Circus for a year, during which time he was one of the highest paid circus performers in the world.

At the outbreak of World War II he returned to England where he tried to enlist in the army. Not surprisingly, he was turned down. During the war he remained in England, donating his services and performing in many stage shows for the troops and for war charities.

After the war he continued to appear in England and on the Continent until his retirement in 1950. He and his wife then moved to a small village in Sussex, where The Great Omi died in 1969 at the age of 77.

The Great Omi succeeded because he was unique. But during the latter part of his career fewer and fewer tattooed people were seen in circuses. One reason was that they were no longer novelties. Circus patrons were losing interest in seeing yet another man or woman covered with traditional American-style tattooing. Another reason was the decline of the freak show, in which tattooed people were usually exhibited. After the war freak shows came under attack from medical authorities and social reformers who objected to the practice of exhibiting deformed individuals as a source of amusement and profit. At the same time, medical advances made it possible to treat or prevent many of the hormonal imbalances and other conditions that had caused the physical deformities seen in freak shows. As a result, fewer people were available and willing to exhibit themselves as freaks.

And the attitude of the public had changed. Circus patrons were better educated and more sophisticated. They no longer believed the ballyhoo and the preposterous stories that were the staple fare of the old-fashioned freak show. The individuals who were exhibited as freaks were considered sick and unfortunate, and fewer parents took their children to laugh at them.

After World War II a few of the larger circuses still included freak shows and tattooed people. But by this time a host of factors had combined to erode circus profits. Competition from movies and television was blamed for declining circus attendance. The cost of transporting equipment, animals and performers increased as profits diminished. Many circus employees joined unions and demanded higher pay. Smaller circuses went out of business. Larger circuses could no longer compete with each other and joined forces to form virtual monopolies.

On July 16, 1956, Ringling Brothers' Greatest Show on Earth, the last giant traveling three-ring circus in the U.S., gave its final performance in Pittsburgh, Pennsylvania. A clown lifted a little girl onto his lap and said, " Put away a lot of memories tonight. This is the last three-ring big-top anyone will ever see." The Greatest Show on Earth had gone bankrupt in the middle of the summer season. The 80-car circus train was packed for the last time and returned to winter quarters in Florida. The next day the headline in the New York Times read: "The Big Top folds it tents for the last time."

Some circuses managed to survive on a greatly reduced scale by putting on their performances in indoor arenas rather than tents. In these circuses freaks and tattooed people were rarely exhibited.

When we look at photographs of traditional circus tattooing, we see that the great tattooing of the past is still great today. Constantine and Omi would create a sensation if they appeared at a modern tattoo convention. And there is still magic in designs. The crosses, flags, hearts, dragons, and sailing ships that made up the dominant themes of the art symbolized the unabashed expression of profound and simple emotions: faith, patriotism, loyalty, love, and courage.

Tattooing has come a long way since Charlie Wagner laid down his machine for the last time in 1953. Tastes have changed. Many of the old designs seem naive to us now. But at the same time, there is a new appreciation of our tattoo heritage. In the course of our progress we will rediscover the past, see it with new eyes, and find much that endures.

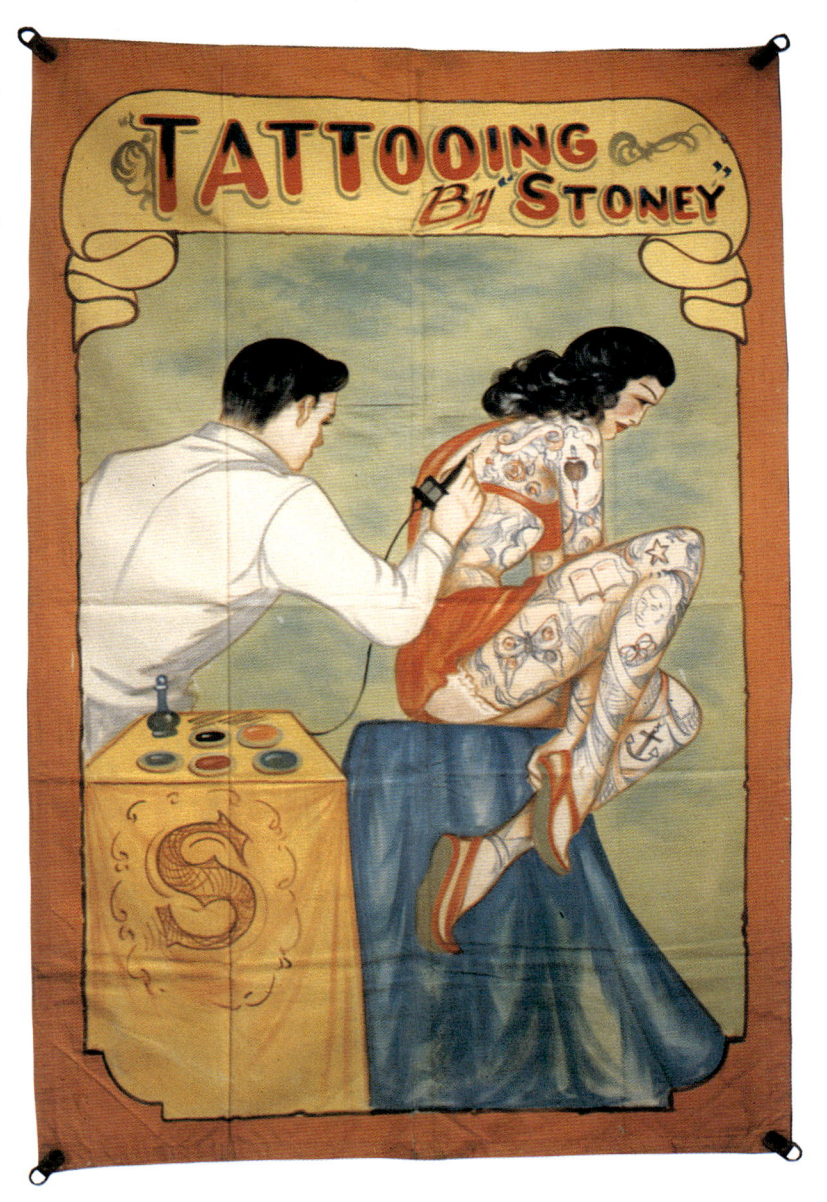

Stoney St Clair (1912-1980) exemplified American tattoo spirit at its best. He traveled with circuses and carnivals for over 20 years and operated a number of successful shops, producing masterly freehand tattoos and beautiful flash, despite being wheelchair-bound from a childhood bout with rheumatoid arthritis. The banner painter took broad liberties in his depiction.

Copyright 1994 by Steve Gilbert. This article was originally published in International Tattoo Art *and is reprinted by kind permission of the publisher.*

Portrait of Banner Artist Tattoo Jack Cripe, Gibsonton, Florida 1988. Photo by Jeff Crisman, Courtesy of Aron Packer Gallery, Chicago
Opposite Page: Self Portrait of Jack Cripe tattooing Marilyn Monroe, Courtesy National Museum of American Art, Smithsonian Institution, Gift of Herbert Waide Hemphill Jr. and museum purchase made possible by Ralph Cross Johnson.

107

108

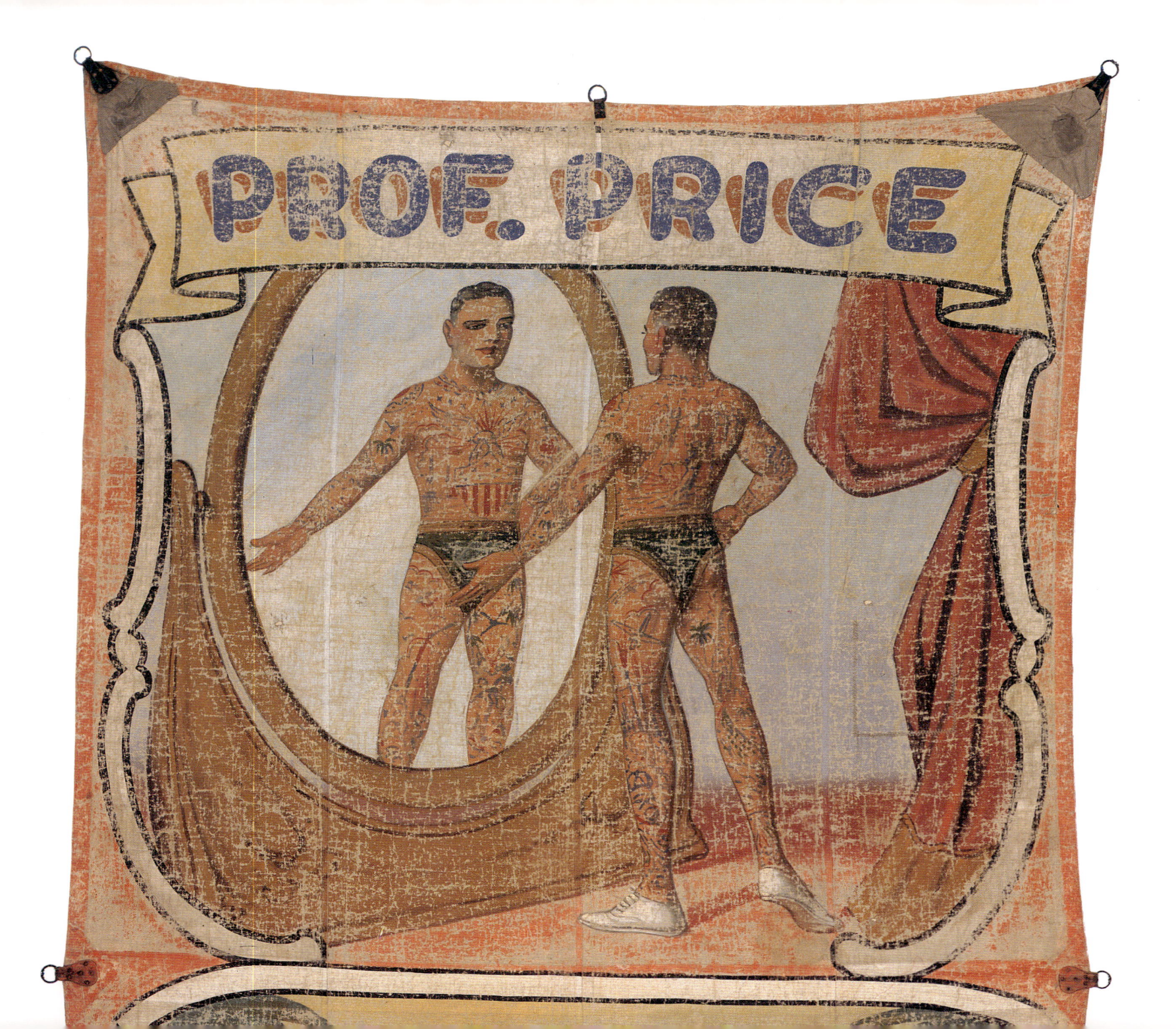

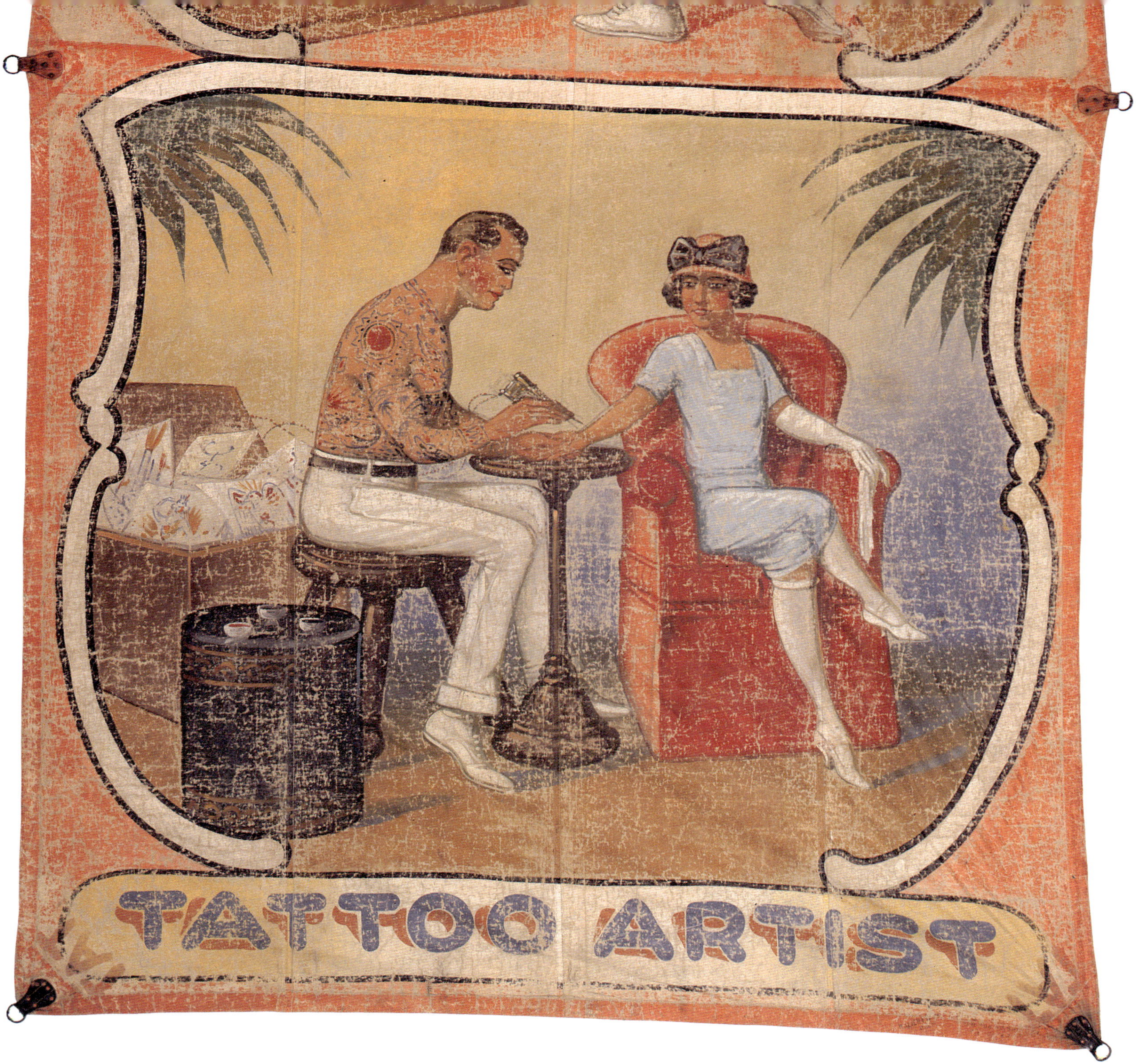
TATTOO ARTIST

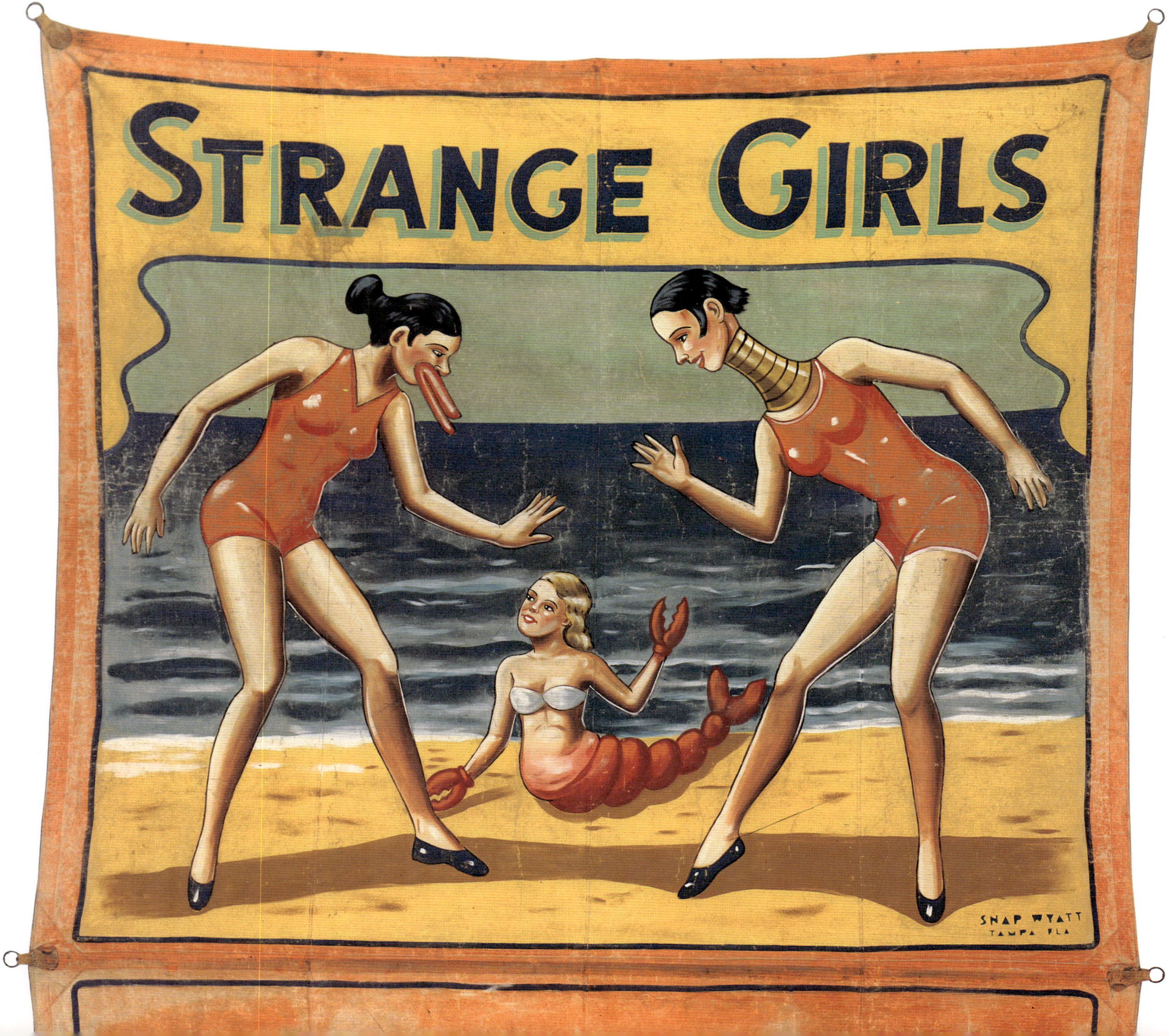
STRANGE GIRLS
SNAP WYATT
TAMPA FLA

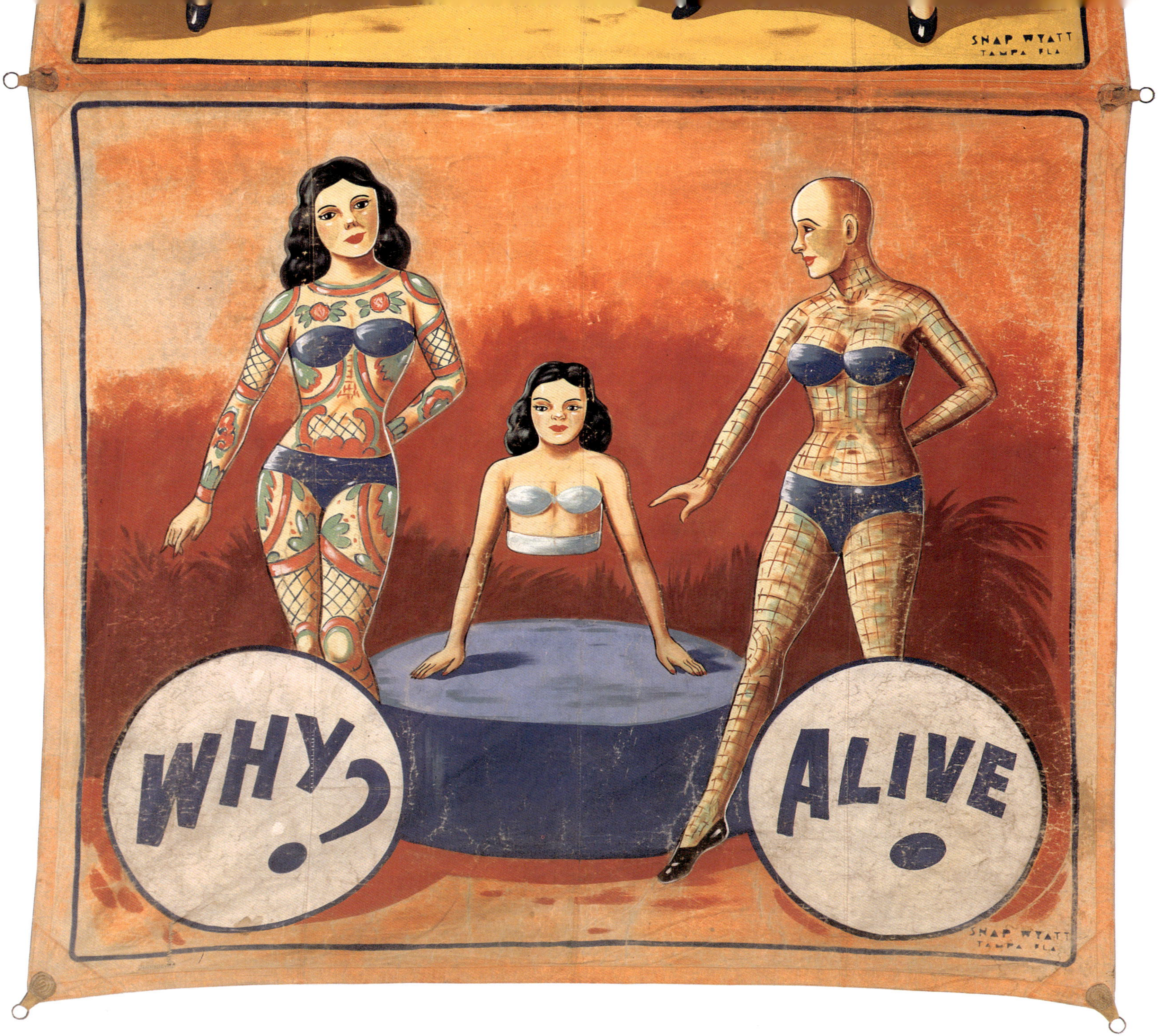
SNAP WYATT
TAMPA FLA
WHY?
ALIVE!
SNAP WYATT
TAMPA FLA

STRANGE GIRLS

CAN THEY
MARRY LIKE OTHER GIRLS
HAVE CHILDREN
BE HAPPY AS THEY ARE
?
WHY?
WERE THEY BORN

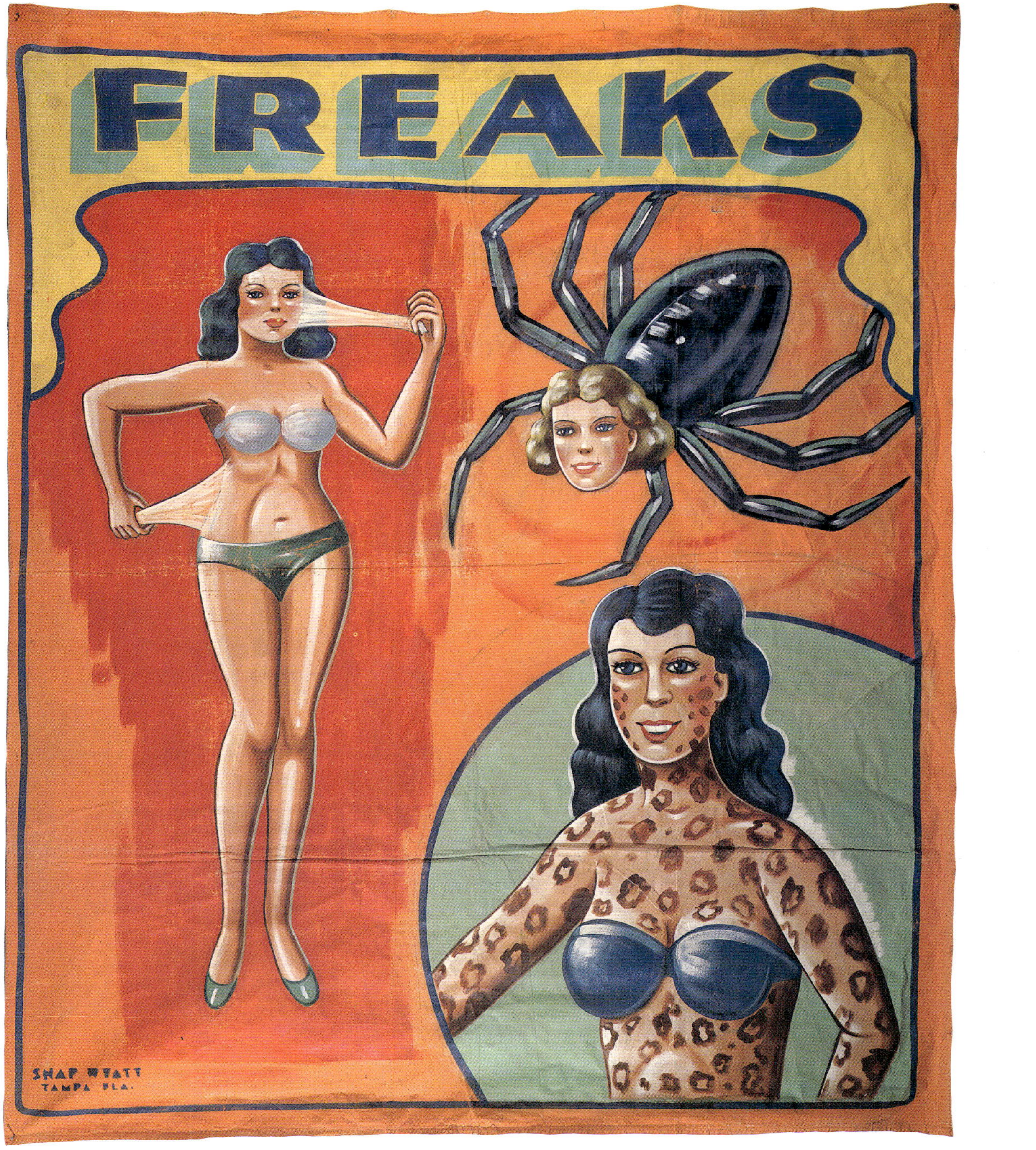
FREAKS
SNAP WYATT
TAMPA FLA.

114

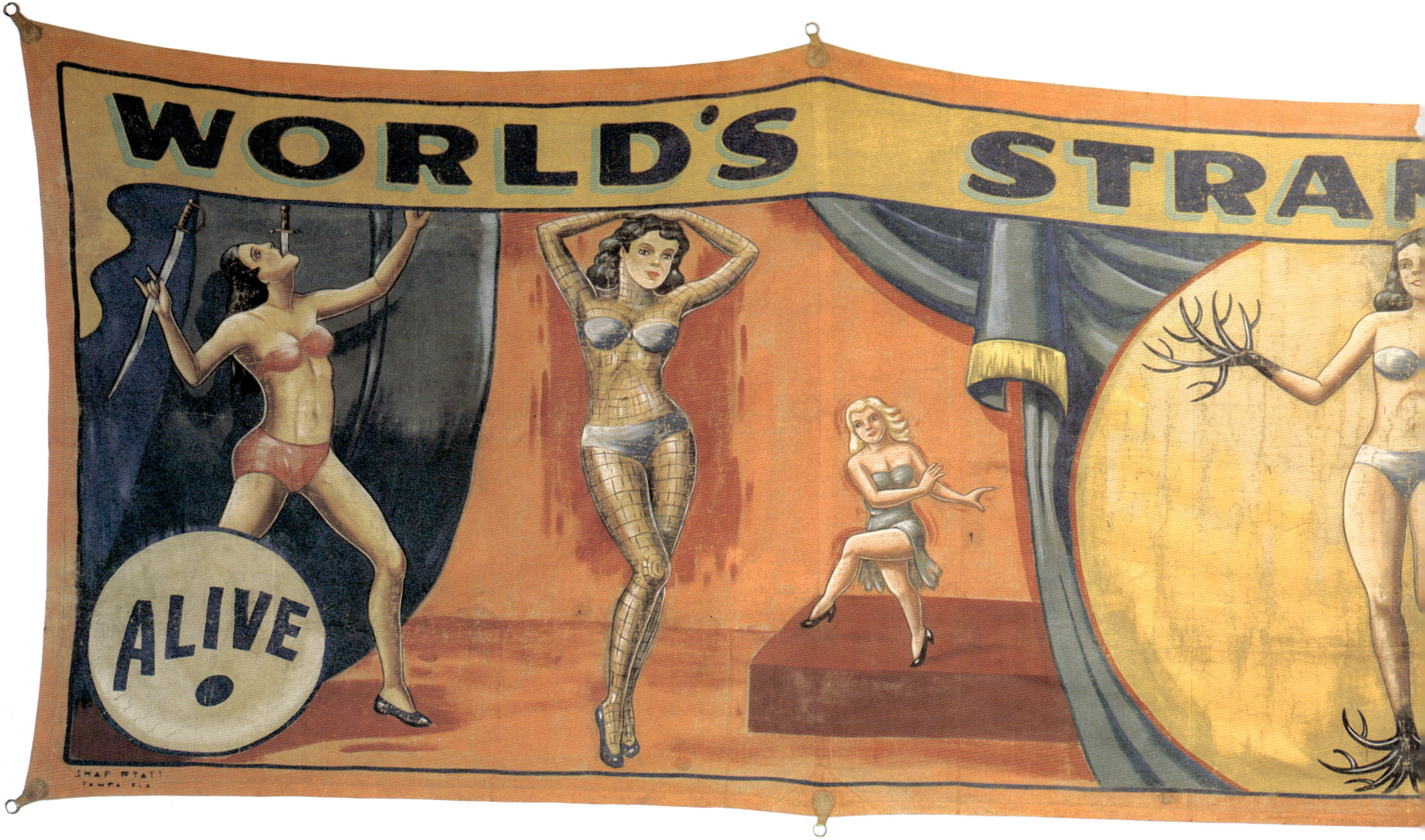

MARTHA.
THE ARMLESS WONDER.

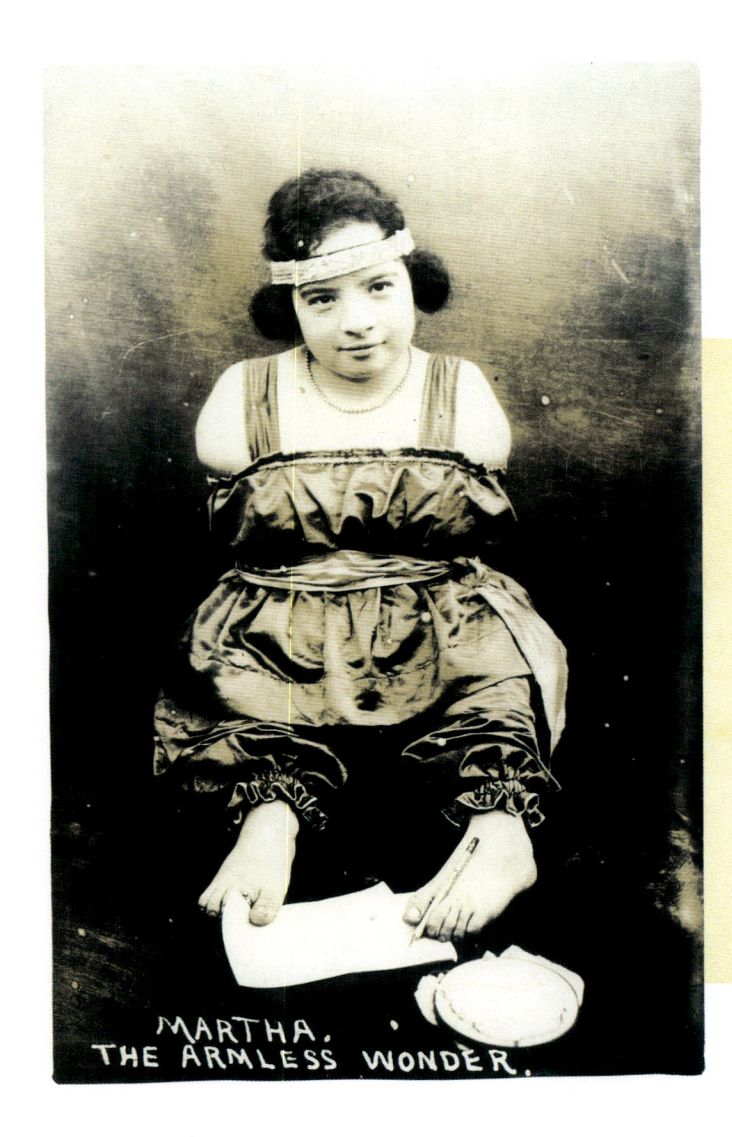

POST CARD

CORRESPONDENCE — ADDRESS — PLACE STAMP HERE

Martha Morris.

117

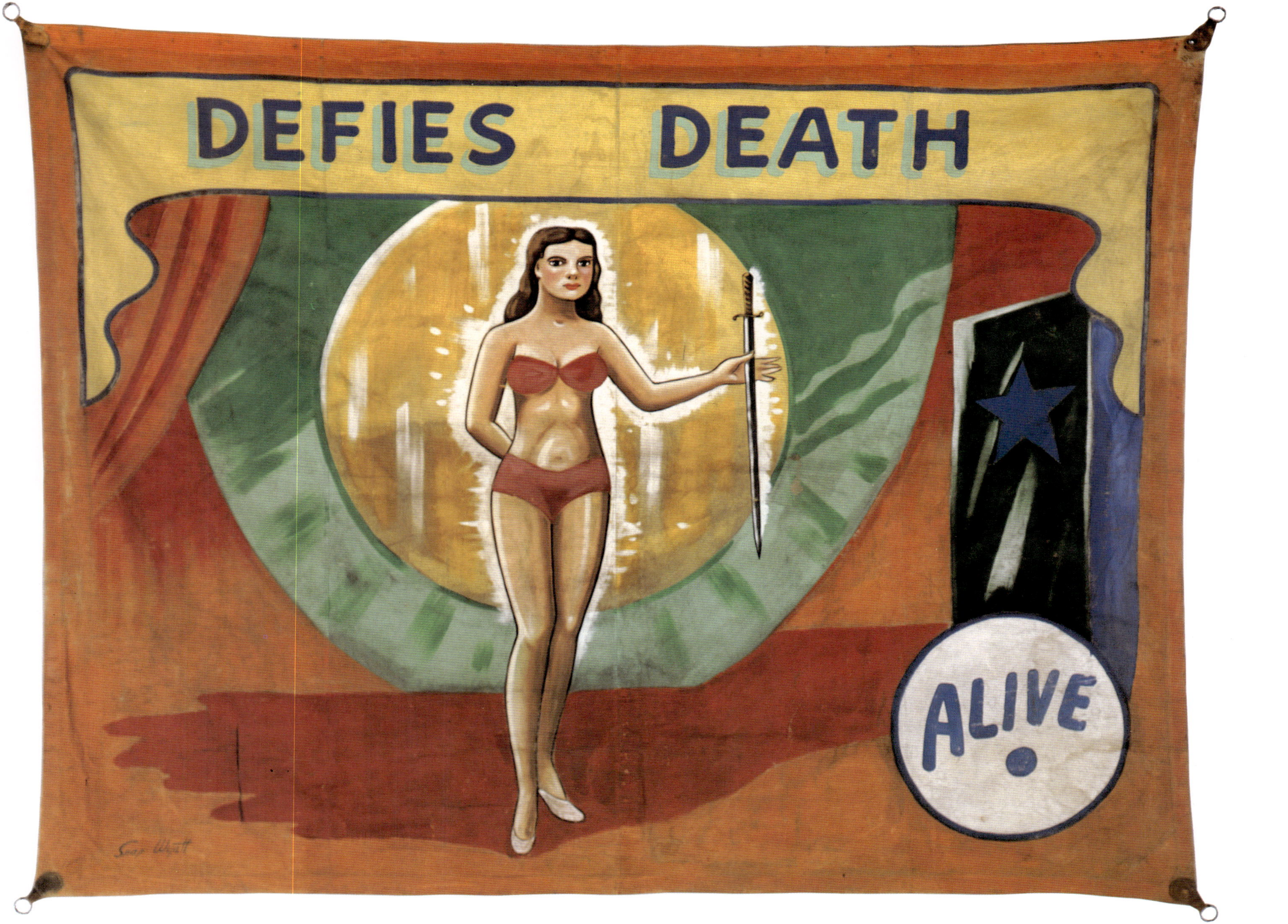
DEFIES DEATH
ALIVE

119

Notes on Alligator Skinned People by Johnny Meah

To understand the whys and wherefores of the popularity of sideshows one would do well to try blocking out current medical and scientific knowledge. In doing so, you can more easily accept many of the attractions at face value. For example, the skin condition known as vitaligo was not widely covered in medical journals back in the '20s and '30s. Doctors who specialized in dermatology were found only in big cities and were far too expensive for the average person.

Vitaligo, basically, is a lack of pigmentation. If your skin is dark, for example, the condition would manifest itself in oddly patterned white splotches. In an extreme version of this condition the entire body would bear these random groupings of splotches.

It's quite possible that you've seen people with this condition and know the medical term for it. That's because you've grown up in an atmosphere of rapid medical advancement and advanced methods of communication.

Now imagine that you're standing in a carnival sideshow in, let's say, 1935. Your world consists of the town you live in and the people who populate it. Aside from the local newspaper your link with the rest of the world is the radio and an occasional newsreel at the theater. Your family doctor has never seen a case of vitaligo. Remember, it's 1935.

A black woman wearing a cape mounts the sideshow platform. The lecturer introduces her as Leona the Leopard Girl. She removes the cape, revealing a body patterned with white and black markings. The lecturer tells you that she was born in Laurens, South Carolina, and that when her mother was pregnant with her she was frightened by a leopard being exhibited at a circus—frightened so badly, in fact, that it permanently marked her unborn child. A woman standing next to you comments, "I've heard of that happening, they talk about it in the Bible."

Someone else murmurs, "Jeez, I thought it'd be painted on or somethin' but you can see it's real!" And you would remember the Leopard Girl for many years, thinking, in all probability, that you'd seen the only person of her kind in the world.

Alligator skinned people were more prevalent on the sideshow circuit than Leopard skinned people, due in part to the fact that a small-time operator lacking the funds to book the real McCoy could manufacture one very inexpensively. The bogus alligator skin effect was accomplished by weakening a solution of Casco glue—a product available in most hardware stores—painting the milky substance onto the body of one of the cast members and, upon drying, having them move and flex causing a patterned cracking effect that was amazingly similar to ichthyosis. Ichthyosis is the condition that the real alligator skinned people were afflicted with.

True ichthyosis, particularly in its advanced stages (i.e., covering the entire body), is a very unpleasant condition. The skin becomes dry, rough and cracks in reptile-like patterns. Oil must be constantly rubbed on to the face, palms of the hands and soles of the feet to stave off the drying, cracking process. Those afflicted with it are unable to perspire, so on hot days frequent immersion in water is their only relief. Constant tearing of the eyes of nearly salt brine quality is another discomfort associated with the heat as, for lack of a more conventional escape route, sweat is eliminated through the tear ducts.

I've pictorialized numerous alligator skinned people. In rendering them one must constantly bear in mind that the banner will be viewed from many feet away, therefore very bold lines and exaggerated light and dark contrast must be used in depicting the unusual skin. As is the case with most banner art, you constantly repress the urge to use softer, more subtle effects as they are lost when viewed from a distance.

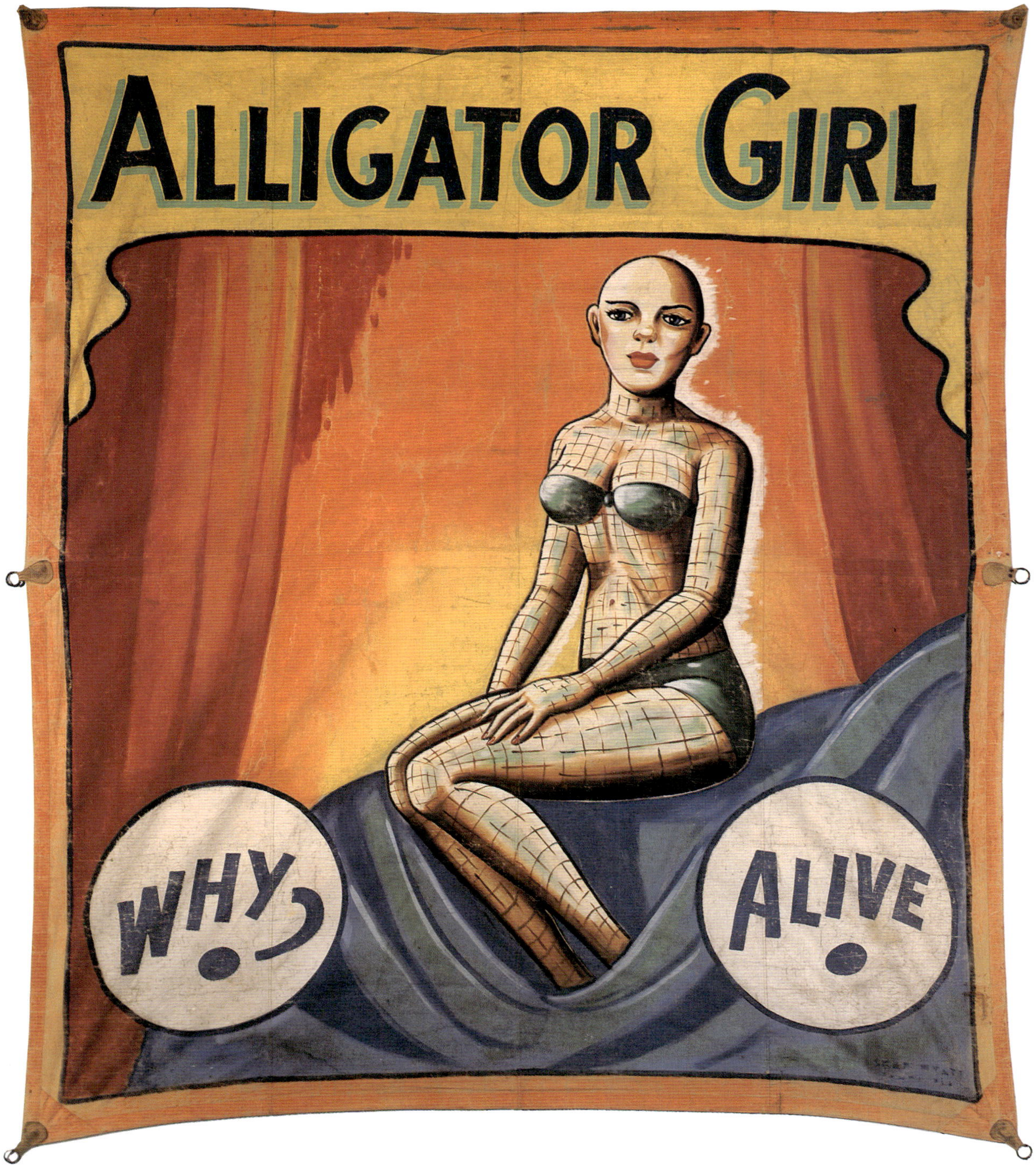
ALLIGATOR GIRL
WHY?
ALIVE!

122

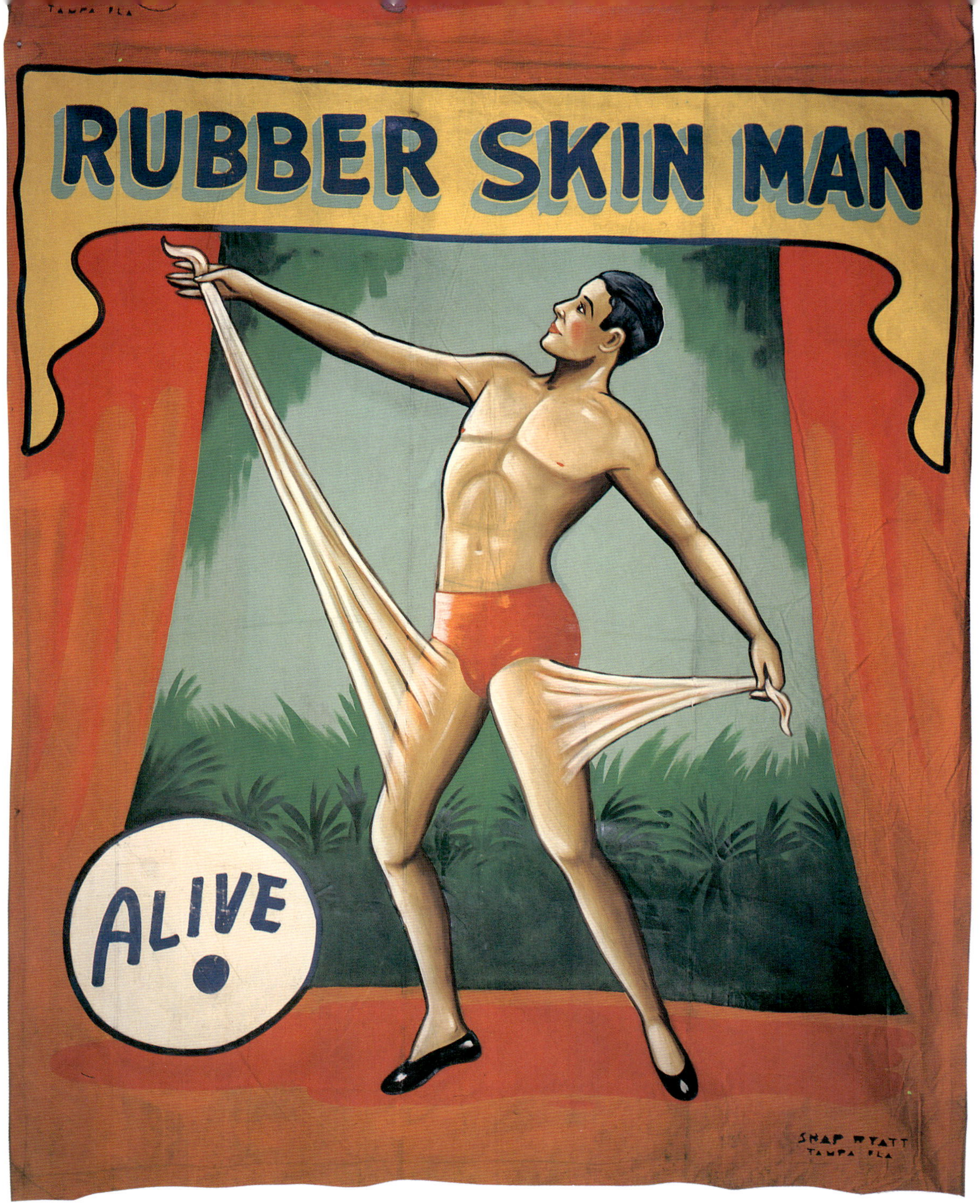
RUBBER SKIN MAN
ALIVE
SNAP WYATT
TAMPA FLA

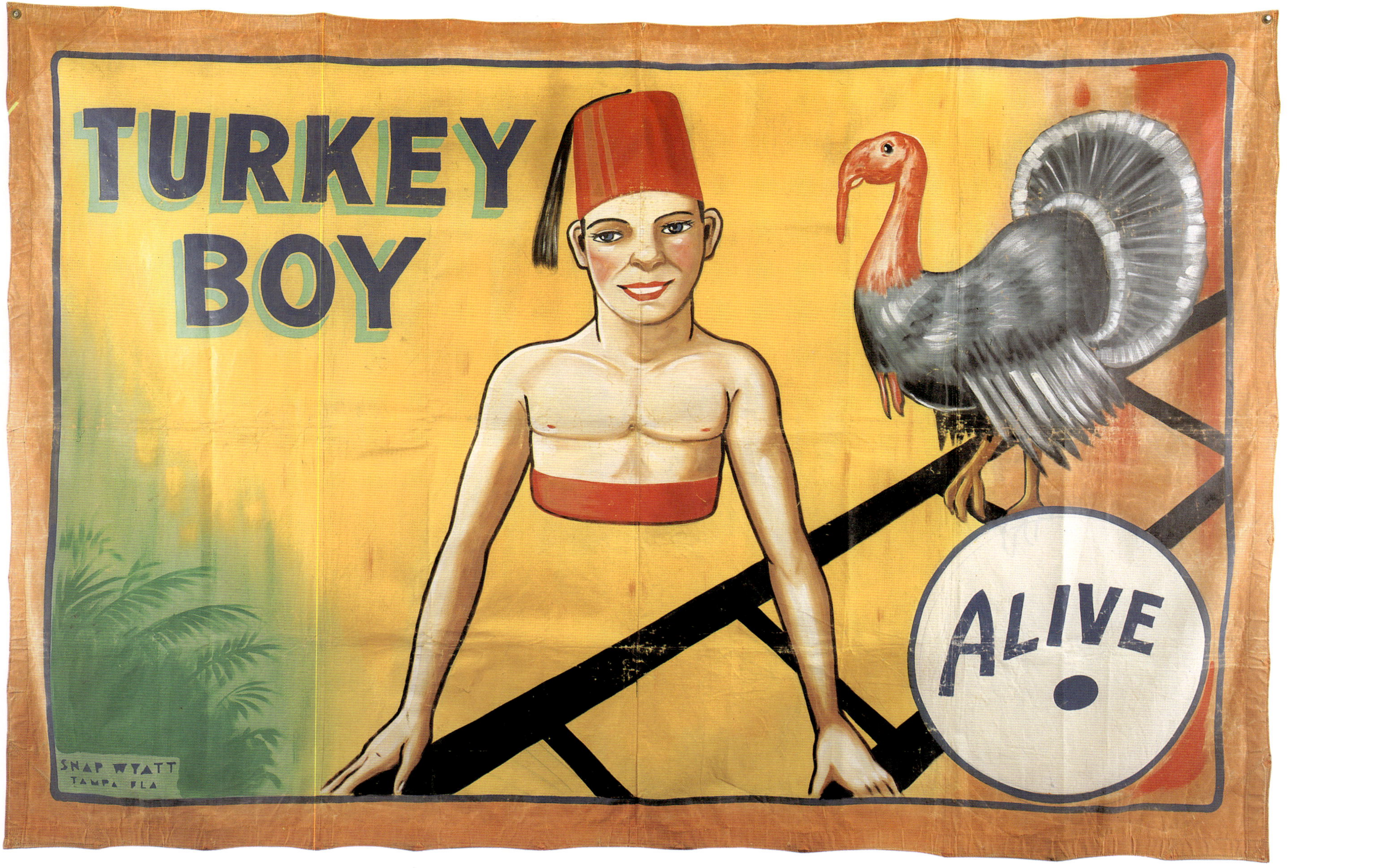
TURKEY
BOY
ALIVE
SNAP WYATT
TAMPA FLA

The LURE of the SIDE SHOW
DENIAL/DESIRE

Dale Slusser

From their inception at the end of the nineteenth century carnivals enjoyed immense popularity in the United States and by the 1920's there were over two thousand carnival companies ranging in size from one to as many as forty train cars crisscrossing the country. One of the largest of these early companies, the Johnny J. Jones Mighty Exposition–"The Show Beautiful," in 1938 offered forty acts, including the Royal Russian Midgets; a Freak Museum; Fat Girl Twins; a Two-Headed Baby; the Temple des Rhumba; and a Palace of Illusions; and rides such as a Merry-Go-Round, Auto Skooter, Hey-Dey, and Lindy Loop, as well as concession stands and games of skill.

Carnival companies and acts varied greatly, yet they all featured amazing wonders which blended elements of the grotesque, bizarre, and erotic in the hope of awakening desire and curiosity in the passerby.

What the carnival offered went beyond mere entertainment; by paying the few cents of the entrance fee one could glimpse a world which transgressed the outer limits of reason and experience. It was a world of overwhelming excess and the exotic "other", inhabited by immensely fat men and women; "Glomming Geeks" who ate live snakes; African witch doctors; alligator girls; three-legged football players; and "The World's Strangest Girls." When the carnival came to town it undoubtedly offered a welcome disruption in the day-to-day pattern of provincial habits and local traditions while injecting a certain degree of cosmopolitanism into the area yet this alone does not account for its great success.

Recently much has been written by scholars on the carnival, particularly on the forms which carnival took in Europe from the seventeenth through the twentieth centuries. Such scholarship adds to the interpretations of its enormous popularity over time.[2] Although there is little concensus on interpreting the sideshow phenomena, it has become clear that forms of entertainment which occur in the carnival are indeed actions which articulate important cultural and political meanings.[3]

Central to the carnival is the interaction between the "high" and "low," the exalted and the base. Those at the "top" of the hierarchies of wealth and power in society continually attempt to reject the "bottom" in order to gain prestige and status. This, of course, proves to be impossible, for as a binary pair the top is dependent upon the bottom for its own construction. A pattern emerges where "the top *includes* that low symbolically, as a primary eroticized constituent of its own fantasy life."[4] Thus the two poles of repugnance and fascination are charged, where the political imperative of those above to eliminate the "low" creates a desire for what has been denied. This process of differentiation through the rejection of certain actions and images which are construed as the debasing "low" does not only occur at the pinnacles of society, but is enacted along the entire spectrum of the social hierarchy

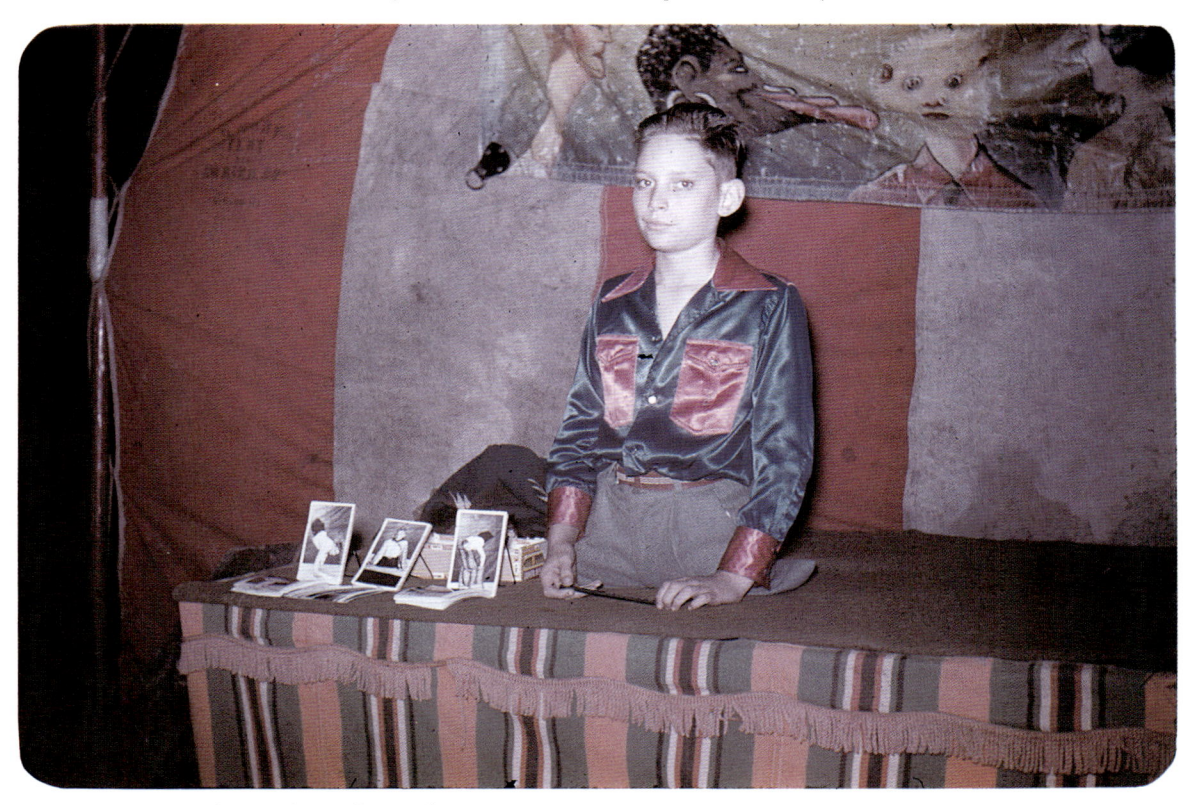

Wesley Upperman at the age of 13, Biller Brothers, 1950

wherever subtle gradations of above and below are imposed. Thus it was not only among the established elite that this pattern of repression and desire emerged, but also throughout the rural population of the United States, which in the early twentieth century, largely through the efforts of the state and church, was increasingly coming to exhibit the characteristics of order, civility and decorum.

It was in the sideshows of the traveling carnivals that the repressed "low" was celebrated and one could gaze upon that which had been denied. As the title of this book suggests, *Freaks, Geeks & Strange Girls* were exhibited on the midway for all who could pay the admission fee. Acts such as "Turkey Boy," "Sealo the Seal Boy" and "Vicki Condor, Four-Legged Tennis Player," by their seeming abnormality assaulted the viewers' assumptions of what was indeed normal in this world. Perhaps these acts even contributed an element of hope that some equally extraordinary, though quite different act of fortune would occur to improve the often harsh lives of the carnival going crowds. Of those who viewed the freak shows, some probably felt guilt over their participation in the spectacle; even more, no doubt, left imagining that, compared to what they had witnessed, they were a bit more superior than they felt when they had entered.

In addition to the extraordinary, the "other" from distant lands was also exhibited. Acts which featured women purported to be from various countries of the world, such as "The Singing Girls of Bagdad," "Oriental Fantasy Girls" and "Streets of Cairo," which included belly dancing, were especially popular, and shows of African Americans and Native Americans were also common.[5] At the carnival Americans could share in the myth of the Orient as the "inferior other" which had played such an important role in the construction of European legitimacy during the colonial era. Moreover, during the middle decades of this century dancing girl or "cooch shows" became increasingly risque as the dancers discarded more and more of their clothing. Beyond the obvious titillation, what was being sold by such acts was the opportunity to participate as an observer in a position of relational superiority over the women and people of color on display.

In considering sideshows, it must be acknowledged that the carnival was often profoundly guilty of exploiting the unfortunate and contributing to models of racism and sexism. Yet, as they did for visitors to the carnivals of old, sideshow banners still evoke the charge between the twin poles of repugnance and fascination that flows strong in us today. While we must question the spectacles that these acts (re)presented, a contemporary view of banners allows us to view their creation more thoughtfully and grasp the sideshow in relation to the ever present interplay between perceptions of "high" and "low" in our culture. As the business of entertainment is transformed through new technology in this century, different modes of recreation are constantly being developed, and images of the "low" continue to fire our imaginations. In this regard the audience has not really changed, for it remains true today that what is denied is desired.

NOTES:

1. Joe McKennon, A Pictorial History of the AMERICAN CARNIVAL, *Vol.1 (Bowling Green, Ohio: Popular Press, 1971), 97, 120. This edition includes both volumes 1 and 2 combined in one binding.*

2. *A seminal work on the subject is found in M.M. Bakhtin,* Rabelais and his World, *Trans. H. Iswolsky (Cambridge, MA: MIT Press, 1968).*

3. *Peter Stallybrass and Allon White,* The Politics and Poetics of Transgression *(Ithaca: Cornell University Press, 1968) 43.*

4. *Ibid p 5.*

5. *McKennon,* A Pictorial History of the AMERICAN CARNIVAL, *Vol.1, pp. 72, 100; Vol. 2, p. 155.*

6. *See Edward Said,* Orientalism *(New York: Vintage Books, 1979) and Edward Said,* Culture and Imperialism *(New York: Knopf, 1992).*

ADDITIONAL SOURCES:

Deborah Donato and Randy Johnson, Fred G. Johnson: Sideshow Banners. Exhibition Catalog *(Chicago: State of Illinois Art Gallery, 1989).*

Frederick Drimmer, Very Special People *(New York: Amjon Publishers, Inc., 1973).*

Arthur H. Lewis, Carnival *(New York: Trident Press, 1970).*

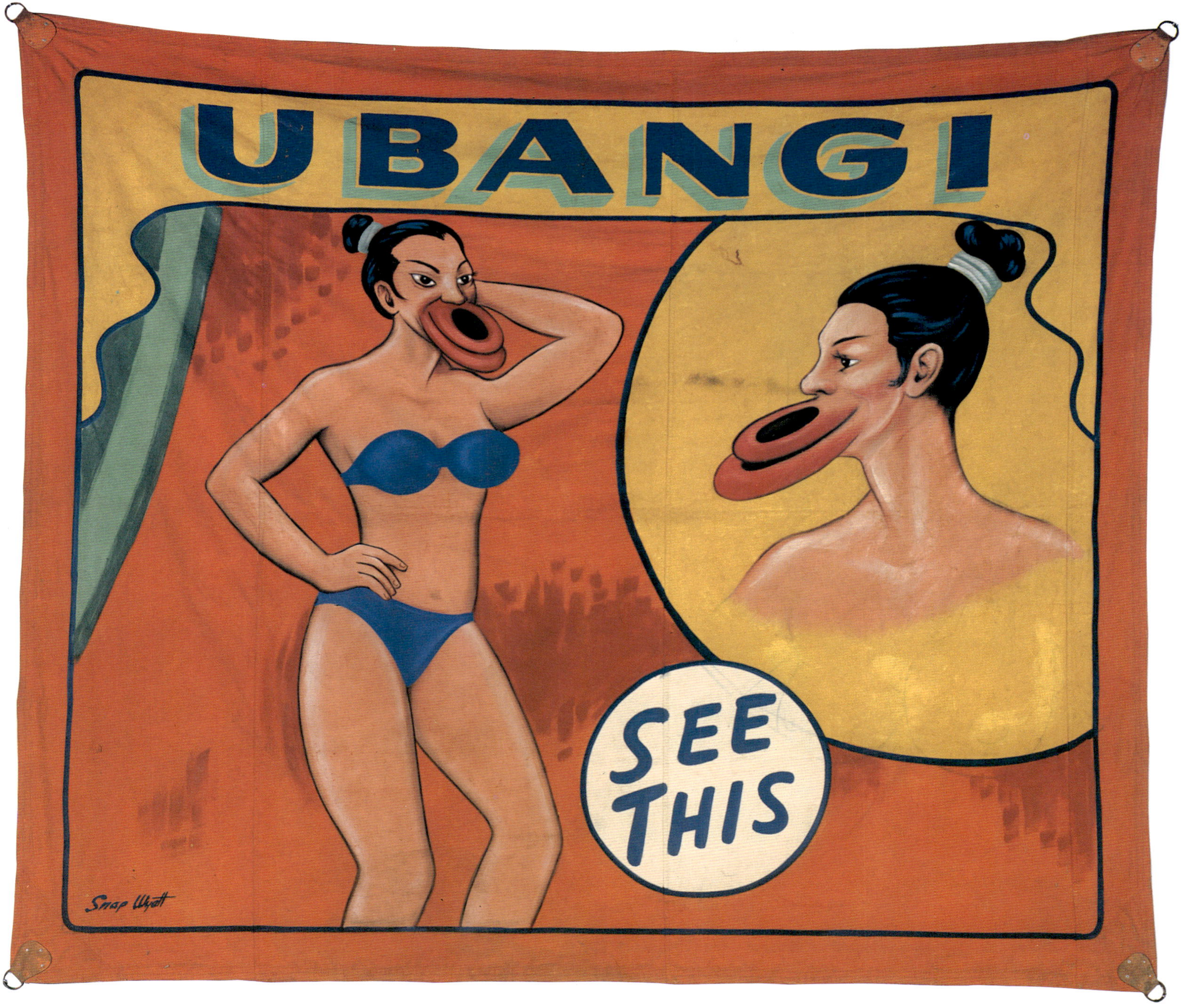
UBANGI
SEE THIS
Snap Wyatt

128

SNAP WYATT
TAMPA FLA
AFRICAN
WITCH DOCTOR
ALIVE
SNAP WYATT
TAMPA FLA

THE
MAGICAL
The GREAT RAFAEL
THE GIRLS of ENCHAN
THE GIRLS of EXCITEM
THE GIRLS of ILLUSIO

130

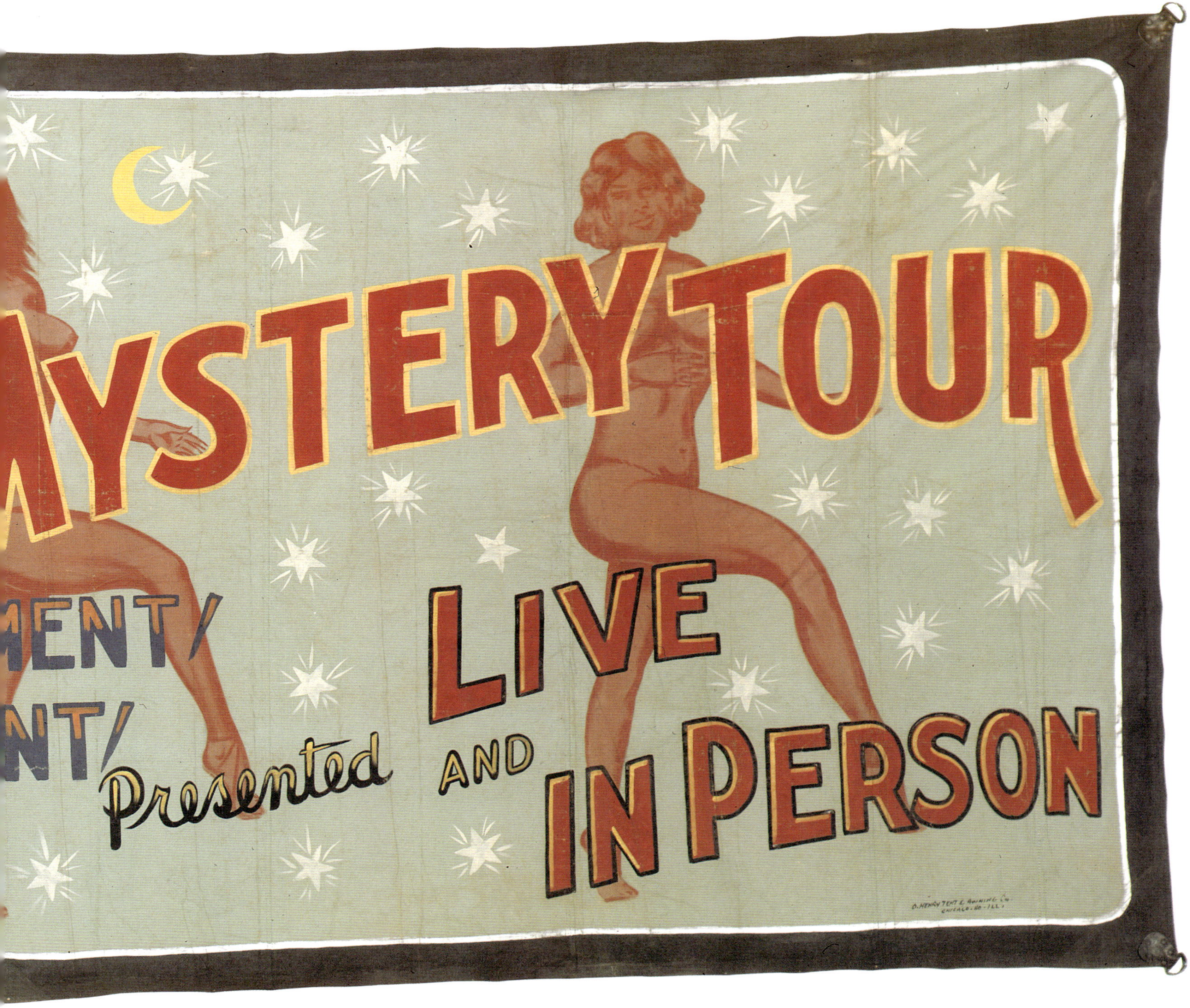
YSTERY TOUR
MENT/
NT/
Presented
LIVE
AND
IN PERSON

THIS EXHIBIT IS
NOT ENTERTAINMENT
SEE THE
SHOCKING
BRUTAL TRUTH
LEARN THE
HEART BREAKING FACTS
about
DRUG
ABUSE!
YOU MUST SEE THESE VICTIMS

The Dope Show

Teddy Varndell

This banner line was commissioned in the early 1970's at the height of the Nixon era drug hysteria and painted by Fred G. Johnson late in his career. Chromosome damage, flying Linkletters, and F.C.C admonitions warning of the direct link between low wattage FM stations and heroin addiction were rampant. White suburban high school virgins were being genetically reprogrammed for life by LSD-25, and boy-howdy we remembered Thalidomide. Returning Viet Nam vets were making methadone clinics a growth industry. Cigarette manufacturers were still pitching their products prime-time, while selling a couple of joints to a minor in Missouri was a capital crime. Speed freaks that weren't killing themselves outright were finding Jesus or winding up in jail, so either way they put on a little weight and their hair grew back. Compared to a clean six hour acid high for $2.00, cocaine was an expensive novelty (*treys, nickels, dimes, half-spoons and spoons* was the chant). The experts of the day described cocaine as only moderately psychologically addictive. With cocaine use perceived as predominant to the African American community, the Feds had other priorities.

These banners are unusual in their lack of orange, a color commonly dominant in sideshow banners. The "dressing gown" green ground, also used in earlier banners of other subjects, the use of a black border, and the metallic silver pin stripe detail gives this show a serious, clinical quality. One can only assume that the artist's early experience as a WW I ambulance painter was responsible for his invocation and interpretation of the "white cross" (also symbol for small meth-amphetamine tablets common at the time) design elements in the upper corners of each banner. While heroin and marijuana are well represented, cocaine is conspicuous in its absence.

Johnson's unique perspective of human proportion gives the thick-trunked, broad-shouldered figures a dwarflike quality. The banner portraying a bearded James Brolinesque doctor admonishes us against illegal thrills lest we propagate a monster baby attraction of our own. A knife wielding zombie warns us that in Charlie and Sharon's case, the combination of LSD and uninvited house guests can be dicey at the least. "Anything can happen if your trip is a bummer. "Take heed children lest you wind up like the sandal-shod, bell-bottom-clad "hippy chick" in Tammy Faye eye shadow. One of those who "dies in vein".

I first saw these banners late in the summer of 1977 at the DuQuoin, IL State Fair. By this time High School kids were the only ones using acid (what was going on in these schools that made a half-a-hit at lunch seem like a reasonable effort at making the situation semi-tolerable?), Jimmy Carter was president, polyester was everywhere, and somehow inflation translated into $30 bags of Santa Marta gold. I was standing out in front of the show wearing the new uniform (Hawaiian shirt, straight leg wash slacks and a Panama hat) in emulation of the guy who was laying out those big lines of 70% borax and wondering whether or not to get off the half a buck, when a sidekick exited the trailer and confirmed that "This Exhibit is Not Entertainment", but a rather fat black guy with a methadone card. He assured me that a beer at the same price was going to be a lot more fun, so off I staggered with the banner image of a slashing, hunchbacked Mansonette burned into the back of my brain.

Fast forward fifteen years and I'm standing in a driveway in Montgomery AL wearing the new, new uniform, (black T-shirt, black jeans, and black Chuck Taylor high tops) and listening to a showman's sad tale of this attraction's evolution from pickled punks to a mobile "Scared Straight" unit. It seems that back in '77, a competitor's show had been popped up in Lake County, Illinois for violating a statute prohibiting the "possession and transportation of a corpse without a license." Scheduled to open in the same state a few weeks later and wishing to avoid a pinch, the dope show was hurriedly reframed as a live single-O, the incarnation I found in Du Quoin. (For a description of a similar show see Spaulding Gray's essay in *In Search of the Monkey Girl* by Randal Levenson). Not only did this new improved version play well in the heartland, but the operator assured me it would still make a ton of dough in the nineties.

Why would anyone pay to see a show that was being given away for free on the streets of any American city? Since the onset of AIDS, the strung out whores of Chicago's North Avenue are scarier than any darkride bogeyman. Twitching crack babies come free with any paid PBS subscription. Bullet holes pockmark street corners where scared teenagers die defending their right to sell dime bags to suburban tourists. Health care costs soar as insurance companies fail to see the folly of thirty day programs.

We can shut down the dope show if we want to. Legalize it, 'cause it sure ain't going away. If someone is so strung out, so dysfunctional, that staying high is the primary motivating factor in their life, give them the drug for free at a cost to the community of a few pennies a hit, rather than having them out on the street sucking hundreds of dollars a day out of the community jacking and thieving. Design effective treatment programs that deal with the whole person and their circumstances, not just their addictions. Tax recreational use, get the profits out of the safe deposit boxes and offshore banks and into the general revenue funds. Take the money spent on ineffective interdiction schemes and spend it instead teaching people respect for each other and themselves. Stop building prisons and start building schools. By educating our children, we empower them to greater career choices than fry cook or drug cartel lackey. Peace.

WILL YOUR NEXT CHILD BE A HOPELESS DRUG ADDICT?

IT'S POSSIBLE

ACTUAL VICTIMS

MARIJUANA   METHADONE   HEROIN MAY THRILL YOU NOW BUT HOW WILL THEY EFFECT YOUR CHILDREN?

IS A RIDE ON A BUS

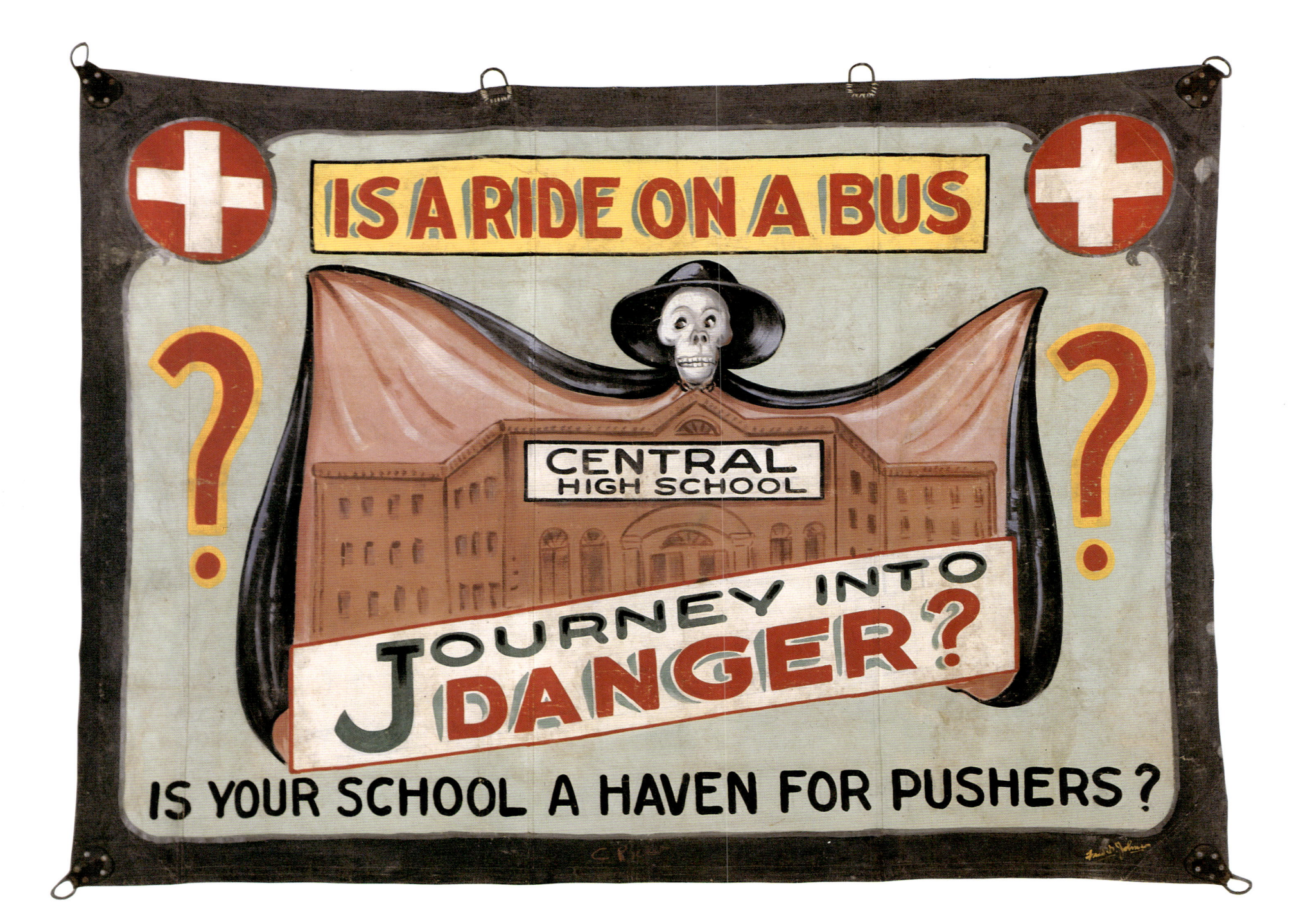

CENTRAL HIGH SCHOOL

JOURNEY INTO DANGER?

IS YOUR SCHOOL A HAVEN FOR PUSHERS?

ANYTHING CAN HAPPEN
IF YOUR TRIP IS A
BUMMER!
Remember
CHARLIE MANSON
AND SHARON TATE!
See
ACTUAL
VICTIMS
O. HENRY TENT & AWNING CO.

PLANNING A TRIP?
WILL IT BE
ONE WAY?
DON'T BE ONE OF
THOSE WHO DIED
IN VEIN

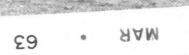

Notes on Geeks by Johnny Meah

    Yes, there really were Geek Shows and yes, they really did bite the heads off of—among other things—chickens. Within these pages are photos of several banners that advertised these individuals.

    Since there were a lot of Geek Shows at one time it follows that there were a lot of career geeks. I will not attempt to delve into the psyche of the professional chicken chomper. A friend of mine, a heavily degreed mind mender who's fascinated with my tales of sideshow folk, asked me about geeks one day. After regaling him with several vivid accounts he commented, "They must be nuts." I'll let that stand as a qualified opinion.

    The Rentons, Chuck and Al, were, if not the best, certainly the most memorable Geek Show operators in the last half century. Chuck Renton's show was titled, "Strange Eeka"—a sort of contraction of geek, freak and eek. The name played well and the show prospered. There were many who appeared in the title role over the years.

    As the years passed, public indignation reared its ugly head, (groups like Citizens Against Chicken Disembowelment I suppose), so we were next treated to a softer, gentler geek. These new-wave geeks no longer performed acts of disgusting depravity, they just looked depraved and disgusting. No longer operating behind a bannerline of carnivorous cannibal images they now worked in pseudo-educational "drug abuse" shows, groveling about in a pit, grunting and acting as weird as possible. "Victims," as the signs told us, "of a lifetime of heroin addiction."

    Somehow this conjures up a vision of a senior geek peering in at one of these new guys, shaking his head sadly and saying, "It's just not the same."

    In my period of time as a banner artist I've rendered my fair share of geek paintings. They weren't my favorite topic, due mostly to the fact that the customers all wanted their canvases to look like Fred Johnson's version of a geek. Johnson, who, incidentally, did most of Renton's work, cranked out so many geek banners that he could probably have done one in his sleep.

    His characters were usually wild-eyed, dark haired little creatures in animal skins, almost always either being captured by or dining on sailors. This may well have been the reason I never enlisted in the Navy. It was definitely the reason I didn't care for geek banners, as I had no desire to mimic someone else's style, as good as they may have been.

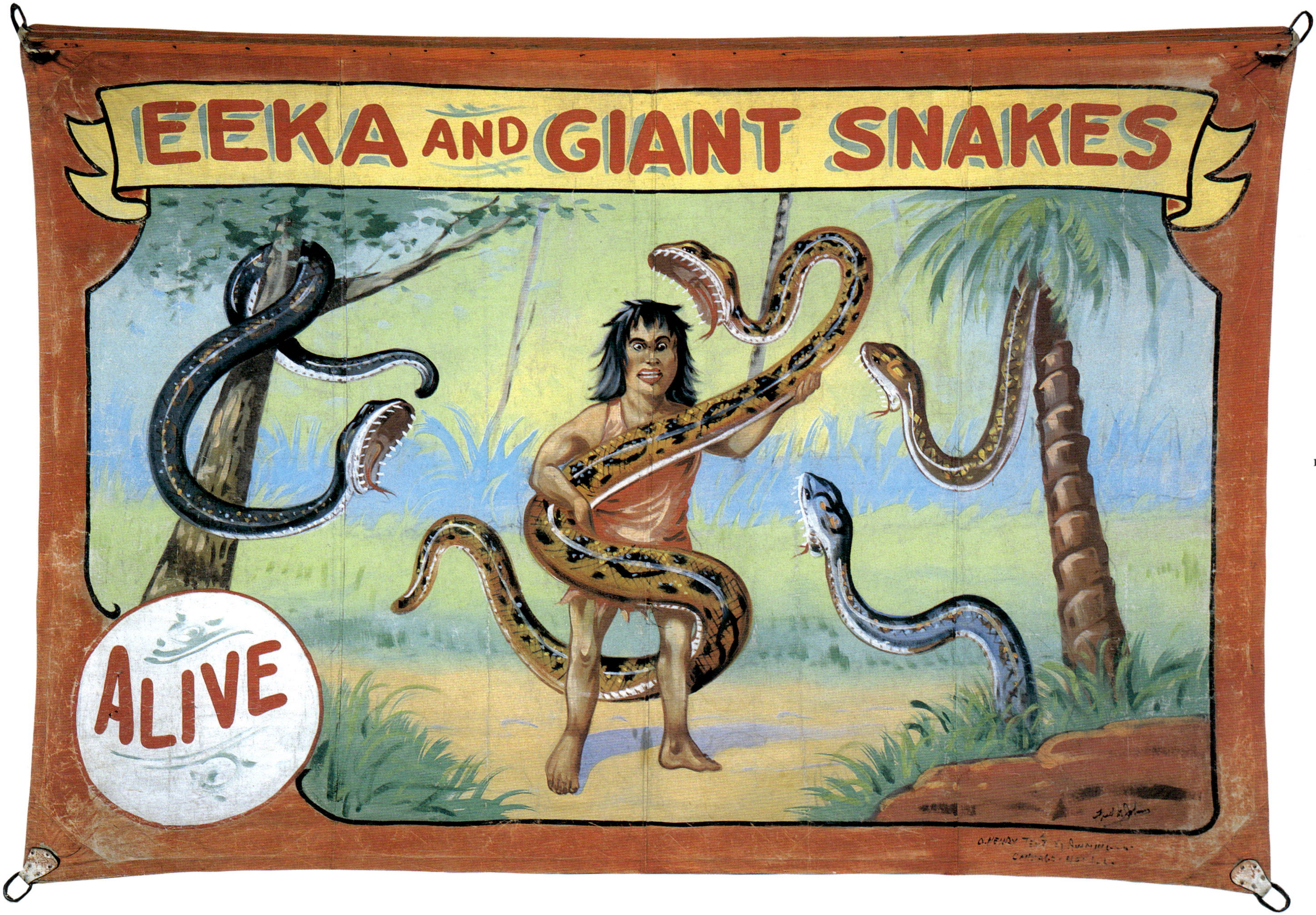
EEKA AND GIANT SNAKES
ALIVE

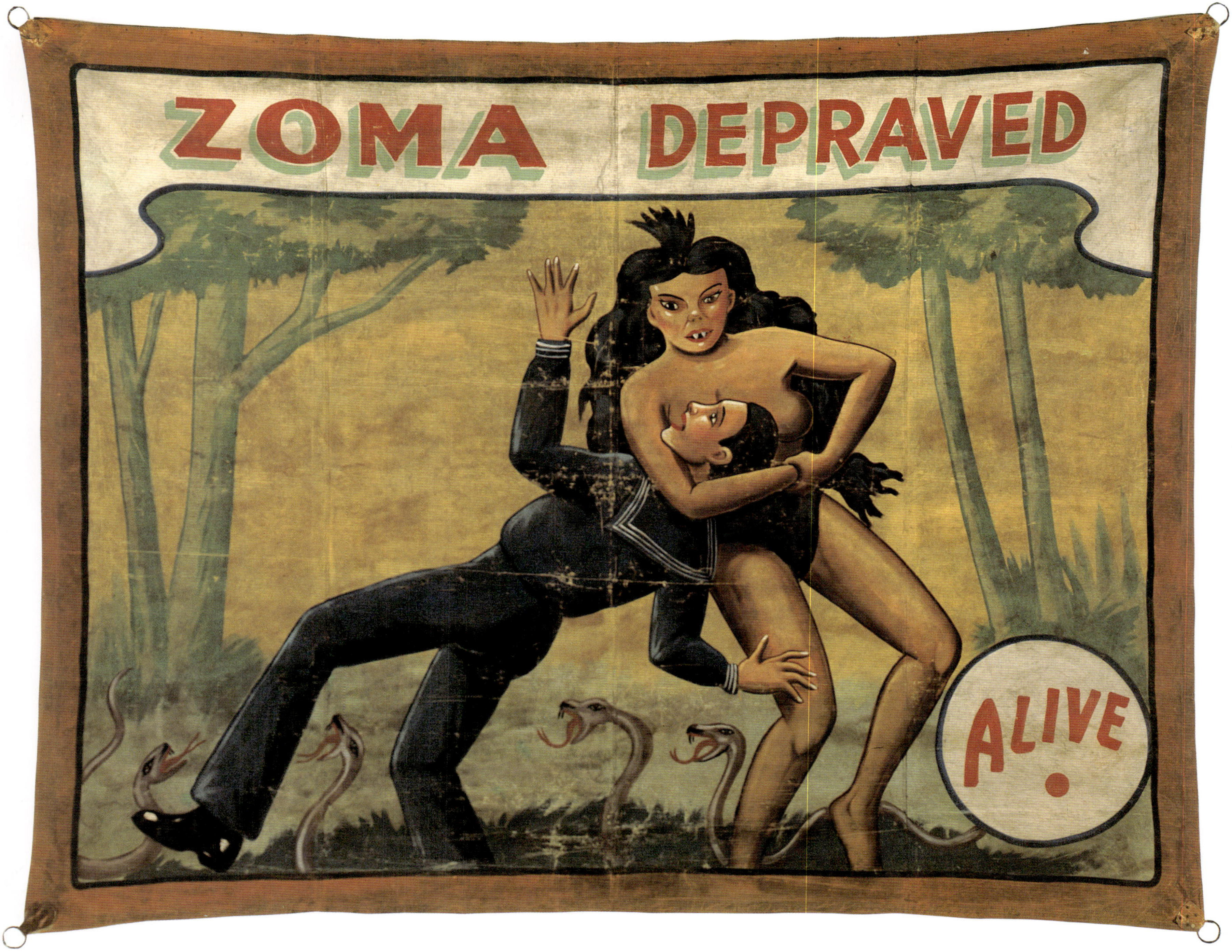

140

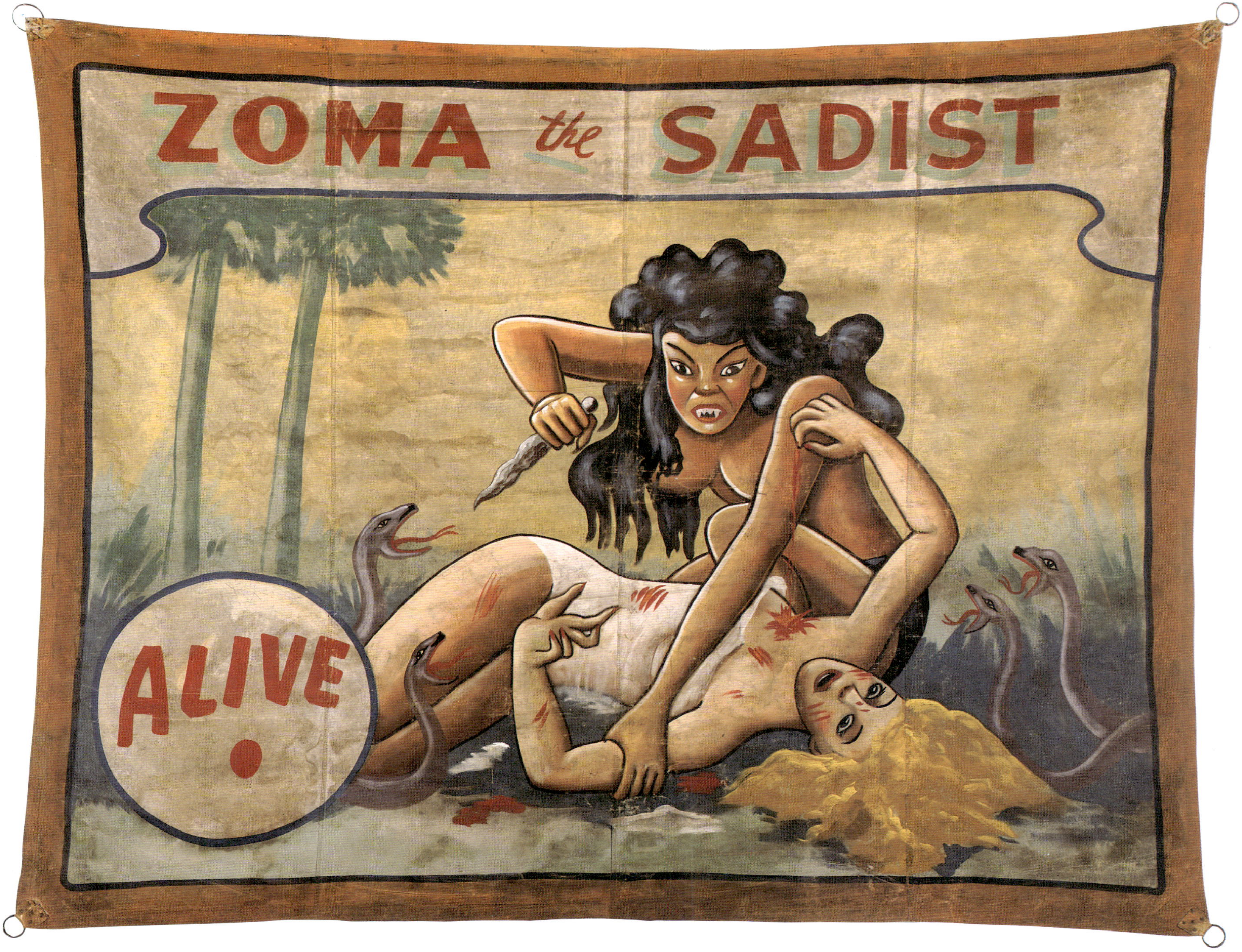
ZOMA the SADIST
ALIVE!

142

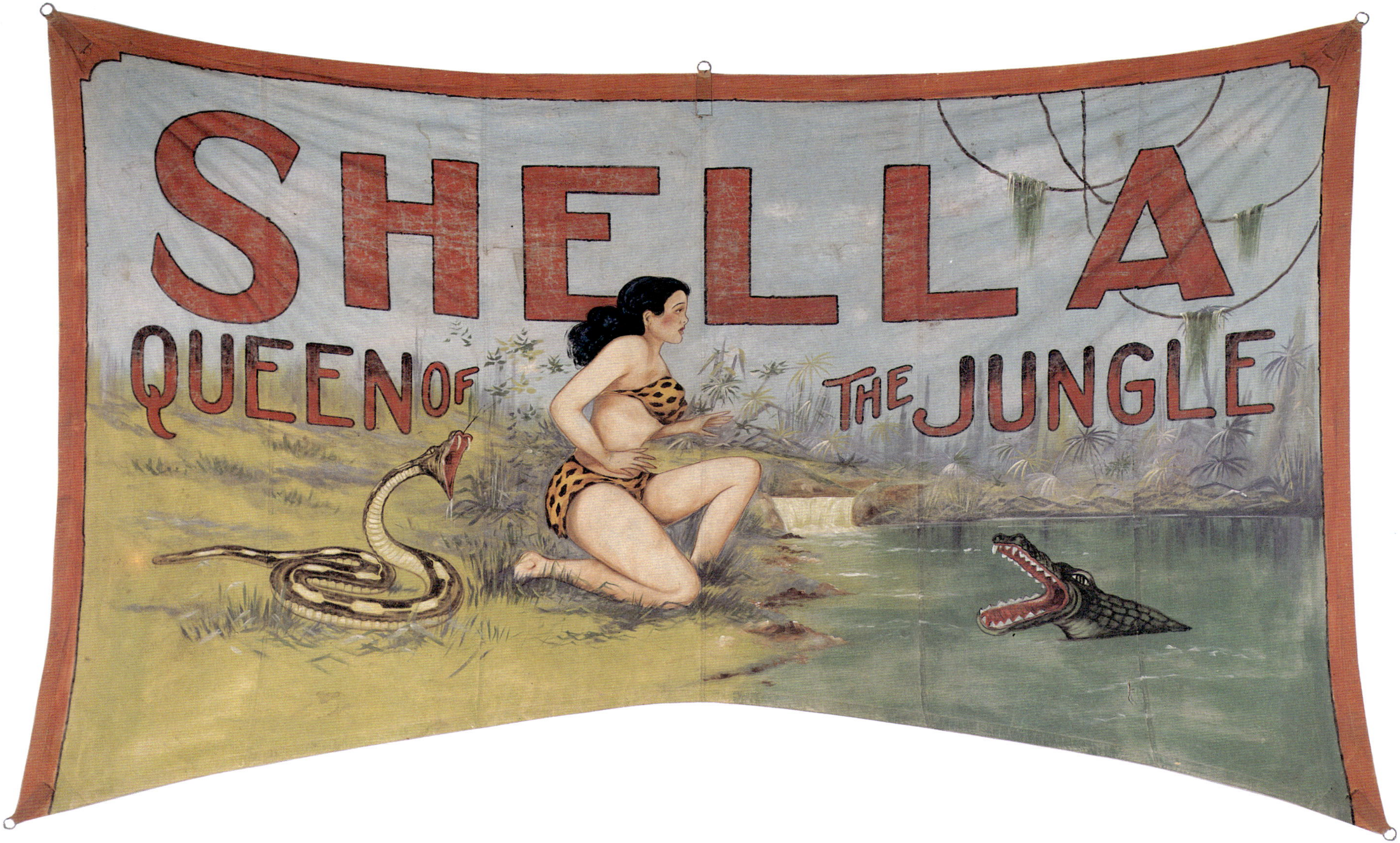
SHELLA
QUEEN OF THE JUNGLE

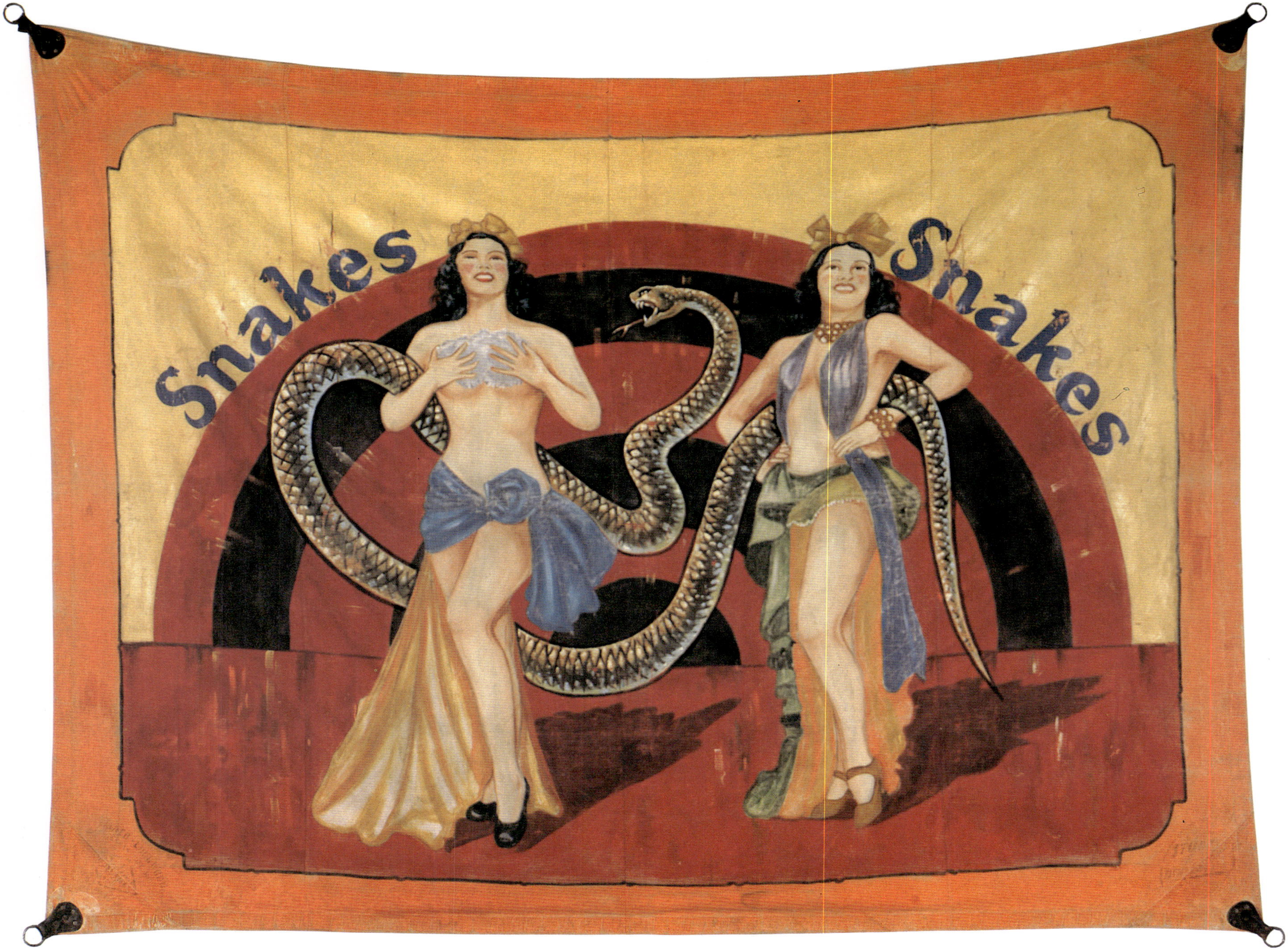
Snakes
Snakes

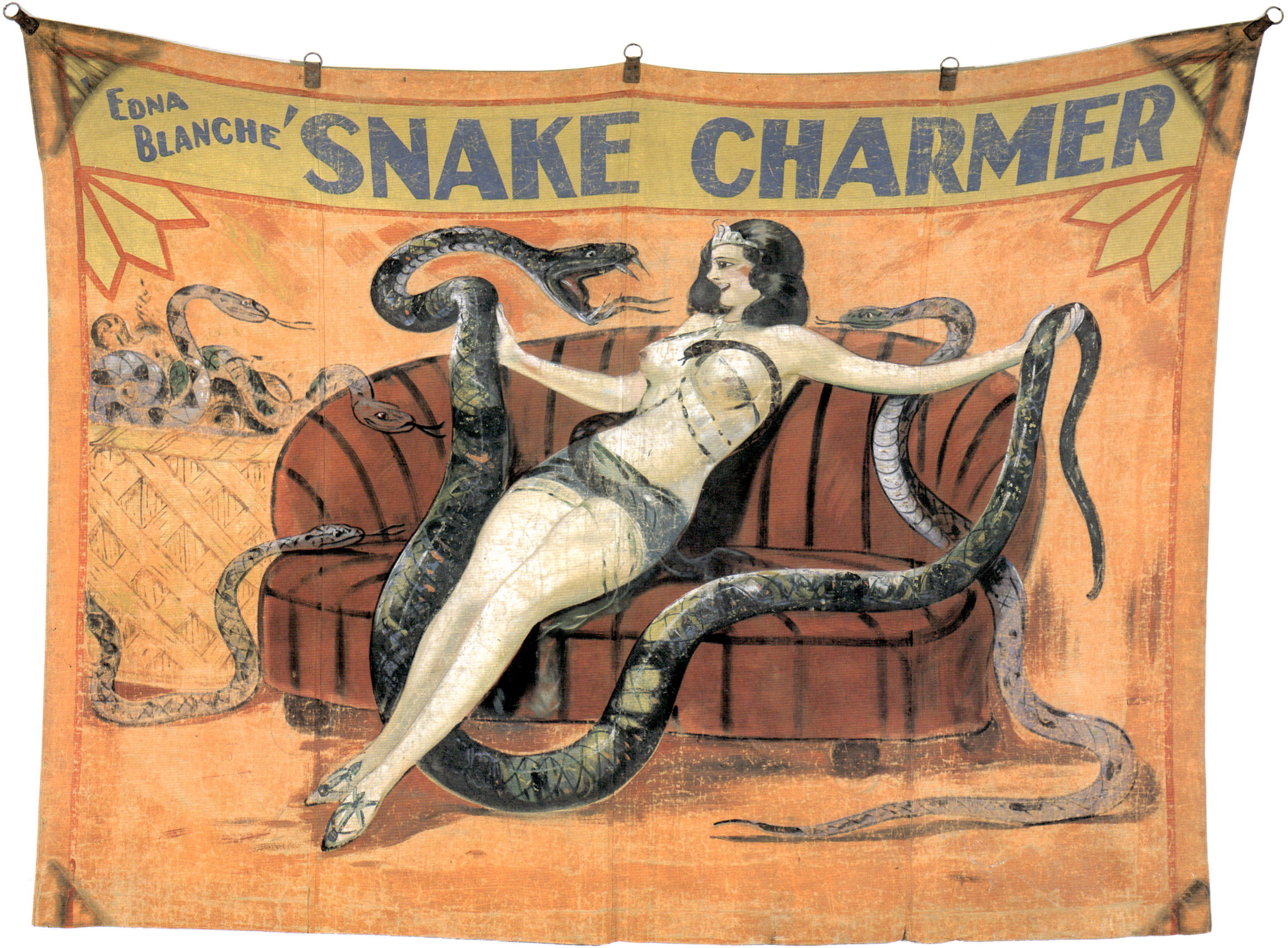
EDNA BLANCHE'
SNAKE CHARMER

SHEEP WITH 4 HORNS
ALIVE
HALF MONKEY-HALF SQUIRREL
ALIVE
COW WITH 5 LEGS
ALIVE
MIDGET BULL
ALIVE
MIDGET HORSE
FREAK ANIMALS
2 HEADED COW
5 LEGGED SHEEP
2 BODIED COW
ALIVE
2 NOSED COW
DAISY MAE
the 2 HEADED COW
POSITIVELY ALIVE
ALL ALIVE
A CONTINUOUS
WELCOME
FAIR
20
FREAK

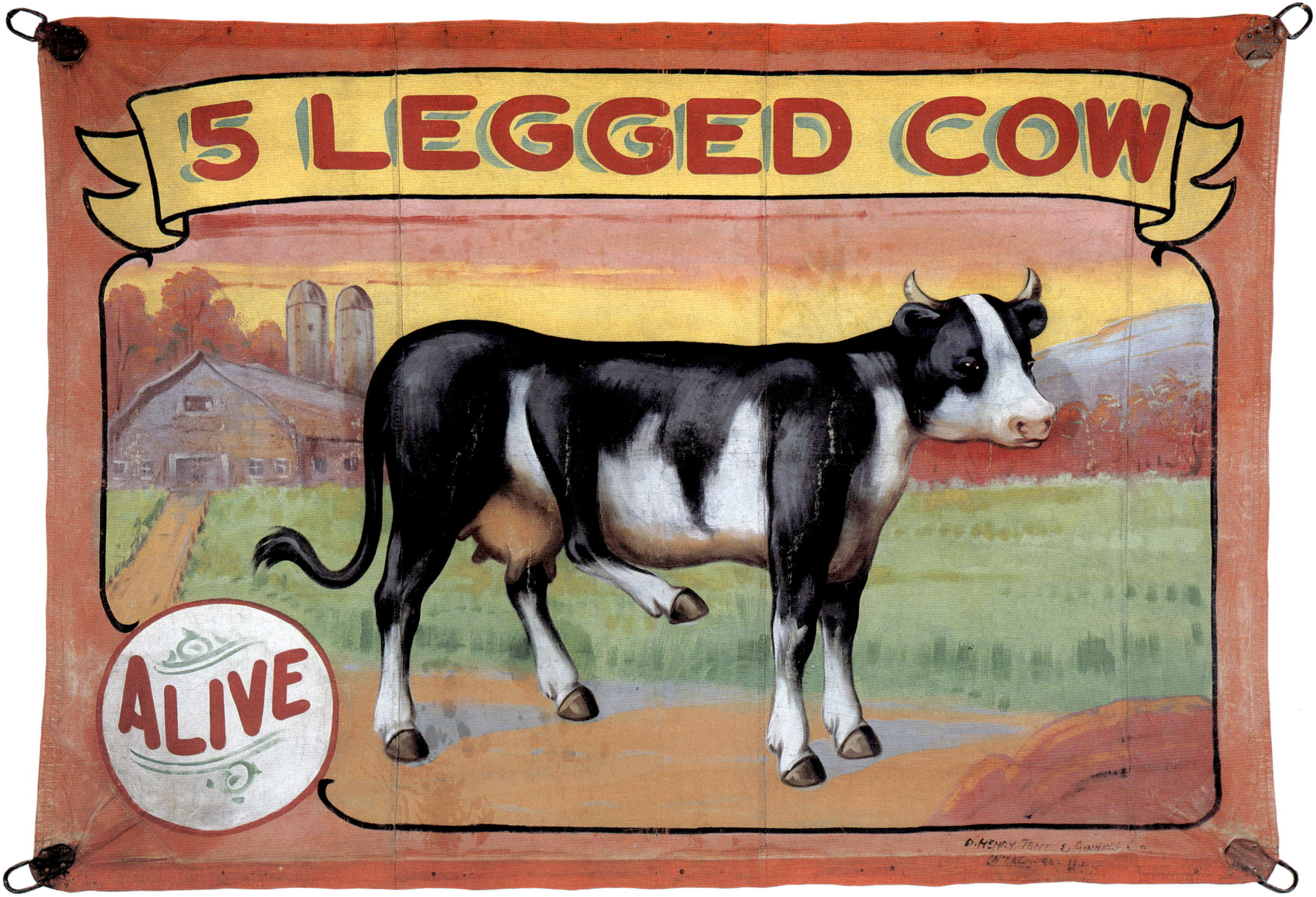
5 LEGGED COW
ALIVE

148

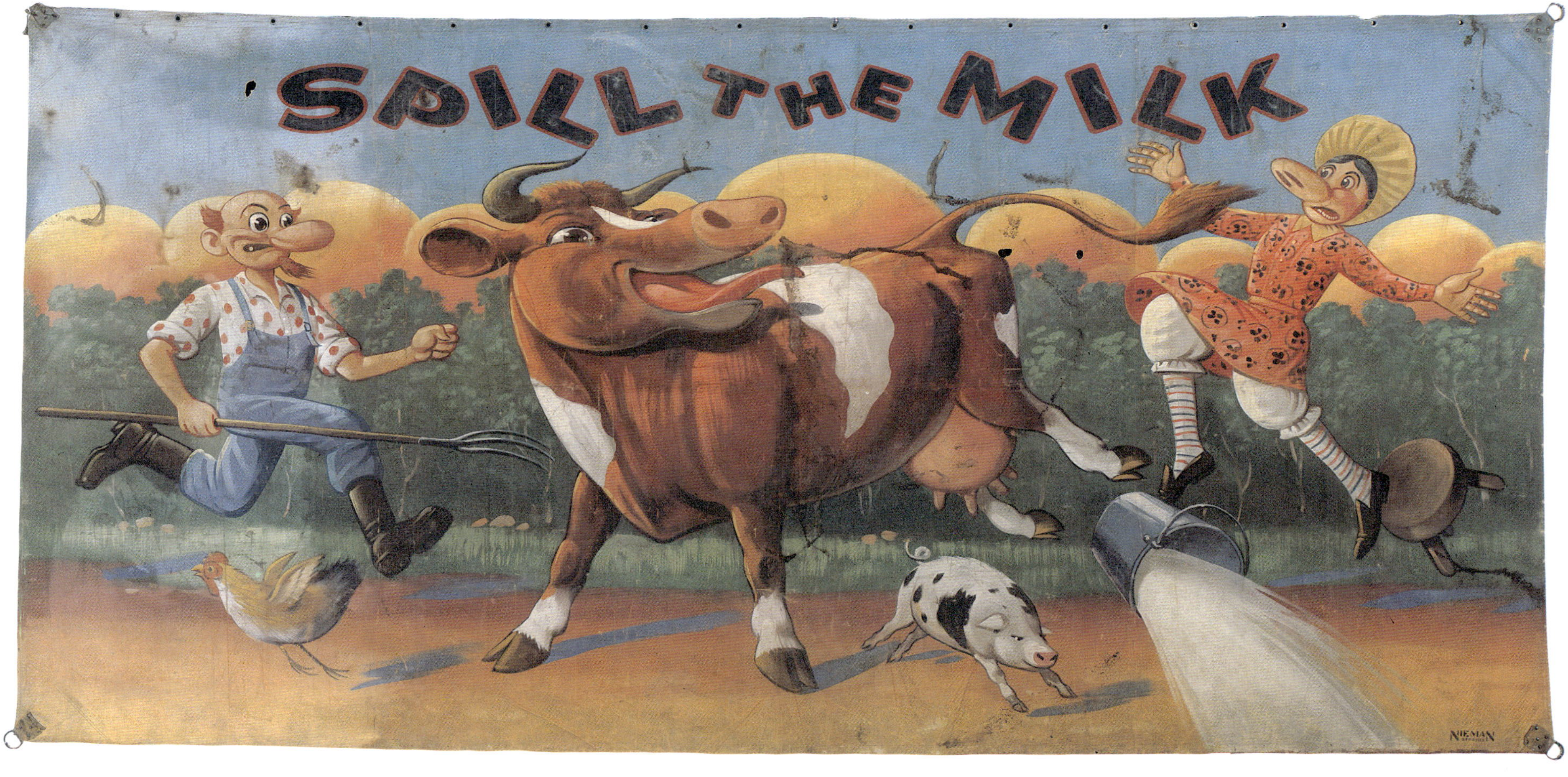
SPILL THE MILK
NIEMAN

150

FEATURED ON T-V PROGRAMS
"KINGDOM OF THE SEA"
" ZOO PARADE"
" YOU ASKED FOR IT"
ALIVE
ALIVE
FEATURED IN "LIFE"
"LOOK" & "TRUE" MAGAZINES

The WINNER
PRESS
1ST PRIZE
$10,000
IN MONKEY MONEY
1 STALK BANANAS
2ND PRIZE
$5,000
1 COCANUT
3RD PRIZE
$1,000
1 BAG PEANUTS
RULES
NO HOLDS
BARRED
5
SIGLER
TAMPA

152

BANNER NOTES & CAPTIONS

We hope this list and description of banners and illustrations in Freaks·Geeks and Strange Girls will be helpful, enjoyable and will enhance your understanding of this genre of art. All banners were painted with oil based paints (white lead) applied with a brush to canvas "blanks." Scientific analysis of pigments and canvas fibers has not been conducted. Dimensions have been rounded off to the nearest half foot and are included to establish a sense of scale and usage rather than for identification purposes. Height precedes width. Dating of the banners, in general, is inconclusive and open to debate. We relied on materials, style, experience, and "vibe" when we could not pinpoint specific dates through provenance. Many unsigned banners are unmistakably the work of a specific hand or studio and are so ascribed. If signed, we assumed the authorship to be that of the signator. Condition is subjective, and was provided by the collector in cases where we did not actually handle the banner in preparation of this book.

Initials after comments indicate author: KD = Kent Danner, RJ = Randy Johnson, JS = Jim Secreto; TV = Teddy Varndell

Cover
Dance with Death, (detail, see p. 60)

Inside Cover
Detail from **Jack Cripe Scrapbook**
Collection: Mike Seculan

p. 1
Detail from **Fred G. Johnson Scrapbook**
Collection: Randy Johnson

p. 2
Photo of **Ackley's Independent Shows**
Collection: John Polacsek

p. 4
Frog Boy (detail)
Artist: Nieman Eisman
Collection: Circus World Museum, Baraboo, WI

p. 7
Tattooed Woman (detail)
Artist: Snap Wyatt
Collection: Circus World Museum, Baraboo, WI

p. 8
Photo of **Sideshow Bannerline**
Collection: John Polacsek

p. 9
Blockhead
Artist: Jack Cripe (Brush) 1960-70
Studio: J. Sigler 9'x12'
Comments: Elsie Sutton Sideshow — KD
Condition: Good
Collection: Jim Secreto
Photo: Jim Secreto Photography

p. 10 (left)
Bee Boy
Artist: Joel-Peter Witkin 1981
Medium: Photograph
Collection: Courtesy Pace MacGill, NYC and Fraenkel Gallery, San Francisco

p. 10 (right)
Melvin Burkhart: Human Oddity
Artist: Joel-Peter Witkin 1985
Medium: Photograph
Collection: Courtesy Pace MacGill, NYC and Fraenkel Gallery, San Francisco

p. 11
Dickie the Penguin Boy
Artist: Fred G. Johnson 1960-1970
Studio: O'Henry Tent & Awning (Stencil) 8'x10'
Collection: Randy Johnson.
Photo: Mercury Studios

p. 12 (left)
Wanda
Artist: Ed Paschke 1973
Medium: Oil on canvas 55.5" x 45.75"
Photo: William H. Bengtson
Collection: Courtesy Phyllis Kind Gallery, Chicago, private collection

p. 12 (right)
Zoma Depraved (detail, see p. 140)
Photo: Jim Secreto Photography
Collection: Sonya Taylor

p. 13 (left)
Spring Carnival (detail, see p. 55)
Photo: Brian Etheredge, Illinois State Museum
Collection: Ellsworth and Shirley Johnson Family

p. 13 (right)
Homo sapiens scurra bozus, (installation detail)
Artist: Randy Johnson 1990
Medium: Backlit computer generated photograph
Collection: Artist

p. 14 (left)
Detail of **House of Mirrors** front (Fred G. Johnson)
Photo: Fred G. Johnson

p. 14 (right)
Digital Presence
Artist: Karl Wirsum 1993
Medium: Acrylic on wood 48" x 35"
Photo: William H. Bengtson
Collection: Courtesy Phyllis Kind Gallery, Chicago, private collection

p. 15 (left)
Pinhead On Stage, (Jack Cripe)
Collection: Mike Seculan

p. 15 (right)
Alan Artner: Ironic Contortionist of Irony
Artist: Roger Brown 1994
Medium: Oil on canvas 20" x 24"
Photo: William H. Bengtson
Collection: Courtesy Phyllis Kind Gallery, Chicago

p. 16
Otis the Frog Boy — Alive
Artist: Jack Cripe (Brush) 1960's-70's
Studio: J. Sigler 9'x12'
Condition: Good
Collection: Jim Secreto
Photo: Jim Secreto Photography

p. 18
London Punch and Judy
Artist: S. Bock (Brush) circa 1915
Studio: Chicago, 11'x7'
Collection: Circus World Museum, Baraboo, WI
Photo: Wilmer Zehr, courtesy Krannert Art Museum, University of Illinois at Urbana

p. 19
Votre Future
Artist: G. M. Caldwell 1930's
Studio: G. M. Caldwell
Condition: Good/fair; repaint over title
Collection: Jim Secreto
Photo: Jim Secreto Photography

p. 20
Artist: Unknown circa 1920
Studio: Unknown 8'x10'
Comments: Possibly a "Diavolo" act bicycle loop performance — JS
Condition: Good
Collection: Jim Secreto
Photo: Jim Secreto Photography

p. 21
Medical Discovery of the Ages — Old Squaw Snake Oil
Artist: G. M. Caldwell 1900's-20's
Studio: G.M. Caldwell (Stencil) 8'x10'
Comments: Medicine shows went out of business in the 30's — KD
Condition: Good
Collection: Jim Secreto
Photo: Jim Secreto Photography

p. 22
Wee Willie Strong Man
Artist: Nieman Eisman
Studio: Nieman Eisman (Stencil) 8'x10'
Condition: Good; slightly faded
Collection: Jim Secreto
Photo: Jim Secreto Photography

p. 23
The Great Marlowe — Strong as a Lion
Artist: Nieman Eisman 1920's
Studio: Nieman Eisman (Stencil) 8'x10'
Condition: Very good
Collection: Jim Secreto
Photo: Jim Secreto Photography

p. 24
Jack Joyce's Performing Horses — World's Finest Trained Equines
Artist: G. M. Caldwell 1920-30
Studio: G. M. Caldwell (Stencil) 8'x10'
Comments: Jack Joyce had his own show, worked subsequently with Craft Show then Ringling Bros. — KD
Condition: Very good
Collection: Jim Secreto
Photo: Jim Secreto Photography

p. 25
Moroccan Moments
Artist: Unknown circa 1930
Studio: Caldwell (Stencil) 8'x10'
Comments: Stenciled verso "Its the front of the show that gets the dough"
Condition: Good; paint loss, in painting, tears, patches
Collection: Edward R. Varndell
Photo: Jim Secreto Photography

p. 26
Tex and Mae
Artist: G.M. Caldwell 1930's
Studio: G.M. Caldwell (Stencil) 8'x10'
Comments: Famous Will Roger's impersonator/ double for Ripley's Believe It or Not sideshows, Wild West shows, etc. — JS
Collection: Jim Secreto
Photo: Jim Secreto Photography

p. 27
Nuba — The Ferocious Black Leopard
Artist: G.M. Caldwell 1930's
Studio: G. M. Caldwell (Stencil) 8'x10'
Comments: Used in a small truck tent circus; possibly Mighty Hagg Circus — KD
Condition: Excellent
Collection: Jim Secreto
Photo: Jim Secreto Photography

p. 28
Oriental Magic
Artist: Unknown circa 1915
Studio: Millard & Bulsterbaum (Stencil) 7'6"x4'
Condition: Good
Collection: Jim Secreto
Photo: Jim Secreto Photography

p. 29
Chief Roongwa — Formerly Witch Doctor of the Ubangi Savages
Artist: Unknown 1930's
Studio: Millard and Bulsterbaum (Stencil) 5'x7'
Condition: Excellent
Collection: Jim Secreto
Photo: Jim Secreto Photography

p. 30
Photo of **Happyland's Main Show**
Collection: John Polacsek

p. 31
Chas. G. Driver Tent Co. (advertisement)
Collection: Ellsworth & Shirley Johnson Family

pp. 32, 33, 34
Panoramic View of Carnival Lot
Collection: Walter Wanous

p. 35
John T. Backman — Artist in Glass
Artist: G.M. Caldwell 1920's-30's
Studio: G.M. Caldwell (Stencil) 5'x7'
Comments: Banner from Venice Beach, CA; John Backman was also Ringmaster for Al G. Barnes Circus — KD
Condition: Excellent
Collection: Jim Secreto
Photo: Jim Secreto Photography

p. 36
Photo of **Mills Bros. Circus** 1953
Collection: John Polacsek

p. 37
Glass Blower
Artist: G.M. Caldwell 1930's
Studio: G.M. Caldwell (Stencil) 8'x10'
Condition: Good
Collection: Jim Secreto
Photo: Jim Secreto Photography

p. 38
Age 38 Years
Artist: Cad Hill (Stencil) circa 1920
Studio: Hill/Shafer 10'x10'
Comments: Groff shows, which was a C.W. Parker unit; second 1/2 of double — KD
Condition: Good; "68 lbs." added later
Collection: Jim Secreto
Photo: Jim Secreto Photography

p. 39
Only 3-Legged Football Player in the World — Alive
Artist: Unknown circa 1930
Studio: Millard and Bulsterbaum (Stencil) 8'x10'
Comments: Francesco A. Lentini worked for Craft 20 Big Show; used on West Coast during the 30's — KD
Condition: Good
Collection: Jim Secreto
Photo: Jim Secreto Photography

p. 40
Hermaphrodite (pitch card)
Collection: Charlie Rudolph

p. 41
Roberta-Ray... Two Bodies and One Head — Alive
Artist: Unknown 1920's-30's
Studio: Millard and Bulsterbaum (Stencil) 8'x10'
Condition: Fair/good
Collection: Jim Secreto
Photo: Jim Secreto Photography

p. 42
Torture of India
Artist: George Bellis circa 1940
Studio: Sunshine Studio (Stencil) 9'6"x8'

Comments: Reverse stenciled: Sunshine Studio 1510 Market St., Wichita Kansas
Condition: Very good; re-lettered.
Collection: Richard Wright
Photo: Jim Secreto Photography

p. 43
Mystic Reader
Artist: George Bellis circa 1940
Studio: Sunshine Studio (Stencil) 13'x8'
Comments: Stenciled reverse: Sunshine Studio 1510 N. Market St., Wichita, Kansas, George Bellis Artist
Condition: Very good; tear lower left.
Collection: Private collection
Photo: Jim Secreto Photography

p. 44
Iron Foot Marvel
Artist: George Bellis circa 1940
Studio: Sunshine Studio (Stencil) 13'x8'
Comments: Stenciled verso same as Mystic Reader.
Condition: Very good
Collection: John D. Coiner, St. Paul
Photo: Jim Secreto Photography

p. 45
Shooting Through A Woman
Artist: George Bellis circa 1940
Studio: Sunshine Studio (Stencil) 9'6"x8'
Comments: String-show banner/illusion-type show — JS
Condition: Very good
Collection: Jim Secreto
Photo: Jim Secreto Photography

p. 46
Fire Worshipper
Artist: J. Meah (Brush) 1994
Studio: Meah Studio 6'x4'
Condition: Mint; never hung
Collection: Dean Jensen Gallery, Milwaukee
Photo: Mercury Studios

p. 47
Secrets of the Swamp/Laloo
Artist: Johnny Meah
Collection: Ward Hall and C.M. Christ
Photo: Randy Johnson

p. 48 (top)
Popeye
Artist: Johnny Meah
Photo: Courtesy Krannert Art Museum, University of Illinois at Urbana

p. 48 (bottom)
Popeye at Riverview
Photo: Tom Palazzolo

p. 49
Little Aboriginies/Strange Girls
Artist: Johnny Meah
Collection: Ward Hall and C.M. Christ
Photo: Randy Johnson

p. 50
The Great Johnny Meah 1994
Photo: Randy Johnson

p. 51
Rhee Flex
Artist: J. Meah (Brush) 1994
Studio: Meah Studio 6'x4'
Condition: Mint; never hung
Collection: Dean Jensen Gallery, Milwaukee
Photo: Mercury Studios

p. 52 (left)
Fred Johnson in his Studio 1970
Photo: Randy Johnson

p. 52 (right)
House of Mirrors at the Illinois State Fair 1970
Photo: Randy Johnson

pp. 53, 54
Clown Show Front
Artist: Fred G. Johnson (Brush "F.J.")
Studio: O'Henry Tent & Awning 47'x18'
Condition: Mint
Collection: Marvin's Marvelous Mechanical Museum, Farmington Hills, MI
Photo: Jim Secreto Photography

p. 55
Spring Carnival
Artist: Fred G. Johnson (Brush) 1962
Studio: Unknown 8'x10'
Condition: Mint
Collection: Ellsworth & Shirley Johnson Family
Photo: Brian Etheredge, Illinois State Museum

p. 56
John T. Hutchins Modern Museum
Artist: Fred G. Johnson
Studio: O'Henry tent & Awning (Stencil) 8'x12'
Condition: Mint
Collection: Ellsworth & Shirley Johnson Family
Photo: Brian Etheredge, Illinois State Museum

p. 57
Mystery Boy – Roberto Russo
Artist: Fred G. Johnson (Brush)
Studio: O'Henry Tent & Awning, 8'x10'
Condition: Excellent
Collection: Randy Johnson
Photo: Brian Etheredge, Illinois State Museum

p. 58
Bone Crushing Anaconda — Alive
Artist: Fred G. Johnson 1960's
Studio: O'Henry Tent & Awning (Stencil) 8'x10'
Condition: Mint
Collection: Jim Secreto
Photo: Jim Secreto Photography

p. 59
Amazon Snake Charmer
Artist: Fred G. Johnson (Stencil)
Studio: Unknown 8'x10'
Condition: Mint
Collection: Ellsworth & Shirley Johnson Family
Photo: Brian Etheredge, Illinois State Museum

p. 60
Dance of Death
Artist: Fred G. Johnson circa 1940

Studio: O'Henry Tent & Awning (Stencil) 8'x10'
Condition: Very good
Collection: Jim Secreto
Photo: Jim Secreto Photography

p. 61
Waltzing Dogs
Artist: Fred G. Johnson
Studio: O'Henry Tent & Awning (Stencil) 8'x10'
Condition: Very good; minor dirt
Collection: Wyatt Landesman/Quantity Postcards, San Francisco
Photo: Mercury Studios

p. 62
Alligator Boy
Artist: Unknown 1960's
Studio: O'Henry Tent & Awning (Stencil) 12'x10'
Comments: Performer possibly Emmet Bajano; rings on center show that banner was next to entrance/gaff banner — KD
Condition: Good
Collection: Jim Secreto
Photo: Jim Secreto Photography

p. 63
Main Entrance to Riverview Park (postcard)
Collection: Charlie Rudolph

pp. 64, 65
Harvey Boswell's Palace of Wonders/Moody Freak Animal Show 1974
Photos: Glen C. Davies

p. 66
Communication Breakdown
Artist: Glen C. Davies 1993
Medium: Acrylic on canvas 56.25'x39.75
Photo: William H. Bengtson
Collection: Courtesy Phyllis Kind Gallery

p. 67
Emmett: The Armless & Legless Boy
Artist: Fred G. Johnson 1960-1970
Studio: O'Henry Tent & Awning 8'x10'
Comments: Emmett was with Ward Hall and Wanous during this period; very good detail and unusual scroll-work — KD

Condition: Mint
Collection: Jim Secreto
Photo: Jim Secreto Photography

p. 68
Dickie the Penguin Boy
Artist: Fred G. Johnson 1960-1970
Studio: O'Henry Tent & Awning (Stencil) 10'x10'
Condition: Good; tears
Collection: Randy Johnson
Photo: Mercury Studios

p. 69
Master of Magic
Artist: Fred G. Johnson
Studio: O'Henry Tent & Awning (Stencil) 9'6"x9'6"
Condition: Very good; tears.
Collection: Richard and Darlene Johnson, Chicago
Photo: Mercury Studios

p. 70
Fat Man
Artist: Fred G. Johnson (Brush)
Studio: O'Henry Tent & Awning 5'x3'
Condition: Mint
Comments: Originally painted for Riply's Believe It or Not – RJ
Collection: Randy Johnson
Photo: Brian Etheredge, Illinois State Museum

p. 71
World's Smallest Man
Artist: Fred G. Johnson (Brush)
Studio: O'Henry Tent & Awning 5'x3'
Condition: Mint
Comments: Originally painted for Riply's Believe It or Not – RJ
Collection: Randy Johnson
Photo: Brian Etheredge, Illinois State Museum

p. 72
Past and Present
Artist: Fred G. Johnson circa 1960
Studio: O'Henry Tent & Awning 12'x10'
Comments: Serves same purpose as gaff (a wide short banner behind the bally) – TV
Condition: Very good

Collection: Mike Seculan, Columbus
Photo: Jim Secreto Photography

pp. 73, 74
The Royal Family of Strange People
Artist: Fred G. Johnson (Brush) circa 1970
Studio: O'Henry Tent & Awning 8'x19'
Comments: Closely related example to gaff illustrated on dust-jacket of Levenson's *In Search of the Monkey Girl* – TV
Condition: Very good; hand sewn tear
Collection: Sonya Taylor
Photo: Jim Secreto Photography

p. 75
Freak Photos
Collection: Jim Secreto/Randy Johnson

p. 76
Vickie Condor — 3 Legged Tennis Player
Artist: Fred G. Johnson
Studio: O'Henry Tent & Awning 10'x10'
Condition: Good; holes
Collection: Randy Johnson
Photo: Mercury Studios

p. 77
Albino Girl
Artist: Fred G. Johnson 1960-1970
Studio: O'Henry Tent & Awning (Stencil) 10'x10'
Condition: Excellent
Collection: Ellsworth & Shirley Johnson Family
Photo: Mercury Studios

p. 78
Huey the Pretzel Man
Artist: Fred G. Johnson (Brush) 1970's
Studio: Unknown 8'x10'
Comments: See hard cover dust jacket of *In Search of the Monkey Girl* – TV
Condition: Fair; hand sewn tears
Collection: Sonya Taylor
Photo: Jim Secreto Photography

p. 79
World's Smallest Mother
Artist: J. Sigler (Brush) 1970's

Studio: Unknown 10'x12'
Condition: Excellent; small holes
Collection: Courtesy Ann Nathan Gallery, Chicago, Deedee Waxter Grant
Photo: Mercury Studios

p. 80
Tiniest Entertainers
Artist: Nieman Eisman 1930's
Studio: Nieman Eisman (Stencil) 8'x10'
Comments: Great detail/color; crisp images
Condition: Mint
Collection: Jim Secreto
Photo: Jim Secreto Photography

p. 81
Alkali Bill
Artist: Nieman Eisman
Studio: Nieman Studios (stencil) 8'x10'
Condition: Excellent
Collection: Circus World Museum, Baraboo, WI
Photo: Wilmer Zehr, courtesy Krannert Art Museum, University of Illinois at Urbana

p. 82
Major Debert — Tiniest Man
Artist: Unknown 1930's
Studio: Millard and Bulsterbaum (Stencil) 14'x7'
Comments: Never been used outside; banner was ordered and never picked up from the studio — KD
Condition: Mint
Collection: Jim Secreto
Photo: Jim Secreto Photography

p. 83
Sweet Marie
Artist: Snap Wyatt 1960's
Studio: Wyatt (Stencil) 8'x10'
Condition: Very good; dirty, over-paint
Collection: Dean Jensen Gallery, Milwaukee, WI
Photo: Mercury Studios

p. 84
Laugh With Dolly
Artist: Fred G. Johnson (Brush)
Studio: O'Henry Tent & Awning 8'x10'

Condition: Mint
Collection: Ellsworth & Shirley Johnson Family
Photo: Brian Etheredge, Illinois State Museum

p. 85
Fred Johnson in his Studio
Collection: Ellsworth & Shirley Johnson Family
Photo: World Wide Photo

p. 86
Fat People Photos
Collection: Jim Secreto

p. 87
Jolly Trixie pitch card
Collection: Charlie Rudolph

p. 88
Giant Baby – 10 Yrs. Old – 390 Lbs.
Artist: Al DeCura   1930's
Studio: Al DeCura   5'x8'
Condition: Good
Collection: Jim Secreto
Photo: Jim Secreto Photography

p. 89
Oh My! But She Is Fat — Positively Alive
Artist: Snap Wyatt   1950's
Studio: Snap Wyatt   10'x10'
Condition: Mint
Collection: Jim Secreto
Photo: Jim Secreto Photography

p. 90
Jolly Trixie pitch card (verso)
Collection: Charlie Rudolph

p. 91
Untitled Banner, Fat Lady in Red Chair
Artist: Fred G. Johnson (Brush)   1960's
Studio: O'Henry Tent & Awning   8'x10'
Comments: Unusual scroll-work with great detail; single banner with wording attached — JS
Condition: Mint
Collection: Jim Secreto
Photo: Jim Secreto Photography

p. 92
Americas Largest Circus Sideshow
Artist: Fred G. Johnson   circa 1960
Studio: Unknown   12'x10'
Condition: Very good
Collection: Sonya Taylor
Photo: Mercury Studios

pp. 93, 94
Main Circus Side Show
Artist: Snap Wyatt (Stencil)   circa 1960
Studio: Snap Wyatt   29'6"X10'
Comments: Central figure is probably Johann the Viking Giant – JS
Condition: Good; minor tears, missing corner ring
Collection: Sonya Taylor
Photo: Jim Secreto Photography

p. 95
Photo of **Bathing Beauty Bally**
Collection: John Polacsek

p. 96
Bathing Beauties
Artist: Unknown   circa 1920
Studio: Unknown   7'6"x12'
Condition: Good
Collection: Jim Secreto
Photo: Jim Secreto Photography

p. 97 (left)
Tattoo Artist
Artist: Jack Sigler
Studio: Unknown   3'6"x3'6"
Comments: Companion piece to untitled tattooed woman.
Condition: Very good.
Collection: Richard and Darlene Johnson, Chicago
Photo: Mercury Studios

p. 97 (right)
Untitled tattooed woman
Artist: Jack Sigler (Brush)
Studio: Unknown   3'6"x3'6"
Condition: Very good; water staining.
Collection: Richard and Darlene Johnson, Chicago
Photo: Mercury Studios

pp. 98, 99 (double high)
Rasmus Nielsen: Scandinavian Strongman
Artist: Fred G. Johnson
Studio: O'Henry Tent & Awning   16'x10 1/2'
Condition: Excellent; minor tears and dirt
Collection: Wyatt Landesman/Quantity Postcards, San Francisco
Photo: Jim Secreto Photography

p. 100
Tattoo Photos
Collection: Don Ed Hardy/Randy Johnson

p. 101
Photo of **Charlie Wagner** tattooing his wife Maude
Collection: Steve Gilbert

p. 102
Rasmus Nielsen postcard
Collection: Charlie Rudolph

p. 103
Photos of **Jean Furella at Riverview**
Photos: Tom Palazzolo

p. 104
Photo of the **Great Omi**
Collection: Jeff Crisman

p. 105
Tattooing By "Stoney"
Artist: Unknown   circa 1960
Studio: Unknown   8'x5'
Condition: Excellent
Collection: Lawrence and Evelyn Aronson
Photo: Courtesy Krannert Art Museum, University of Illinois at Urbana

p. 106
Photo of **Tattoo Jack Cripe**   1988
Photo: Jeff Crisman
Collection: Courtesy Aron Packer Gallery, Chicago

p. 107
Tattoo Artist in Person
Artist: "Tattoo Jack" Cripe   circa 1950
Studio: Sigler & Son (Stencil)   12'x10'
Condition: Very good
Collection: National Museum of American Art, Smithsonian Institution, Gift of Herbert Waide Hemphill Jr. and museum purchase made possible by Ralph Cross Johnson
Photo: Smithsonian Institution

pp. 108, 109 (double high)
Professor Price
Artist:: Unknown   circa 1925
Studio:: Driver Brothers (Stencil)   17'x 9' 6"
Comments: Verso- Driver Brothers. 500-504 Green St. Chicago, Ill. Driver Brand. Best on Earth. Walter F. Driver Pres.
Condition: Fair; paint loss, tears. (handstitched)
Collection: La Chapelle Collection. Courtesy W. E. Channing and Co. Santa Fe. NM
Photo:: Jim Secreto Photography

pp. 110, 111 (double high)
Strange Girls
Artist: Snap Wyatt (Stencil each panel) circa 1965
Studio: Snap Wyatt   17'x10'
Condition: Very good; sewn repairs.
Collection: Sonya Taylor
Photo: Jim Secreto Photography

p. 112
Strange Girls
Artist: Unknown   circa 1965
Studio: Unknown   12'x10'
Comments: Probably Wyatt Studios – TV
Condition: Very good
Collection: Sonya Taylor
Photo: Jim Secreto Photography

pp. 113, 114 (Gaff)
Strange Girls
Artist: Snap Wyatt (Stencil)   circa 1965
Studio: Snap Wyatt   9'x30'
Comments: During one season Dick Best had all woman freaks on working acts – KD

Condition: Very good; some tears.
Collection: Sonya Taylor
Photo: Jim Secreto Photography

p. 115
Freaks
Artist: Snap Wyatt (Stencil)   circa 1960
Studio: Unknown   12'x10'
Condition: Excellent
Collection: Courtesy Phyllis Kind Gallery, private collection
Photo: William H. Bengtson

p. 116
Photo of **Martha the Armless Wonder** postcard front and back
Collection: Charlie Rudolph

p. 117
Marie Armless Girl
Artist: Snap Wyatt (Brush)   1970's
Studio: Snap Wyatt   11'x10'
Condition: Excellent
Collection: Sonya Taylor
Photo: Jim Secreto Photography

p. 118
Defies Death
Artist: Snap Wyatt (Brush)   1950's
Studio: Snap Wyatt   8'x10'
Condition: Good/fair
Collection: Jim Secreto
Photo: Jim Secreto Photography

p. 119
FEEJEE Mermaid
Artist: Snap Wyatt (Brush)   1970's
Studio: Snap Wyatt   9'x9'
Comments: Rigged mermaid of monkey torso sewn to fish tail – TV
Condition: Mint
Collection: Private collection
Photo: Jim Secreto Photography

p. 120
Suzy Nature's Enigma pitch-card
Collection: Randy Johnson

p. 121
Alligator Girl
Artist: Snap Wyatt   1970's
Studio: Snap Wyatt (Stencil)   11'6"x10'
Condition: Very good; small patch.
Collection: Sonya Taylor
Photo: Jim Secreto Photography

p. 122
Alligator Girl
Artist: Snap Wyatt (Stencil)   circa 1965
Studio: Unknown   12'x10'
Condition: Excellent
Collection: Courtesy Phyllis Kind Gallery, Chicago, private collection
Photo: William H. Bengtson

p. 123
Rubber Skin Man
Artist: Snap Wyatt (Stencil)   circa 1965
Studio: Unknown   12'x10'
Condition: Excellent
Collection: Courtesy Phyllis Kind Gallery, Chicago private collection
Photo: William H. Bengtson

p. 124
Turkey Boy
Artist: Snap Wyatt (Stencil)   circa 1965
Studio: Unknown   6'x10'
Condition: Excellent
Collection: Courtesy Phyllis Kind Gallery, Chicago, private collection
Photo: William H. Bengtson

p. 125
Photo of **Wesley Upperman**   1950
Collection: John Polacsek

p. 126
Photo of **Hell-Drivers**
Collection: Ellsworth & Shirley Johnson Family

p. 127
Ubangi – See This
Artist: Snap Wyatt (Brush)   circa 1960
Studio: Snap Wyatt   8'x10'

Comments: Captain Harvey Boswell, Palace of Wonders; bullet "See This" means this was not a live act, but a mannequin made by Snap Wyatt — JS
Condition: Mint; never used outside
Collection: Jim Secreto
Photo: Jim Secreto Photography

pp. 128, 129 (double high)
Tirko the Monkey Boy – African Witch Dr.
Artist: Snap Wyatt (Stencil)   1970's
Studio: Snap Wyatt   17'x10"
Comments: Snap Wyatt, Tampa , Fla. stencil
Condition: Very good; machine stitch repair.
Collection: Sonya Taylor
Photo: Jim Secreto Photography

p. 130, 131 (gaff)
The Magical Mystery Tour
Artist: Fred G.Johnson (Brush)   circa 1970
Studio: O'Henry Tent & Awning   8'x19'
Condition: Excellent
Collection: Sonya Taylor
Photo: Jim Secreto Photography

p. 132
Shocking Brutal Truth
Artist: Fred G. Johnson (Brush)   circa 1970
Studio: O'Henry Tent & Awning   6'x8'
Condition: Very good
Collection: Sonya Taylor
Photo: Jim Secreto Photography

p. 133
Journey into Danger
Artist: Fred G. Johnson (Brush)   circa 1970
Studio: O'Henry Tent & Awning   6'x8'
Condition: Very good
Collection: Sonya Taylor
Photo: Jim Secreto Photography

p. 134
Will Your Next Child Be a Hopeless Drug Addict?
Artist: Fred G. Johnson   circa 1970
Studio: O'Henry Tent & Awning   6'x8'
Condition: Very good

Collection: Sonya Taylor
Photo: Jim Secreto Photography

p. 136

Anything Can Happen If Your Trip is a Bummer
Artist: Fred G. Johnson   circa 1970
Studio: O'Henry Tent & Awning   6'x8'
Comments: Johnson was still using Chicago 40, Ill. postal code at this late date – TV
Condition: Very good
Collection: Sonya Taylor
Photo: Jim Secreto Photography

p. 137

Planning a Trip?
Artist: Fred G. Johnson (Brush)   circa 1970
Studio: O'Henry Tent & Awning   6'x8'
Condition: Very good
Collection: Sonya Taylor
Photo: Jim Secreto Photography

p. 138

Photos of **Geek Bannerlines**
Collection: Rick and Darlene Johnson

p. 139

Eeka and Giant Snakes
Artist: Fred G. Johnson (Brush)
Studio: O'Henry Tent & Awning   7'x10'
Condition: Very good
Collection: Randy Johnson
Photo: Brian Etheredge, Illinois State Museum

p. 140

Zoma Depraved
Artist: Unknown   circa 1950
Studio: Unknown   9'x10'
Condition: Good; dirty, repair and inpainting.
Collection: Sonya Taylor
Photo: Jim Secreto Photography

p. 141

Zoma the Sadist
Artist: Unknown   circa 1950
Studio: Unknown   9'x10'
Condition: Good; dirty, water staining

Collection: Sonya Taylor
Photo: Jim Secreto Photography

p. 142

Shella
Artist: Unknown   1940's
Studio: Unknown
Comments: Geek-show; used with Queen of Jungle entrance banner – JS
Condition: Very good
Collection: Jim Secreto
Photo: Jim Secreto Photography

p. 143

Shella Queen of the Jungle
Artist: Unknown   1940's
Studio: Unknown
Comments: Geek-show type; possibly used as an entrance banner – JS
Condition: Good

Collection: Jim Secreto
Photo: Jim Secreto Photography

p. 144

Snakes/Snakes
Artist: Manuel   1930-40
Studio: Baker-Lockwood   8'x10'
Comments: Corners and lack of scroll-work make this a stock banner type – JS
Condition: Very good
Collection: Jim Secreto
Photo: Jim Secreto Photography

p. 145

Edna Blanche- Snake Charmer
Artist: Unknown
Studio: Millard and Bulsterbaum (Stencil)   8'x10'
Comments: Top half, cut from a double high – RJ
Condition: Good
Collection: Circus World Museum, Baraboc, WI

Photo: Wilmer Zehr, courtesy Krannert Art Museum, University of Illinois at Urbana

p. 146

Photo of **Moody Freak Animals** banner line
Photo: Glen C. Davies
Collection: Glen C. Davies

p. 147

5 Legged Cow
Artist: Fred G. Johnson
Studio: O'Henry Tent & Awning (Stencil)   6'x8'
Collection: Circus World Museum, Baraboo, WI
Photo: Brian Etheredge, Illinois State Museum

p. 148

Mickey Mouse Circus
Artist: Unknown
Studio: Unknown   6'x9'
Comments: Flea Circus
Condition: Good
Collection: Private collection
Photo: Jim Secreto Photography

p. 149

Spill the Milk
Artist: Unknown   circa 1945
Studio: Nieman Studios (Stencil)   8'x16'
Condition: Very good; paint retention excellent, stains. minor holes
Collection: Amy C. Graller
Photo: Jim Secreto Photography

p. 150

Kingdom of the Sea
Artist: Fred G. Johnson   circa 1970
Studio: O'Henry Tent & Awning   11'x9'
Comments: Chicago, 40 Ill.
Condition: Excellent, finish is glossy
Collection: Sonya Taylor
Photo: Jim Secreto Photography

p. 151

The Winner
Artist: Sigler (Brush)   circa 1950
Studio: Unknown   8'6"x8'6"
Condition: Very good

Collection: Courtesy Gasperi Gallery, New Orleans, Mr. & Mrs. Dorian Bennett
Photo: Gasperi Gallery, New Orleans

p. 152
Photo of Monkey Hippodrome
Collection: John Polacsek

p. 155
Gorilla Girl — Alive
Artist: Unknown 1960's
Studio: Unknown 4'x4'
Comments: All three banners (pp. 155, 157, 159) painted by same artist in Ohio area; Possibly from a Dime-show – JS

Condition: Good
Collection: Jim Secreto
Photo: Jim Secreto Photography

p. 157
Armless Wonder — Alive
Artist: Unknown 1960's
Studio: Unknown 4'x4'
Collection: Jim Secreto
Photo: Jim Secreto Photography

p. 159
Pin Cushion Man — Alive
Artist: Unknown 1960's
Studio: Unknown 4'x4'

Collection: Jim Secreto
Photo: Jim Secreto Photography

p. 160
Christian Bros. Circus Sideshow
Collection: John Polacsek

p. 164
Photo of Strong Man
Collection: John Polacsek

p. 166
Keep Smiling with Big Jumbo
Collection: Jim Secreto

p. 167
Closed
Photo: Jim Secreto Photography

p. 168, Inside Back Cover
Detail from **Fred G. Johnson Scrapbook**
Collection: Randy Johnson

Back Cover
Two-Headed Cow (detail)
Photo: Brian Etheredge, Illinois State Museum
Collection: Circus World Museum, Baraboo, WI

Other Publications of Consequence

Fred and Mary Fried's *America's Forgotten Folk Arts* (New York: Pantheon Books, 1978) was the first mainstream book to present the painted banner as an American folk art form. It was soon followed by Geoff Weedon and Richard Ward's *Fairground Art* (New York: Abbeville Press Inc., 1981). These two books can be considered the primer texts on the subject, and come highly recommended. Both have extensive bibliographies which we have chosen not to duplicate. Following is a list of other books that may be of interest.

Bogdan, Robert. *Freaks Shows*. Chicago, University of Chicago Press, 1988.

Donato, Debora Duez & Randy Johnson. *Fred G. Johnson: Sideshow Banners*. Chicago: State of Illinois Art Gallery, 1989.

Drimmer, Frederick. *Very Special People*. New York: Amjon Publishers Inc. 1973.

Gray, Spalding and Leverson, Randal. *In Search of the Monkey Girl*. Millerton: Aperture, 1982.

Hall, Ward. *My Very Unusual Friends*. Gibsonton: Ward Hall, 1991.

Hall, Ward. *Struggles and Triumphs of a Modern Day Showman, An Autobiography*. Sarasota: Carnival Publishers, 1981.

Jay, Ricky. *Learned Pigs & Fireproof Women*. New York: Warner Books, Inc., 1986.

Lewis, Arthur H. *Carnival*. New York: Trident Press, 1970.

McKennon, Joe. *A Pictorial History of the American Carnival*. Vol. III. Sarasota: Carnival Publishers, 1981.

Mannix, Daniel P. *Freaks: We Who Are Not as Others*. San Francisco: Re/Search Publications, 1990.

Monestier, Martin. *Human Oddities: A Book of Nature's Anomalities*. Secaucus: Citadel Press, 1978.

Ray, Fred Olen. *Grind Show – Weirdness as Entertainment*. Hollywood: American Independent Press, 1993.

Sloan, Mark, Roger Manley and Michelle Van Parys. *Dear Mr. Ripley*. Boston: Little Brown and Company, 1993.

Sotheby's Inc. *The Smith Collection of Penny Arcade Machines and Related Memorabilia*. (Catalogue: auction 6594). New York: Sotheby's, Inc., 1994.

St. Clair, Leonard L. & Alan B. Govenar. *Stoney Knows How: Life as a Tattoo Artist*. University Press of Kentucky, 1981.

Wlodarczyk, Chuck. *Riverview: Gone but not Forgotten*. Chicago: Riverview Publications, 1977.

RANDY JOHNSON

JIM SECRETO

TEDDY VARNDELL

JOHN POLACSEK

GLEN C. DAVIES

STEVE GILBERT

DALE SLUSSER

LISA STONE

DON ED HARDY

JOHNNY MEAH

LITERARY FREAKS · COMPUTER GEEKS & STRANGE CONTRIBUTORS

GLEN C. DAVIES has traveled with circuses and carnivals for over twenty years, painting showfronts and documenting and lecturing on circus and carnival life. After attending the School of the Art Institute of Chicago from 1968-1972, Davies received his BFA in 1978 from Drake University and his MFA in painting from the University of Illinois in 1981. He now divides his time between working in his Champaign, IL painting studio and life on the road painting murals and working as a visiting artist and artist in residence in schools, museums and colleges.

STEVE GILBERT is a writer and illustrator with a lifelong interest in tattooing. His articles on the history of tattooing have been published in *Outlaw Biker Tattoo Review* and in *International Tattoo Art*. He is currently working on a revised edition of the tattoo classic *Art, Sex and Symbol* by Ronald Scutt and Christopher Gotch.

DON ED HARDY first gained international recognition as a tattooer, working since 1966 to expand the potential of the medium. In recent years he has resumed painting, drawing and printmaking, exhibiting works that play off the visual vocabulary of tattooing and other popular art forms. In addition to curating several museum shows he has written, edited and published 13 books documenting the tattoo world. This book expands his commitment to champion powerful art forms previously ignored by "high culture"

RANDY JOHNSON is an amazing artist, brilliant graphic designer, incredibly shy person, and is also the grandson of premier banner painter Fred G. Johnson. He maintains the family tradition of exploring the under-side-show aspects of humanity in artworks of greatness and agility. He earned his MFA from University of Illinois at Urbana and has curated two sideshow banner exhibitions, *Palace of Wonders* at Krannert Art Museum and *Fred G. Johnson: Sideshow Banners*, State of Illinois Art Gallery.

JOHNNY MEAH – *Meah On Meah*
I can't think of anything nicer than doing something well and being recognized for it. I feel quite honored to be included in this book because, frankly, there are so many banner artists who've preceded me and gotten little or no recognition for their efforts that it tends to make me feel like I've won something rather than having achieved something. (Am I really that good at what I do or have I simply outlived the rest of the gang?)

At any rate, here I am in printed and pictorial form, sharing my thoughts on various subjects with your and giving you a glimpse at my artwork.

For the collectors of facts and figures, I'm fifty-eight years old, was born in Bristol, Connecticut and now I live in Riverview, Florida with my lovely wife, Joan. I also work as a sword swallower, fire eater, circus clown and lecturer. And I paint banners — lots and lots of banners. Actually, looking at my paintings will give you a far batter understanding of me than a page full of words. There are little pieces of me in all of them.

Generally speaking, banner artists are as different from one another as the subjects they portray. There is, however, some common ground. One afternoon Jack Synrex and I were discussing how we felt about our paintings. In the course of the conversation Jack, who is, by the way, a marvelous show painter and story teller, made an observation that really hit home. "You know," he said, looking up at the clouds through half closed eyes, "When I'm working on a painting I really like I can't wait to run out and look at it first thing in the morning. No coffee, no newspaper — just gotta go look at that painting." He looked at me with a knowing grin. "You too, huh?" "Yeah." And for a long time we said nothing enjoying the mutual comfort in knowing that there were at least two peas in what moments ago seemed like a single occupancy pod.

End of story — now go play! Run through the book as though it was your own personal playground because that's what a sideshow bannerline is — a playground for the mind.

JOHN F. POLACSEK is currently Curator of Marine History for the Detroit Historical Museum and Director of the Dossin Great Lakes Museum. In 1974 he received an M.A. in American History from Bowling Green State University, Bowling Green, Ohio. His thesis topic was "The Development of the Circus and Menagerie in Ohio Prior to 1860." He is Past President of the Circus Historical Society, 1990-1993.

JIM SECRETO works as an automotive advertising photographer. Over the course of many years he has collected Fairground Art, beginning with carousel objects and later acquiring art and artifacts from the circus. His initial attraction to the sideshow was visual. This interest later inspired him to pursue the history of its forms, feeling that "the painters of the midway were the artists of the common man."

DALE SLUSSER is employed as an instructor of the Japanese Art of Tea. He has spent a number of years in Japan and recently received a Master of Arts in East Asian Languages and Cultures from UCLA. His interests also include literary theory and modes of cultural production. He currently lives and writes in Los Angeles.

LISA STONE is a free-lance snake handler in Spring Lake, Wisconsin.

TEDDY VARNDELL a product of the industrial Midwest, resides in Chicago with his wife Lynn and daughter Taylor. After graduating from Southern Illinois University-Carbondale with a degree in art, he took the career path of many fine art baccalaureates, from fry cook to bench jeweler, dishwasher to construction laborer, gem merchant to dealer of connoisseur-quality wild American ginseng. For the last ten years he has been pursuing a career as a dealer in Pan-primitive art from the Americas.

Teddy would like to give all propers and thanks to the following people who gave him help and encouragement along the banner trail. Lynn Varndell, Randy and Karen Johnson, Jim and Mel Secreto, Lisa Stone, Ed Hardy, Paul Dickman, Willie Huzyk, Walter Wanous, Rob Adams, Ann Nathan, Carl Hammer, Rick and Darlene Johnson, Johnny Fox, Paul and Joan King, Burns and Micky, Richard Wright, John Coiner, Will Channing, Diana Powell, Kent Anderson, Juan, Shirley, Iris, Ariel, Deborah, Jeannine and Goo-Goo.

164

UNBELIEVABLE BEINGS of STRENGTH
WORLD'S GREATEST

It's impossible to acknowledge all the people who truly deserve thanks for contributing to *Freaks·Geeks & Strange Girls*. Much information was gathered on the run at studios and fairs, in conversations with people in the sideshow world – with whom we had amazing encounters but never got their names. I hope you know who you are. Many thanks.

This book was unquestionably inspired by the creative vision of my grandfather – Fred G. Johnson. His incomparable legacy is shared by the rest of my family: Ellsworth and Shirley, Darrell, Diane, Jarrett and Jillian Johnson, Judy, John, Jocelyn and Justin Paris and my wife Karen and daughter Kendy, all of whom I would like to thank for their incredible assistance, patience and support.

To the artists and contributors who filled this book and made it happen I extend my sincere gratitude: Teddy "Total Knowledge Man" Varndell; Jim "Image Man" Secreto, who is largely responsible for the quantity and quality of photographs in this book; The Great Johnny Meah – Master Artist, Tales-Man and Human Sideshow; Glen "True Friend and Great Artist" Davies; John Polascek; Steve Gilbert; Dale Slusser; and Lisa "Hatchet Girl" Stone, who accepted the task of organizing and editing the book and whose brilliance and energy made this project come alive.

In the years since side show banners have been recognized as art history in America, a number of museum and gallery people have been involved in documenting, preserving, exhibiting and interpreting this art form. Special recognition goes out to Ann Nathan and Mary Donaldson at Ann Nathan Gallery, Chicago; Phyllis Kind, William T. Bengtson, David Russick and Jack Ludden at Phyllis Kind Gallery, New York and Chicago; Aron Packer Gallery, Chicago; Dean Jensen Gallery, Milwaukee; Richard Gasperi Gallery, New Orleans; Carl Hammer Gallery, Chicago; Fred Dallinger at Circus World Museum, Baraboo, Wisconsin; Krannert Museum of Art, University of Illinois at Urbana; Illinois Art Gallery and the Illinois State Museum; friends and colleagues at Intuit: The Center for Intuitive and Outsider Art, Chicago, and Lynda Roscoe Hartigan at the National Museum of American Art, Smithsonian Institution, Washington D.C.

For all manner of information, inspiration, ideas and especially for use of original art and permission to reproduce images, I thank Terry Allen, Lawrence and Evelyn Aronson, (Art)[N], Sherry Band, Mr. and Mrs. Dorian Bennett, Roger Blakely, Capt. Harvey Boswell, Roger Brown, David Byrne, John D. Coiner, Jeff Crisman, David and Toni Damkoehler, Kent Danner, Paul Dickman, Liam Durnan, Dr. Herbert Eisman, Brian Etheredge, Ellen Fisher, Fraenkle Gallery, Fred and Mary Fried, Amy C. Graller, Ward Hall and C.M. Christ, Herbert Waide Hemphill, Jr., Don "Barnacle" Howlett, Faye & Earl Johnson, Richard and Darlene Johnson, Joe Johns, Sang Lee-Kuczura, Gordon Makely, Ariel Martin, Marvin's Marvelous Mechanical Museum, Joan Meah, Mercury Studios, Pace MacGill Gallery, Tom Palazollo, Ed Paschke, Wyatt Landesman/Quantity Postcards, Bobby Reynolds, Mike and Bette Rogers, Andy Roski, Bob, Sam & RPCH, Charlie Rudolph, Jack Sarcona, Bryan Schuetze, Melanie and Jim Secreto Jr., Mike Seculan, Sonya Taylor, Lynn and Taylor Varndell, Walter Wanous, Deedee Waxter-Grant, Robt. Williams, Karl Wirsum, Joel-Peter Witkin, Richard Wright, Sandy Wolf, Jim Zanzi, Wilmer Zehr, private collectors, Eugene and Marie, Smokey the Devil Dog, Carl das Wunder Hund, Starbucks and Bozo.

Last, but not least, deep thanks to Don Ed Hardy, whose dedication and vision allowed a loose idea to become a project, and now a book.

Randy Johnson
January 1995

KEEP SMILING WITH BIG JUMBO

"ACTUAL SCENE MIDGET WEDDING SAVANNAH, GA.
APRIL 8TH 1926."
MIKE----IKE---MRS. IKE

PEOPLE ATTENDED   FIRST MIDGET WEDDING IN 43 YEARS

NEW YORK...MIKE AND IKE
MIDGETS ARRIVE HERE ON
THEY WERE ACCOMPANIED BY
PHOTO SHOWS GENE TUNNEY
AND IKE IN HIS ARMS.

Mike & Ike Midgets — 1927